SOCIOLOGY OF HEALTH AND HEALTH CARE

An Introduction for Nurses

Edited by

STEVE TAYLOR

BA, LL.B, MPhil, PhD
Lecturer in Medical Sociology and Medical Law
King's College, London, The London School of Economics
and Coventry University

DAVID FIELD

BA, AM, MA, PhD
Senior Lecturer in Medical Sociology
Department of Epidemiology and Public Health
University of Leicester

Blackwell Science

Blackwell Science Ltd
Editorial Offices:
Osney Mead, Oxford OX2 0EL
25 John Street, London WC1N 2BL
23 Ainslie Place, Edinburgh EH3 6AJ
238 Main Street, Cambridge
  Massachusetts 02142, USA
54 University Street, Carlton
  Victoria 3053, Australia

Other Editorial Offices:
Arnette Blackwell SA
1, rue de Lille
75007 Paris
France

Blackwell Wissenschafts-Verlag GmbH
Kurfürstendamm 57
10707 Berlin
Germany

Blackwell MZV
Feldgasse 13
A-1238 Wien
Austria

First published 1993
Reprinted 1994, 1995

Set by DP Photosetting, Aylesbury, Bucks
Printed and bound in Great Britain by
Hartnolls Ltd, Bodmin, Cornwall

DISTRIBUTORS

Marston Book Services Ltd
PO Box 87
Oxford OX2 0DT
(*Orders:* Tel: 01865 791155
    Fax: 01865 791927
    Telex: 837515)

North America
  Blackwell Science, Inc.
  238 Main Street
  Cambridge, MA 02142
  (*Orders:* Tel: 800 215-1000
       617 876-7000
       Fax: 617 492-5263)

Australia
  Blackwell Science Pty Ltd
  54 University Street
  Carlton, Victoria 3053
  (*Orders:* Tel: 03 347-5552)

A catalogue record for this book is
available from the British Library

ISBN 0-632-03402-5

Library of Congress
Cataloging in Publication Data

Sociology of health and health care: an
  introduction for nurses / [edited by]
  Steve Taylor, David Field.
    p.   cm.
    Includes index.
    ISBN 0-632-03402-5
    1. Nursing—Social aspects.
  2. Nursing—Social aspects—Great
  Britain. 3. Social medicine. 4. Social
  medicine—Great Britain. 5. National
  Health Services (Great Britain)
  I. Taylor, Steve (Steve D.) II Field,
  David, 1942-
    [DNLM: 1. Delivery of Health Care—
  Great Britain—nurses instruction.
  2. Sociology, Medical—nurses'
  instruction. 3. State Medicine—Great
  Britain. W 84FA1 S67 1993]
  RT86.5.S67   1993
  306.4'61'0941—dc20

                              93-7900
                              CIP

Contents

List of Contributors

KEN BLAKEMORE BA, MSocSci, PhD, Lecturer in Social Policy, University of Swansea.

DAVID FIELD BA, AM, MA, PhD, Senior Lecturer in Medical Sociology, Department of Epidemiology and Public Health, University of Leicester.

NICKY JAMES RGN, MA, PhD, Senior Lecturer, Department of Nursing and Midwifery Studies, Faculty of Medicine, University of Nottingham.

NICK JEWSON BSc, MA, Lecturer, Department of Sociology, University of Leicester.

PAM SMITH BNurs, Cert Ed., MSc, PhD, RGN, DN, HV, RNT, Lecturer in Nursing, Institute of Advanced Nursing Education, Royal College of Nursing, London.

ANTHEA SYMONDS BSc, MSc, PhD, Lecturer in Social Policy and Health Care, University of Swansea.

STEVE TAYLOR BA, LL.B, MPhil, PhD, Lecturer in Medical Sociology and Medical Law, King's College, London and The London School of Economics.

Foreword

In this beautifully written text, the authors make sociology seem interesting, accessible and above all centrally relevant to nursing. It is therefore a great pleasure to consider how nurses may exploit the discipline and strengths of the sociological mind. Objective evidence is clearly presented here in a natural literary style and this has the effect of persuading the reader that sociology is indispensable to the understanding of health and health care.

Perhaps it is the very choice of chapter topics which makes this so useful and provides a liberal view of applied sociology. Here social commentary and interpretation establishes a basis for assessing which factors affect health and illness, and also provides an example of how information and research findings can strengthen the influence of sociology. Convincing evidence and explanation so well presented should win over those who may not have realized how significant this can be.

In congratulating the authors, it is not only the topicality and provocative insights offered, such as 'sickness can never be prevented only postponed' but the easy integration of demography and epidemiology which is refreshing. Finally, readers will not be blind to assumptions by the authors that nurses have an awareness of health problems as well as the ability to help people. I would like to return this compliment to all those who contributed to this successful work.

Jenifer Wilson-Barnett
Professor and Head of Nursing Studies
King's College, London

Preface

This book aims to provide a clear, easy to understand sociological text which is specifically oriented towards nursing. As teachers of sociology on nursing courses we were aware of the need for such a book, especially with the introduction of Project 2000. Existing texts were either dated or directed towards the requirements of medical or sociology students.

We have organized the text around four distinct areas. In the introductory section, we first explain what sociology is, how sociological research is undertaken, and its applications to health and health care. We then look at how fundamental changes in British society influenced the organization and delivery of health care.

The second section is concerned with social structure and health. Britain, like other developed countries, has invested massively in medical technology and research on the assumption that the 'conquest' of disease through advances in the treatment of the sick was the key to better health. However, despite some spectacular achievements, the major diseases of modern societies, such as heart disease and most cancers, remain stubbornly resistant to medical cure. In recent years the attention of health professionals, including many nurses, has returned to examining some of the sources of good or bad health and the task of health promotion. In this context we examine the various ways in which health is shaped by social factors.

Despite this renewed interest in health and its maintenance, the major part of nursing work is, and will remain, the care of people who are sick and disabled. Section three therefore examines the contribution of sociological research to understanding people's experiences of illness, disability, mental disorder and death.

The final section examines the organization and delivery of health care in modern Britain. It considers the informal care given in families and communities and the formal provision of care in the National Health Service. The final chapter looks at the development of nursing and at the relationships between nurses and their patients.

The contributors are experts in the sociology of health and health care and have experience of teaching on nursing courses. While the book is organized to ensure continuity between chapters, each chapter can also be read on its own.

Steve Taylor and David Field

Part I
Introduction

Chapter 1
Sociology, Health and Health Care

What is sociology?

The simplest view of sociology is that it is about understanding human societies. However, that does not take us very far. While we will know very little about say, physics, without studying it, most people will feel they know a great deal about the society in which they live simply from their experience of it. People have views on how society is changing, what is wrong with it, what to do about it and so on. In what ways are sociologists' interpretations different? We could perhaps answer this by arguing that sociologists are taught about the study of society, engage in research and, therefore, define sociology as the academic study of society. However, even if we take this view, we are still confronted by the fact that there are other academic disciplines – history, economics, anthropology for example – that also study human society. As sociologists have no monopoly over the subject of society, it is better to ask what is distinctive about the way in which they study societies.

There is no clear and simple answer even to this because, as we shall see, there is no single agreed sociological approach but rather, a number of competing perspectives. However, it is possible to draw some common threads together by looking at some of the key questions that stimulated the development of sociology as an academic subject and still underpin a great deal of sociological thought today.

Sociology developed in Europe in the nineteenth century at a time of unprecedented social upheaval. Agricultural production was giving way to industrialization, increasing numbers of people were moving from the land to urban areas, traditional institutions of power, such as the Church and the nobility were losing much of their influence and new sources of power, such as the power of organized labour, were beginning to emerge. The fact that societies could be transformed so quickly led people to start asking certain fundamental questions about the nature of social order and social change. For example, how is society possible at all? What is it that prevents chaos and gives social life a sense of stability and order? What is it that brings about social change and development? What is the relationship between the individual and society and to what extent does the nature of the society into which people are born shape their behaviour as individuals? In this chapter we shall examine these questions in a little more detail, then look at how sociologists undertake research and, finally, consider the application of sociological perspectives to health and health care.

The problem of order

It is sometimes said that sociology is about the study of social problems, that is, about what people feel is 'wrong' with society: crime, poverty, drug abuse and so on. However, sociology is about rather more than this. Sociologists are interested in what people in a given society say is wrong with it, but that does not define for them the scope of their enquiries. Sociologists are just as interested in things that are considered to be 'good', 'normal' or 'healthy' for example, as they are in what is seen as 'bad', 'abnormal' or 'unhealthy'. Sociological problems, then, are about how societies work in the way they do (Berger 1968). In this sense, sociology is closest to politics and philosophy.

Relationships between people and between different parts, or institutions, of society do not occur randomly, but tend to be regular or patterned. For example, birth and death rates remain relatively stable in a given country year after year; some groups within a country have consistently higher life expectancy than others; some groups regularly commit more crimes than others and so on. Even when sociologists engage in detailed, firsthand observation of behaviour such as nurse-patient, teacher-pupil or police officer-suspect interaction, they still find regular and consistent patterns of behaviour. It is the regularities, rather than the exceptions, that the sociologist seeks to explain. Taylor (1989), wrote about child abuse both as a sociologist and as a journalist and explained some of the differences between the two:

'In approaching the identification and management of child abuse as a journalist my attention would probably be focused on a few sensational cases where something had gone dramatically 'wrong' and which are subject to an enquiry. I would place a great deal of emphasis on my own impressions and the comments of people in authority. I would focus on 'key personalities' in the 'drama'. However, as a sociologist, I was interested in observing routine cases over a period of time in order to look for regular and recurring patterns of action and interaction that might allow certain generalizations to be made. The emphasis would be less on workers and families as individuals and more the roles they play, and how those roles are constrained by certain formal and informal rules.'

Sociology is concerned with the puzzle of why social life appears to be structured and shaped by particular sets of rules. Of course, some of these rules are obvious to most people. There are laws and moral values prescribing certain types of conduct. But some sociologists go further, arguing that many of the rules of social life are latent, or hidden, and that people are unaware of the extent to which collective social life is shaping their behaviour. In a famous pioneering sociological study, Durkheim (1897, trans. 1952) argued that even such an apparently 'individual' and anti-social act as suicide could be explained socio-logically. He showed that differences in the suicide rates of various social groups not only remained constant over time, but could be explained in terms of some of the social characteristics of those groups. In industrial societies, the more the lives of members of a social group were woven, or tied in, with each other, through kinship bonds or membership of organizations for example, the lower the suicide rate of that group would be. Thus, according to Durkheim, the motivation for suicide was, in part at least, socially caused.

Social change

We have already observed that sociology began as a discipline in modern western society, and one of the questions it asked was how and why the modern world had developed in the way it did. Some theories see eco-nomic factors as the main source of social change. One of the founders of modern social theory, Karl Marx, argued that contradictions between the way goods were produced (forces of production) and the way goods and services were organized (relations of production) led to conflicts which brought about social changes and the emergence of a new 'type' of social order. Marx identified three types of society: ancient, feudal and industrial capitalist. He argued that under industrial capitalism the workers, concentrated in towns and factories, would become increas-ingly conscious of their common predicament and this would lead to the development of 'working-class' political movements and pressure for revolutionary change. Another group of economic theories saw social change in evolutionary rather than revolutionary terms. They argued that fundamental social changes, such as the movement from extended to nuclear families, 'mass' education, the growth of the professions and the spread of democracy were brought about by the 'needs' of industrial economies for a trained and mobile workforce.

Other theorists gave more prominence to the independent role of ideas and belief systems (such as religion) in producing social change. According to Max Weber, another of the founders of sociology, the major developments in modern and modernizing societies, including economic developments, were made possible by the changes in the way in which people thought about the world. According to Weber, the major change in modern societies was increasing rationalization of life. By rationalization Weber meant the replacement of traditional ways of doing things by calculable rules and procedures, the displacement of religion by science and the substitution of a hierarchy based on birth by one based on training and expertise. These changes brought about what Weber termed the 'disenchantment of the world'.

Today, modern sociologists, especially those engaged in research, are much more likely to be looking at developments within particular organizations or societies rather than trying to construct general theories of social change. However, some of the same issues remain. For example, there is still a debate in sociology between 'materialist' theories, which argue that the economic conditions of people's existence shape their social experience of the world, and 'idealist' theories which place more emphasis on the independent role played by cultural and social influences in historical change. However, despite different theoretical approaches, classical sociology correctly recognized that societies are constantly changing and that little sense can be made of the present without understanding what came before. In this sense sociology is closest to history.

The individual and society

In the individualistic modern world, most people assume that societies are merely a consequence of the activity of individuals. From this point of view it is the study of the individual, through psychology and biology for example, that provides the key to understanding social behaviour. For example, the fact that in most societies women have traditionally played a much larger part than men in nurturing the young and caring for the sick and elderly while men have tended to dominate positions of political influence and economic power, has been explained in terms of differences in the 'natural' instincts of women and men.

In challenging the assumption that social behaviour can be reduced to the study of the individual, sociologists are not, as is sometimes suggested, rejecting the study of the individual in favour of the group. Rather, they are arguing that one cannot be understood without the other. Sociologists are thus interested in the *relationship* between individuals and societies. Societies are obviously the product of individuals but, in important respects, individuals are also the products of their societies.

As social life evolves, certain types of conduct and belief – codes of behaviour or religious practices for example – become reproduced by successive generations as accepted or proper ways of doing things. In sociological terms, they become *institutionalized*. Language is a good example of a social institution. We all learn it, use it for our purposes, but none of us created it. The ways by which the practices of a society are transmitted to people, which begins from the time they are born, is called *socialization* and the various pressures placed on people to conform to the practices and values of a society is called *social control*. To return to our example of the differences between male and female roles in society, sociologists, without necessarily rejecting all biological explanation, have drawn attention to the different child-rearing experiences of boys and girls. For example, aggressive and boisterous behaviour is tolerated more in boys, while girls are encouraged to take on more domestic chores. In short, to an extent, boys and girls are socialized into 'masculine' and 'feminine' roles. Becoming a man or a woman is not simply a product of biology, it is also a process of social learning. In exploring the relationship between the individual and society, sociology is closest to psychology and social psychology.

The institutional practices of a society, and the values and beliefs into which people are socialized, tend to reflect the interests of the most powerful groups in that society. Sociologists are interested in the sources of power and how it is maintained and legitimized. In this context, sociology is closest to politics. For example, Marxist sociologists have argued that the laws and the government institutions of modern western societies, although in principle reflecting the wishes of the majority, in practice have served the interests of the ruling capitalist class in maintaining its exploitation of the rest of society. More recently, feminist sociologists have argued that, despite legislation and social change aimed at sex equality, many of the institutions of modern society still function to preserve power differentials between men and women. In the spheres of employment and family relations, for example, most women still tend to be subject to male control. Feminists have used the concept of *patriarchy* to examine the subordination of women to men and the values underlying this (Walby 1990). The implications of this for nursing, which is still predominantly a female profession, are examined in Chapter 12.

Doing sociological research

Introduction

In attempting to explain how societies, or parts of societies, work in the way they do, sociologists attempt to go beyond opinion, speculation and political debate. They provide evidence to support, or at least illustrate, what they are saying and they try to make their accounts as systematic and objective as possible. This involves the careful accumulation and interpretation of data. At certain points in this section we shall use the specific example of undertaking research in child abuse to illustrate more general points.

Concepts

If a nurse was asked to write an account of a working day on her ward, the account would necessarily be selective. For example, she simply would not know about every conversation and every decision made that day. There would also be things she would choose not to write about because she did not feel they were important. Any account, whether by a nurse, a journalist or a social scientist is necessarily a selective reconstruction of the complexity of a real set of events. Selection is governed partly by the availability of evidence and partly by the judgements of the person writing the account which, in turn, are shaped by wider social influences. All accounts, to a greater or lesser extent, reflect social and individual values.

One of the ways in which social scientists try to make this selection process a little more systematic and objective is to use clearly defined and explained categories, or concepts. For example, sociologists have been interested in the relationship between the economic status of people and their health (Townsend, Davidson & Whitehead 1988). A sociologist studying this would have to find indicators of the concepts of 'economic status' and 'health'. Economic status could, for example, be based on type of occupation or income, and health could be 'measured' in terms of life expectancy or vulnerability to long-standing illness. This would enable data to be collected in a relatively consistent fashion, which could also be checked or developed by other researchers. A positive relationship between relatively low average life expectancy and unskilled manual work might suggest links between stresses or dangers of certain types of manual work and poor health. This may then guide further observations for which new conceptual categories may have to be developed.

Comparative method

Sometimes sociological research may produce a theory of some aspect, or aspects, of human life. However, a major problem for the social sciences is that they are usually unable to 'test' theories in 'closed', or controlled, conditions. As far as sociology is concerned, it would normally be unethical, if not impossible, to conduct 'social experiments' on large groups of people. Sociologists have to employ a technique called the comparative method or 'natural experiment'. This involves collecting information from different social contexts and identifying similarities and differences. For example, in his study of suicide cited above, Durkheim looked at the suicide statistics of different social groups and showed that rates, or levels, of suicide were systematically related to other social factors such as religious belief, marital status and political change.

Sometimes changes in a social group or an organization, such as the introduction of a new policy in a local authority or a new working procedure in a factory, can create a 'quasi-experimental' situation, the effects of which the sociologist can monitor. For example, many studies have suggested that being unemployed is associated with worsening physical and mental health. But what about people put on short term work? McKenna and Fryer (1984) compared factory A, where the workforce was made redundant, with a broadly similar type of factory B, which was operating a rota of lay-offs. They found the perceived health of the unemployed workers from factory A was generally worse than that of those from factory B who were working part-time.

Sources of data

All aspects of human life are of potential interest to sociologists, and data is gathered from a wide range of sources. Sociologists may make use of *secondary* data which is already in existence including data from previous research, collect their own *primary* data, or use a combination of both. An important distinction is between *quantitative* data, such as rates of mortality or unemployment, and *qualitative* data, such as observations of people's behaviour or documentary evidence.

Quantitative data

Official statistics

The term 'official statistics' refers to the mass of data collected by the State and its various agencies. For example, a national Census is held in

Britain every ten years. This provides information about the composition of the population in terms of factors such as age, gender, ethnicity, educational qualifications, nature of residences and so on. State sources also regularly produce domestic data on things like births, deaths, marriages, and divorces. There are economic statistics on employment, unemployment, income and expenditure for example, as well as rates of crime, illnesses, suicides and so on. In addition to state data, other organizations, such as the Stock Exchange or the National Society for the Prevention of Cruelty to Children, are also important sources of statistical information for researchers.

Official statistics are readily available, comprehensive, allow for trends to be monitored over time and are widely used by sociologists and other researchers. A great deal of the information used by studies discussed in this book comes from various forms of 'official statistics', particularly on patterns of health and their relationship to other factors. While much of this data is generally accepted as reliable information, just because something is 'official' and expressed in statistical form does not necessarily make it reliable. First, statistics are not self-evident 'facts', they are only reflections of the conceptual categories through which they are collected. Thus, if we read that the working-class people are twice as likely on average to die before retirement age than the middle-class people, we need to ask, for example, what concept of 'class' was being used and what proportions of the population are in these classes?

Secondly, there may be problems in the collection of some sets of statistics which make their value for research questionable. For example, statistics of children who have been abused or at risk of abuse are kept on Child Protection Registers. This data is used to monitor trends in child abuse and show the areas of society in which it appears most likely to occur. However, there are many reasons why an act of child abuse might not be recorded as such. For example, the child may not be old enough to tell someone what is happening or may not be believed. Even if the child is believed the family may still 'conceal' the abuse from others, or the authorities may feel they do not have enough evidence to record a case on the Register (Fig. 1.1). The official statistics on child abuse may, therefore, seriously under-represent the extent of the problem (Taylor 1992). Similar arguments have been made about the unreliability of 'official statistics' in other areas, such as poverty, crime, suicide, and mental illness. Research on official statistics, then, is not simply about interpreting statistical trends, but also about exploring how the data is produced and evaluating its use for research purposes.

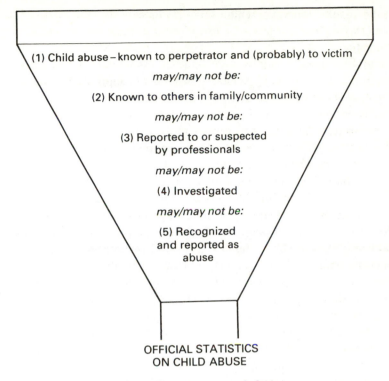

(1) Child abuse – known to perpetrator and (probably) to victim

may/may not be:

(2) Known to others in family/community

may/may not be:

(3) Reported to or suspected by professionals

may/may not be:

(4) Investigated

may/may not be:

(5) Recognized and reported as abuse

OFFICIAL STATISTICS
ON CHILD ABUSE

Fig. 1.1 Child abuse – from abuse to reported abuse.

Surveys and interviews

One of the ways in which sociologists generate their own (i.e. primary) data is to ask people questions. The social survey is a method researchers use to obtain large amounts of data in a relatively short time. It is usually administered in the form of a questionnaire, where a number of set questions are asked in exactly the same way to each respondent. The questions may be asked directly by a researcher or distributed to a group of people, sometimes through the post.

Surveys cannot just be distributed to anyone who happens to come along. The researcher has to calculate the population who could be included in the survey and then construct a sample which is representative of that population. For example, supposing a researcher wanted to find out nurses' opinions of new changes in the organization of the National Health Service (NHS). The more the sample of nurses interviewed or surveyed reflected the general population of NHS nurses in terms of age, class background, ethnicity, gender, professional status and so on, the more the researcher could feel confident in generalizing from the results. 'Surveys' which have no proper sampling procedure, such as those done in the street or by popular magazines have no scientific value.

Surveys are usually used to investigate areas which are not covered, or covered inadequately, by available official and semi-official data. For example, we have observed that official statistics on child abuse (and on crime generally) may not reflect the extent of the problem (Fig. 1.1). One way researchers have tried to obtain more reliable data is to use the 'victim survey'. This involves contacting representative samples of the general population and asking questions about possible experiences of abuse in their childhood. Baker and Duncan (1986) used this method to estimate the prevalence of child sexual abuse in Britain.

The survey is one of the most common tools of social research. It allows large numbers of people to be questioned relatively quickly and cheaply and, because the range of permitted responses is specific and limited, the results can be easily quantified and analysed. However, the survey has limited application. While it is relatively reliable in the collection of simple factual information (such as asking people their occupation), it is of little use in extracting the range of *meanings* that events can have for people. For example, Baker and Duncan asked their respondents if the effects of being abused had 'permanently damaging effects'. Two respondents could both tick that it did but could mean very different things by 'damaging'. Some researchers have tried to account for the problem of meaning by using more open, or unstructured, questions that allow people to answer in their own words. However, the results are then much more difficult to quantify. The major problem in all interviews and surveys is that the resulting data is simply based on what people say they do or think in an artificial situation. When naturalists want to study animal behaviour they tend not to go to a zoo, but to the animals' natural habitats. Similarly, if sociologists want to know more about how people actually behave in real situations, then they may have to go and look for themselves.

Qualitative Research

Ethnography

Ethnography, or field work, simply means studying human behaviour in its natural context. The most common method is participant observation, where researchers join the group or organization they are studying. This technique was used by western anthropologists who joined tribal societies, learning their language and customs in order to observe and document ways of life that were in danger of disappearing with the approach of industrialization. Similarly, in the study of contemporary society, sociologists have to find ways of gaining access to the groups or organizations they wish to study. Then, like the anthropologists, they observe and make detailed records of the 'way of life' of those they are studying.

One of the major problems with ethnographic research is the 'observer effect', where the subjects of inquiry may change their behaviour simply because they are being studied. Some researchers, therefore, attempt to disguise their identity. For example, in his classic study of patient experiences of a state mental hospital, Goffman (1991) worked in the hospital as a games teacher, while Humphreys (1970) in his study of homosexual encounters in public toilets, acted as 'Watch Queen', or lookout. More dramatically, in the cause of research, sociologists have joined delinquent gangs, religious cults and had themselves shut up in mental hospitals.

There is a richness of detail in ethnographic accounts which comes from the fact that sociologists have got out of their offices and studied people at first hand. However, like all research methods, ethnography has its limitations. Not only is the data usually difficult to quantify, it is also hard to test, or replicate, as it is usually one researcher's account of a particular situation. Furthermore, there are many aspects of social life – historical events for example – which cannot be studied this way.

Documentary data

Documents provide a rich source of material for sociologists. They may include the documents of various government institutions, records from schools, hospitals, law courts and so on, as well as reports from journals, magazines and the press. A great deal of historical work is based on careful collection and analysis of documentary evidence.

Qualitative researchers may also make use of personal documents, such as case histories, letters, diaries, and autobiographical works that may help to tell the 'inside story' of how people have interpreted given situations (Plummer 1983). Sometimes documentary evidence can be used to help study experiences where observation is not possible. For example, researchers can neither observe acts of child abuse nor interview the victims. Therefore, accounts written by adults who may have been abused can provide valuable information. Similarly, people researching patient care (as well as health care professionals themselves) can learn a great deal about the experience of being a patient from autobiographical and semi-autobiographical novels, such as Solzhenitsyn's *Cancer Ward* or Kesey's *One Flew Over the Cuckoo's Nest*. In interpreting documentary evidence it is important for the sociologist to

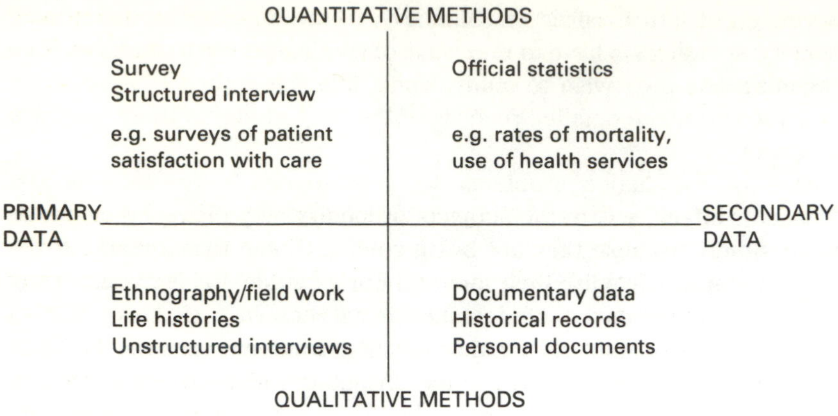

QUANTITATIVE METHODS

Survey	Official statistics
Structured interview	
e.g. surveys of patient	e.g. rates of mortality,
satisfaction with care	use of health services

PRIMARY_____|_____SECONDARY
DATA   DATA

Ethnography/field work	Documentary data
Life histories	Historical records
Unstructured interviews	Personal documents

QUALITATIVE METHODS

Fig. 1.2 Sources of data in social research.

bear in mind that much of it is written to justify, or rationalize, the actions of an individual or organization.

In a research project sociologists are likely to use a variety of sources of data. For example, an ethnographic study may suggest certain questions which the researcher then pursues further with formal interviews. Selection of research strategies will be shaped by the theoretical preferences of the researcher and by the nature of the problem. As we have tried to show, each methodology has its advantages and its limitations. The relationship between different sources of data is illustrated in Fig. 1.2.

It is also important to bear in mind that in doing research sociologists are not merely standing back and observing and analysing what is going on 'out there' in society. There is no such thing as 'pure' data (Pawson 1989). As we have seen, researchers have to define concepts, write questions and select research strategies, and the choices they make have an important bearing on what finally emerges as data. In studying a social science, it is not simply a question of looking at what researchers have discovered, but also at how they went about discovering it.

A Science of society?

So far we have been looking at things which are common to sociology. However, when we look in a little more detail at sociological work, we are confronted by the fact that there is no general agreement in sociology about what societies are or how they should be studied. There is not, then, a unified sociological approach but rather a number of sociological perspectives (Swingewood 1991). Analysis of the different sociological theories cannot be undertaken here, but it is important to understand that there is a major division in social theory about the extent to which the study of society can be objective, or scientific.

Societies as objective realities

Many of the earliest social theorists were optimistic that, by diligently applying the principles and techniques that had been so successful in the natural sciences, sociology would ultimately be able to discover laws of social behaviour and historical change. Social scientists are not so optimistic today. However, many believe, or at least assume, that it is possible to study social life in an objective quasi-scientific manner. This normally involves trying to explain some of the regularities of social life in terms of various 'causal' influences. Sociologists adopting this view tend to have a preference for apparently 'hard' quantifiable data. Thus the sociologists studying child abuse this way might start by looking at the statistics on child abuse from official data, or surveys, and – using the comparative method – look for factors which appear more common amongst families whose children have been abused. From this perspective child abuse is seen as an 'objective' fact whose statistical distribution is to be explained by reference to other social factors such as poor housing or unemployment. The researcher might then go on to develop theories which could explain this relationship and the findings might then be used to help professionals predict which families are more or less likely to abuse their children (e.g. Browne *et al.* 1988).

Societies as subjective realities

Other sociologists are much more sceptical about the very idea of a science of society. They argue that there are differences between the study of the natural world and the social world. Unlike the atoms studied by physicists for example, human beings engage in conscious intentional activity and, through language, attach meaning to their actions. As social life is essentially subjective, sociologists should be less concerned to explain behaviour than to understand how people come to interpret the world in the way they do. This approach is sometimes called interpretive, or subjectivist. The interpretive sociologist would tend to argue that what makes something a case of 'child abuse' is not simply certain behaviour towards a child, but how that behaviour is viewed by other members of society. Child abuse is thus a product of *social definition*. For example, a hundred years ago giving children regular beatings was not only acceptable but in some cases seen as a positive virtue. Today, as values have changed, beating is much more likely to be seen as child abuse. The interpretive sociologist would be more interested in examining how certain forms of behaviour come to be identified as 'child abuse' and how certain families came to be labelled as abusers (e.g. Dingwall *et al.* 1983).

Interpretive sociology has a preference for qualitative research methodologies which bring researchers as close as possible to the world of the subjects they are studying. In looking at the differences between what we have called scientific and interpretive sociology, it is not a question of choosing which is 'right' or 'wrong'. Both give particular insights into social life and both (like all perspectives in the behavioural sciences) have their limitations. Some of the differences between quantitative and qualitative methods are outlined in Fig. 3.1.

Sociology applied to health and health care

Research into health and health care in modern societies tends to be dominated by the biological sciences and the application of various highly technical treatments. In what ways, then, might sociological perspectives be relevant?

QUANTITATIVE	QUALITATIVE
Focuses on a relatively small number of specific concepts	Attempts to understand the entirety of some phenomenon rather than focus on specific concepts
Begins with preconceived ideas about how the concepts are interrelated	Has few preconceived ideas and stresses the importance of people's interpretation of events and circumstances, rather than the researcher's interpretation
Uses structured procedures and formal 'instruments' to collect information	Collects information without formal, structured 'instruments'
Collects the information under conditions of control	Does not attempt to control the context of the research but, rather, attempts to capture it in its entirety
Emphasizes objectivity in the collection and analysis of information	Attempts to capitalize on the subjective as a means for understanding and interpreting human experiences
Analyses numerical information through statistical procedures	Analyses narrative information in an organized, but intuitive, fashion

Fig. 1.3 The differences between quantitative and qualitative approaches. (*Source* D.F. Polit & B.P. Hungler (1991) *Nursing Research: Principles and Methods,* (4th edn). Lippincott, Philadelphia. (Reproduced by permission of J.B. Lippincott Company.))

In this book we shall answer that question by considering the relevance of sociology to three main issues:

- the major influences on health
- people's experiences of illness, disability, mental disorder and dying
- the organization of health care resources and the care of the sick.

Part II, using research mainly from the more 'scientific' theories and quantitative methodologies, examines the role of social influences on health and disease. In the relatively recent past it was accepted almost without question that the best way to improve health in modern societies was through more and improved forms of treatment. Now people are beginning to realize that better health cannot be bought in this way, and that life expectancy and health are determined largely by factors outside the control of the health care system. In this context it has been argued that social influences play an important part. For example, examination of the past shows that significant improvements in health appeared to owe more to various social changes than to medical intervention (Chapter 3). Similarly, social factors such as occupation, ethnicity, culture and life style play an important part in explaining variations in health between different groups in contemporary society (Chapter 4). On another level of analysis, sociological research has suggested that the quality of people's social relations, especially the extent to which they are 'supported' by others, can have a significant effect on their health (Chapter 5). In general, sociological research in this context has attempted to show the extent to which the health and illness episodes of individuals are linked in various ways to the organization of wider society.

Sociologists who are more inclined to interpretive theories and qualitative methods have been interested in explaining how certain biological states and types of behaviour come to be labelled as 'healthy' or 'sick'. The ideas that a society has about what constitutes health and illness do not exist in a medical vacuum, but change in response to social changes. Sociologists are interested in the development of these ideas and in the effect of illness labels on patients. In Part III, we shall look at how people come to define themselves as ill (Chapter 6), people's experiences of chronic illness and disability (Chapter 7), the application of illness labels to various behavioural and mental disorders (Chapter 8) and people's experiences of death and dying (Chapter 9).

The ways in which people respond to sickness and organize health care cannot be divorced from the organization of wider society. This is considered in Part IV. Most health care does not take place in professional settings but is undertaken in the family, usually by women. The role of the family in health care and the implications for health policy cannot be understood without examining how the family is changing in modern societies (Chapter 10). In Britain, most professional health care is provided by the State through the NHS. The origins, 'costs' and 'benefits' of a state funded health care system, and the impact of recent government changes, both for nurses and their patients, can only be understood by looking at changes in wider society (Chapter 11). The largest group of health workers are nurses. Their relationships with their patients are social as well as technical. Sociologists have examined the development of nursing as an occupation, and the social influences on the nurse-patient relationship (Chapter 12).

Summary

Sociology begins by asking certain fundamental questions about the nature of social order and the relationship between social order and individual behaviour. Sociological research involves systematic collection and interpretation of data from a variety of sources, but the social sciences cannot attain the objectivity and predictive power of the natural sciences. The application of sociological perspectives to health and health care suggests that social influences play an important part in helping to explain the distribution of health, experiences of illness and disability, and how health care is organized and delivered.

References

Baker A. & Duncan S. (1986) Prevalence of Child Sexual Abuse in Great Britain. *Child Abuse and Neglect,* **9** 457–69.

Berger P. (1968) *Invitation to Sociology.* Pelican, Harmondsworth.

Browne K., Davies C. & Stratton P. (Eds) (1988) *Early Prediction and Prevention of Child Abuse.* Wiley, Chichester.

Dingwall R., Eekelaar J. & Murray T. (1983) *The Protection of Children.* Blackwell, Oxford.

Durkheim E. (1897/1952) *Suicide: A Study in Sociology.* Routledge, London.

Goffman E. (1991) *Asylums: Essays on the Social Situation of Mental Patients and Other Inmates.* Penguin, London.

Humphreys L. (1970) *Tea Room Trade.* Duckworth, London.

McKenna S. & Fryer D. (1984) Perceived health during layoff and early unemployment. *Occupational Health,* **36**, 201–206.

Pawson R. (1989) *A Measure for Measures: A Manifesto for Empirical Sociology.* Routledge, London.

Plummer K. (1983) *Documents for Life.* Allen & Unwin, London.

Polit D.F. & Hungler B.P. (1991) *Nursing Research: Principles and Methods*, (4th edn). Lippincott, Philadelphia.

Swingewood A. (1991) *A Short History of Sociological Thought*, (2nd edn.) Macmillan, London.

Taylor S. (1989) Researching child abuse. In *Investigating Society*, (Ed. by B. Burgess). Longman, Harlow.

Taylor S. (1992) How prevalent is it? In *Child Abuse and Neglect*, 2nd edn (Ed. by W. Stainton Rogers, D. Hevey, J. Roche & E. Ash). Batsford/Open University Press, London.

Townsend P., Davidson, N. & Whitehead M. (1988) *Inequalities in Health: The Black Report/The Health Divide*. Penguin, London.

Walby S. (1990) *Theorising Patriarchy*. Blackwell, Oxford.

Further Reading

Introductory Sociology Texts

Giddens A. (1986) *Sociology: A Brief but Critical Introduction*. Macmillan, London.

Worsley P. (Ed.) (1987) *The New Introductory Sociology*. Pelican, London.

Sociological research

Burgess B. (Ed.) (1989) *Investigating Society*. Longman, Harlow.

McNeil P. (1985) *Research Methods*. Tavistock, London.

Health and nursing research

Abbott P. & Sapsford R. (Eds) (1992) *Research into Practice: A Reader for Nurses and Caring Professions*. Open University, Milton Keynes.

Sapsford R. & Abbott P. (1992) *Research Methods for Nurses and Caring Professions*. Open University, Milton Keynes.

Chapter 2
Health and Health Care in Modern Britain

Patterns of health and systems of health care do not exist in a vacuum, but are influenced by the nature of the societies from which they emerge. This chapter locates health and health care in the context of modern British society. A number of the issues raised in it will be discussed more fully in other chapters, but the aim of this chapter is to provide an overview of the factors which influence health and health care in modern Britain. To understand the patterns of health and illness and the system of health care in modern Britain some knowledge of British society is necessary. We begin by looking at relevant aspects of modern Britain as an industrial society. Next, implications of demographic changes and associated changes in family and household structures are discussed. This is followed by a consideration of State involvement in health care, leading to the establishment of the National Health Service (NHS). The increasing pressures placed upon the NHS are then examined, followed by a discussion of the NHS in the 1990s. Finally, the chapter looks at implications of these for nursing.

Britain as an industrial society

Britain was the first society in the world to industrialize, and despite subsequent changes, many of its characteristics and problems are best understood as a result of its status as an industrial society.

Political aspects

The present structures of political power and influence emerged during the process of industrialization. The Tory/Conservative party increasingly came to represent the views and power of commercial and business interests (while retaining the loyalty of landowners and farmers), while the fluctuating power of manual workers has been reflected by the emergence and fortunes of the Labour party. Conservatives disagree about this, but in the 1980s the dominant group in the Party has emphasized the importance and responsibility of individuals in shaping their own life and destiny and want the State to intervene as little as possible in everyday affairs. By contrast, and reflecting the experience of the 'working classes' that collective efforts achieve improvements in wages and lifestyle, Labour emphasizes the responsibility of the State for a range of individual 'rights' such as health, housing and minimum levels of income.

Occupational structure

Present divisions of wealth and privilege in British society can be traced to the transformation of Britain from a predominantly agrarian to an industrial society. Towards the end of the last century, an increasing proportion of the urban working population were employed in factories. Subsequently, changes in technology and the increasing openness of world markets have led to the decline of industry, especially 'heavy' industry, in Britain and the expansion of 'service' occupations not directly involved in the manufacture of goods. Since the Second World War there has been a growing shift from manufacturing to service industry, with the growth in personal services particularly prominent. Alongside this, and as part of the process, has been the expansion of the 'public sector', including such basic services as health care, education and other aspects of the welfare state.

These changes have had a number of important consequences for different patterns of unemployment by labour market sector and region, summed up by the over-simplified picture of the 'North/South' divide. Regions with concentrations of heavy industry (the North and Wales) experienced higher levels of unemployment and worse health than the more affluent (mainly southern) regions where commerce, new technology industries and service industries flourished. Despite a general and appreciable rise in living standards over the century, changes in the distribution of wealth have been minor, and there are continuing differentials, with substantial numbers of unemployed and underprivileged people (Chapter 4).

One effect of the shift from heavy industry and other associated changes has been the steady rise of female participation in the labour force. Currently most adult women work, although many married women are part-time employees. Part-time work is particularly common in the service industries. Demographic changes also contribute to the inclusion of women in the labour force, and with the shortage of young males entering the labour market the range of work open to women has expanded, as has the feasibility of pursuing a career. This has implications for nursing as it faces increasing competition for its traditional source of (female) entrants throughout the 1990s. Nursing has always had a problem in retaining its work-force, and this too is likely to become exacerbated by the increasing demand for female labour throughout the economy as employers compete by providing a range of perks and services such as creche facilities, planned career breaks, job-sharing and flexitime to attract mothers with young children to work for them.

Economic changes

Health and health care are tied to the fortunes of the economy in important respects, and changes in the economy and available resources for health care significantly influence health provision in Britain as in other societies. For example, declining growth creates greater demand for state services, including health services, and also pressures for them to be more efficient and to economize.

The NHS was conceived and initially implemented during the period of economic difficulty following World War II, and greatly expanded and consolidated its key role in British society during the late 1950s and 1960s. This expansion came partly in response to demographic need, consumer demand and medico-technological developments, but was made possible by the buoyant national and international economic climate, memorably encapsulated in the Conservative party slogan 'You've never had it so good'. In the 1960s approximately 6% of Britain's gross national product (or wealth) had been spent on health services. Subsequently, as we shall see, the less buoyant and more uncertain state of the British economy has restricted the increase in real expenditure on health (Flynn 1990).

Changes in the British population

Changes in the composition of the British population have exerted a profound influence upon the changing nature of the NHS. Britain, in common with other advanced industrial societies, is characterized by an ageing population. A decline in death rates and increases in life expectancy have been continuing for over a century, with the reduction in infant mortality rates being particularly marked. In 1850, less than 5% of the population was aged over 65, whereas today it is 15% with a projected increase to 19% over the next 40 years. The main reasons for this change in demographic composition have been the 'bulge' in the number of births which occurred after the 1914–18 World War and, to a lesser extent, a decline in mortality rates, especially at birth and in the first years of life. Declining mortality has resulted primarily from better nutrition and higher standards of living, with the impact of modern medicine being a secondary contributor (Chapter 3). At all ages mortality of males is greater than that of females (Tinker 1992).

The burden of disease

Strongly related to these changes has been a shift in the nature and pattern of disease. Acute infectious diseases have been largely superseded by long term chronic conditions as the major sources of illness in society. Acute infectious diseases rarely have fatal outcomes in modern Britain (unlike earlier times, and current 'third world' countries), and the primary causes of death are chronic and degenerative diseases of the circulatory and respiratory systems and cancers. These are conditions which primarily affect middle-aged and older adults. Two important consequences of this changed pattern are that chronic degenerative diseases have become major aspects of health care and that the age at which people normally die has been pushed back to beyond retirement age. However, the problems of infectious disease have not disappeared as concern about HIV/AIDS, the reappearance of TB and recurrent outbreaks of food poisoning amply demonstrate.

The 1988 OPCS survey of the prevalence of disability among adults in Great Britain estimated that there were 6 million adults and 300 000 children with disabilities in society. Almost 14% of adults living in domestic homes (as distinct from residential homes) have at least one disability. The majority of disabled adults have more than one disability, and the likelihood of becoming disabled increases with age – 60% of all disabled people are over the age of 65. One of the main sources of increasing demands upon the NHS is the increasing numbers and proportion of the British population who are above the age of 75. Great concern has been expressed about the costs to the NHS and Social Services as a result of the needs of older people. During the life time of the NHS the percentage of its expenditure spent on people 65 and over has risen from 5% to the current level of just above 30%. Even though most old people regard themselves as in satisfactory health and care for themselves except when they are seriously ill, the majority of hospital beds are occupied by people over the age of 65.

Despite the contributions from the NHS, local authorities and voluntary agencies the majority of the care and social support provided for sick and disabled elderly people is provided not by the State but by 'informal care' from families and neighbours, especially by women (Parker 1990).

Family patterns

Changes in family and household structures towards a more fragmented and less communal pattern have occurred since the introduction of the NHS (Chapter 10). Modern Britain is characterized by a range of family and household structures. In some communities patterns of extended kinship can still be found, although the extended family does not necessarily live together. Elsewhere the 'isolated nuclear family' of two parents and their children is the main family unit, although even here the ties to the families of origin are unlikely to have been completely severed. It is, however, a myth to think that the nuclear family constitutes the typical British family. Since the 1960s there has been a sharp increase in divorce, typically accompanied by remarriage or cohabitation. Divorce rates are especially high among manual workers. Such marital breakdown is associated with increased levels of mortality and morbidity among divorcees and their children. There are a range of potential problems, e.g. jealousy, stress, associated with stepfamilies where not all members have the same shared past and loyalty to each other.

Remarriage leads to complex family relationships and household structures, which may affect the capacity to deliver informal care. Another variation from the nuclear family is the increase in the number and proportion of one parent families, typically headed by a women, and most common in inner city areas. One parent families are associated with illegitimacy, but illegitimacy is not confined to one parent families. An increasing number of illegitimate births are found among those couples who form a 'stable relationship' without marriage. In these couples the association of illegitimacy with greater health risks to the infant and child are not apparent. Associated with these structural changes in family patterns has been a reduction in family size. Although there is no evidence that modern families are abandoning their familial responsibilities of care, the reduction in family size and the fragmentation and complexity of modern family structures identified above means that there are fewer people available to provide such care. The current pattern of deferral of child-bearing is likely to continue, and in interaction with the increasing involvement of women in the labour market is likely to lead to a further reduction in the availability of unpaid lay carers.

Migration

Another important change has been immigration from Britain's ex-colonies and Europe. During the 1950s and early 1960s Britain recruited migrants from the Caribbean and the Indian subcontinent to meet demands for labour during the economic expansion of that time. In the 1970s Asian refugees and other migrants came from East Africa. Altogether 6% of the British population came from these countries, with another 6% of immigrants from Europe and Australasia. New migrants tend to be healthier than the host population, although over time they come to assume the health profiles of the host community. This is true of migrants to Britain, with the exception of migrants from Eire who have less stringent entry requirements placed upon them. Some ethnic groups may be characterized by higher incidence of particular diseases (e.g. sickle cell among Afro-Caribbeans). The pattern of visiting between their country of origin and Britain may also have a slight impact on the disease profile of the host country, as can be seen by the appearance of infectious diseases (e.g. malaria) found in the ex-colonial countries among returners and their ethnic communities.

The 1981 Census revealed a traditional extended household structure to be typical of New Commonwealth or Pakistan (NCP) headed households, although elderly people from ethnic minorities comprised only 4% of people in NCP households, compared with about 17% in the population as a whole. People from NCP groups may adhere more strictly to the cultural attitudes and practices of their country of origin and recent migrants and older people may be less than proficient in their use of English. With the assimilation of younger members of these communities into the round of British life some inter-generational tensions and conflicts have arisen. These groups are also likely to experience discrimination and possibly harassment as a result of racial prejudice in British society. These factors may mean that they have greater difficulty in their use of health and other statutory services than members of the white majority.

State involvement in health care

Historical context

One of the major developments in all industrial societies is the growth of state involvement in health and welfare provisions. In Britain in the mid-nineteenth century the most important area of state intervention was in public health reform, aimed at combating diseases like cholera and typhoid which were flourishing in the newly created urban squalor. The 1848 Public Health Act laid down the foundation for the provision of better water supplies and sewage disposal, while a series of further reforms in the 1870s led to the creation of local authority sanitary boards and the appointment of medical officers of health.

In the early twentieth century state involvement was extended to personalized health care. Concern about the health of children in particular led to a series of reforms, such as the provision of school meals (1906), a school medical service (1907) and the establishment of health visiting as a local authority service (1907). In 1911 the State partially funded GP care for some low paid workers through the introduction of a National Insurance Scheme. These kinds of developments marked the beginnings of the modern welfare state (Fraser 1984). In the inter-war years state responsibility for primary health care was extended, and the 1929 Local Government Act brought many hospitals under local authority control.

There were many reasons for increasing state provision of health care. Some of the earliest measures were, in part, due to the work of reformers such as Edwin Chadwick, whose famous *Report of an Inquiry into the Sanitary Conditions of the Labouring Population of Great Britain* (1842) led to the establishment of a Board of Health and subsequently to the 1848 Public Health Act. However, not all reform was so philanthropically inspired. Governments and employers came to realize the benefits of a healthier workforce. For example, the reforms to improve child health at the beginning of this century were a direct result of a report into the poor health of army recruits to fight in the Boer War. There was also pressure from 'below' for increased state funding of health care. The concentration of large sections of the working population into towns and cities led to increasing 'working-class' consciousness resulting in the development of trade unions and the foundation of the Labour Party. The various branches of the socialist movement used their growing power and increased political representation to campaign, amongst other things, for better health care provision for working people.

Political context

In 1942 the Beveridge Report recommended a massive increase in the provision of state welfare, including a state funded health service. The Labour Government elected in 1945 was committed to implementing these reforms and the National Health Service (NHS) came into being in July 1948. The NHS was the product of a distinct set of socialist ideas called collectivism. Collectivist social policies argue that all citizens have certain social and economic (as well as political) rights, and that the opportunity to realize these rights should be guaranteed by the State. As Aneurin Bevan, Labour Minister of Health when the NHS was created, put it: 'Homes, health, education and social security – these are your birthright'.

In Britain expenditure on the welfare state has grown dramatically in real terms since the Second World War and now accounts for about 30% of national expenditure. The NHS is the largest organization in the welfare state employing over 1 million people, including 415 000 nurses. Each year the NHS treats over 6 million people in hospitals, deals with 37 million out-patient visits, and community nurses visit another 7 million in their homes (Klein 1989). In 1949 the NHS consumed under 4% of Britain's gross national product, today the proportion is approximately 6%. Although successive governments in Britain have struggled to control the costs of the NHS in various ways, including having some patients pay for the costs of their medicines, both Labour and Conservative governments (as well as most health care professionals and the majority of the British public) have remained, with varying degrees of enthusiasm, committed to the collectivist principle of providing a health care service for all which is free at the point of access. However, in recent years, as the cost of the NHS has continued to rise and the rate of Britain's economic growth declined, there have been those inside and outside government who have wondered whether the country can still afford a 'free' health service.

Professional context

As near monopolizers of the right to treat the sick, doctors were in a very powerful position in their negotiations with the architects of the NHS. The medical profession, and especially the senior consultants at the top of medicine's hierarchy of power, were able to extract a number of important concessions from the Labour government. For example, the government guaranteed special funds for high status teaching hospitals and agreed to finance 'merit awards' to those consultants recognized as experts by their professional colleagues. Consultants were also allowed to use NHS facilities and staff, including NHS nurses, to treat their private patients.

The final agreement between the government and the medical profession guaranteed professional autonomy and clinical freedom of doctors, as well as giving them a major voice in the allocation of health care resources. Thus, while the NHS was a new way of financing health care, the major proportion of health care resources remained directed into high technology, hospital based medical care. The NHS thus confirmed the power of the medical profession, especially the medical hierarchy, over other health professionals, including nurses.

Throughout the life of the NHS the medical profession has largely managed to maintain its control over other occupational groups involved in health care through three main strategies. Some groups, such as nursing, have been subordinated to medical control and their activities largely delegated to them by doctors with little scope for autonomy, independence or self-regulation. This is particularly true in hospital settings, although medical control is more light handed elsewhere. Other groups, such as dentists and pharmacists have had their activities limited to a specified range of activities, with the medical profession playing a key role in their registration procedures. Finally, practitioners of 'alternative medicine' have been successfully excluded from the state run and financed health system, although they may be widely used within the community.

Pressures on the NHS

The founders of the NHS believed that its costs would stabilize once a pool of sickness had been 'mopped up'. This expectation proved to be hopelessly naive and NHS costs have quadrupled in real terms since 1948 (Table 2.1).

Despite continuing and increased government investment over its life, the 1980s and 1990s have seen a range of complaints about the NHS and its functioning. Consumers and the Government have complaints about the length of NHS waiting lists and about the quality of care. Nurses and doctors have complaints about lack of resources (including pay) and increased workloads which are preventing them from delivering the care they see as desirable. Thus we have the apparent paradox of the British people paying more for a deteriorating service. However, it is important

Table 2.1 The cost of the NHS: public expenditure on the NHS as a proportion of the Gross National Product (GNP).

Year	NHS expenditure		Total NHS cost
	as % of GNP	£ million	Index 1949 = 100
1949	3.9	437	100
1959	3.8	792	126
1969	4.4	1 733	200
1979	5.3	9 082	303
1988	5.9	22 960	411

Source Adapted from Table 2.3, p. 19 of Office of Health Economics (1989) *Compendium of Health Statistics*, (7th edn). Office of Health Economics, London. (Reproduced by permission of Office of Health Economics.)

Note This table excludes charges to patients. The 1949 index represents the 'real' cost, at 1949 prices, assuming 1949 = 100, i.e. a fourfold 'real' increase by 1988.

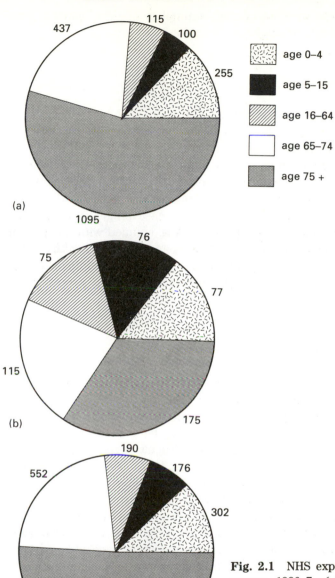

Fig. 2.1 NHS expenditure (£) per person 1986–7. (a) Hospital and community health services. (b) Family Practitioner services. (c) Total NHS. (*Source* Adapted from Tables 2.3 and 2.4, p. 19 of Office of Health Economics (1989) *Compendium of Health Statistics*, (7th edn). Office of Health Economics, London. (Reproduced by permission of Office of Health Economics.))

to recognise that over its lifetime a number of developments have
increased pressures on the NHS.

An ageing population

NHS expenditure per head is highest at birth and in old age (Fig. 2.1), and
a major pressure upon the NHS is the increasing numbers of older
people in Britain. A common estimate is that the NHS will require an
annual increase of 1% in its real income over the rest of the century to
keep pace with the additional costs resulting from the increased number
of old people in the population. On average people aged 75–84 cost the
health service more than four times the national average, with those over
85 nearly seven times more expensive. This, coupled with diminishing
resources for lay care, has important implications for the health service.
There are also significant costs to local authorities providing statutory
social services for old people, and to the families and 'lay carers' of sick
and disabled old people.

Medical technology

Within the medical sphere the continuing development of medical, surgical, and pharmacological technology has led to more powerful and
sophisticated mechanical interventions into matters of life and death. At
the same time that medical intervention has become more powerful, it
has also become more complicated and difficult to co-ordinate the various elements of treatment (Strauss *et al.* 1985). The development of
such techniques has been partly responsible for both the concentration
of secondary medical practice in large general hospitals since the mid-
1960s and the increasing resource demands upon the NHS, especially the
ever increasing costs of hospital medicine (Fig. 2.2). Advances in medical specialization and high technology medicine have increased the
demands on nursing staff while taking resources (including nurses)
away from the long-term care settings elsewhere in hospitals. Even
technological developments which reduce the costs of treatment (e.g. by
allowing day-care hospital treatment instead of hospitalization) and
initially reduce overall costs to the health service may in the long run
increase overall costs as the simpler and cheaper treatments become
more widely available, and more patients are treated. For the nursing
profession such innovations may shift nursing care from the hospital to
the domestic home or community.

	Currently available	On stream	Possibilities for the future
Increased costs to NHS	Coronary artery bypass grafts	Heart/Heart and lung transplant	Neuronal transplant
	Hip replacement	Liver transplant	
		Knee replacement	
	Treatment of end-stage renal failure	Magnetic resonance imaging (MRI)	
	Cataract surgery	Positron emission tomograpgy	
		Diagnostic kits for GPs	
		Subtraction angiography	
Cost neutral	Cimetidine (gastric ulcer drug)	Laser surgery	Developments in laser surgery
		Lithotripter	
		Coronary artery angioplasty	Biotechnology-biosensors monoclonal antibodies as treatment for cancer
	Improved anaesthesia		Cytotoxic
	Computerized diagnosis	Drugs	Stone dissolving
			Mental illness
Reduced cost to NHS			Dementia

Fig. 2.2 Cost implications of medical technology. (*Source* C. Ham (1992) *Health Policy in Britain,* (3rd edn). Macmillan, London. (Reproduced by permission of Macmillan Press Ltd.))

Labour costs

Health care is labour intensive and 70% of the NHS budget now goes on wages and salaries. This means that even relatively low wage increases have a profound effect on the overall costs of the health service. In most industries increasing costs can be offset by trying to increase production and profits, or by passing the burden of higher costs on to the consumer in the form of higher prices. Both these avenues are closed to the NHS. Therefore, it has to go back each year to the government for more money not to improve the service, but simply to try to maintain existing standards. In recent years with economic recession and a prevailing view that public expenditure must be controlled, governments have been increasingly anxious to find alternative ways of organizing the health service and making it more 'efficient'. The recent reforms of the Conservative government have sought to extend managerial control over doctors and nurses and increase competition within the health service (Ham 1992). The implications of these changes for nurses are discussed in Chapter 11.

Expectations of health and health care

The apparent success of modern medicine has had a number of consequences. The health expectations of the British population have risen with the general increase in standards of living and quality of life since the 1960s. Whereas older generations appear to have lower expectations of health and functioning, especially as they become older, those born since the advent of the NHS expect better levels of health, and demand more from the health services. For the majority of Britain's population health for all has come to be seen as a right, rather than as a matter of social status or chance. The introduction and success of the NHS has been seen by the lay public and others as a major factor leading to such raised expectations. Yet despite the well-publicized and real benefits to individual patients of procedures such as renal dialysis, hip replacements and cataract surgery, it is unclear exactly what contributions changes in medical technology have made to the improved health and increased longevity of the British population since the establishment of the NHS (Chapter 3).

The 'iceberg' of illness

It is now realized that there is no fixed level of ill-health to be 'mopped up', and that the demand for health care is potentially limitless. Once one set of disease problems are solved, a new set of problems appear. As we

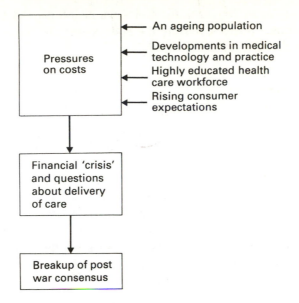

Fig. 2.3   Pressures on the NHS.

have observed, developments in medical technology have made new forms of treatment possible, such as heart surgery and transplants, and patient expectations of the health service have obviously increased. Developments in medicine therefore tend to push up costs. It has been estimated that NHS spending has to be increased by 0.5% a year in real terms simply to allow for developments in medical treatment.

The NHS in the 1990s

The welfare state, and the NHS in particular, rapidly became an accepted and central feature of British life, supported by the major political parties, doctors and nurses and the bulk of the British population. However, since the 1980s there has been increasing critical comment about the continued growth of the welfare state and the collectivist principles underlying it (Chapter 11). Some argue that state welfare is inefficient and as many services as possible should be 'farmed out' to private companies. Others claim that the high taxes needed to fund the welfare state are 'draining' the private sector of the economy and diminishing the capacity for more 'productive' investment. A third argument suggests that state welfare undermines the 'moral fibre' of the nation by discouraging individuals from taking more responsibility for their own health and welfare. From this point of view, more people should be encouraged to make provision for their own health care by taking out private insurance policies, leaving the state system for those in need, such as the unemployed and low paid.

Value for money?

A popular view is that the NHS wastes money, particularly on expensive and unnecessary bureaucracy. However, in spite of rising costs, the NHS appears much more cost-effective than the health services of other western countries (Klein 1989). Another explanation which is popular in some circles is that because the service is free, people make unnecessary demands on it. However, studies by sociologists of how people behave when they are ill show how rarely, not how often, they consult a doctor (Chapter 6). Neither producer waste nor consumer greed can explain the problems of the NHS. As we have seen, the most important causes of increasing health care costs lie outside the control of both producers and consumers of health care.

Private health care

A consequence of the NHS's inability to meet the demands placed on it has been a growth of private health care in Britain. In 1955 only 1% of the British population had private health subscriptions, by 1985 the figure was 8%, and in 1992 it is almost 10% (Office of Health Economics 1989). While most private health insurance schemes are non-profit-making, one of the major developments in the past decade has been the growth in Britain of profit-making health services. Profit-making hospital corporations increased their share of the British private health market from 29% to 51.5% in just seven years (1979–86). This is largely due to an influx of American owned private hospitals. In 1979 American groups owned just 2% of private beds outside the NHS, by 1986 they owned 22.5%. There has also been growth in the privately run nursing and residential homes for elderly people.

Higgins (1988) argues that the development of private health in Britain will increasingly be determined by the interests of the American corporations, 'who have none of the sensitivities about making profits from ill health which are often felt in Britain. In their view health care is a product which can legitimately be bought and sold like any other product' (p. 229). Some welcome the introduction of market economics into health care and are optimistic that the growth of private health care will lift some of the burden from the NHS. Others fear that the drift of patients and staff away from the NHS to the private sector will be followed by massive cuts in state funding, and health care in Britain will come to resemble that in the United States where there is a high level of service for those who have insurance and a very inadequate system for the remainder of society.

Individual responsibility for health

In the 1990s individuals are being encouraged by government and health professionals to accept more responsibility for their health. This is partly because the diseases of modern society are attributed to life style and behaviour. Areas of everyday life such as normal pregnancy, diet, alcohol consumption, exercise, and a broad range of psychosocial problems are increasingly subject to medical intervention. The clients of medicine are no longer simply people who are ill, but potentially all of us, as witnessed by the health education and health promotion campaigns which exhort us to 'look after ourselves' to eat and drink 'sensibly', and to lead healthier lives. Responsibility for maintaining health and preventing illness have become more explicitly defined by government and doctors as the active responsibility of individuals whose own actions are increasingly seen as major factors in patterns of ill-health. These developments are affecting the work of nurses and other health professionals, especially those working in the community, who are becoming increasingly concerned with monitoring and regulating the life style and behaviour of their clients (Chapter 3).

Alternative/complementary medicine

In Britain alternative or complementary therapies receive less recognition than in most other developed countries. Whereas therapies such as osteopathy and acupuncture are respectable in North America and many European countries, it is difficult, if not impossible, to receive such treatments as part of the NHS. However, alternative medicine appears to be popular with the public. In the mid-1980s it was estimated that these therapies involved about 6000 practitioners and were used by 1.5 million people each year at a cost of £250 million. A survey conducted by MORI in 1989 for *The Times* found that 27% of the respondents had used alternative medicine, and that 87% 'would seriously consider' doing so (Sharma 1992). An increasing number of doctors and nurses are taking such non-orthodox therapies seriously, with some GPs incorporating them into their practice.

In the 1990s it is likely that alternative and complementary therapies will continue to be an important source of health care. The popularity of alternative medicine is partly due to the failure of modern health care to offer effective and appropriate treatment for many chronic conditions

(Chapter 7). Some medical practices which are unorthodox in terms of modern medical practice are part of the culture and beliefs of some ethnic minority groups (Bhopal 1986). It has also been suggested that the impersonal nature of high technology medicine and a desire for more patient-centred treatment is another factor contributing to the growing popularity of alternative and complementary therapies among the British population.

Community care

One important area of change in the 1990s is the changes in community services. Structurally, health care in the community is now much less dependent upon 'single handed' medical general practitioners, and there has been a great expansion of community health teams since the 1970s (Jefferys & Sachs 1983). Indeed, by far the greatest increase in the number of community based health workers has been in the number of community nurses. For example, the number of district nurses increased from 6000 in 1949 to 19 500 in 1984 (an increase of 325%), while the number of GPs increased from 21 000 to 29 000 (138%) in the same period (Fry *et al.* 1984). The implications of the shift towards community care and other changes in health policy affecting nursing are discussed in Chapter 11. Here it is important to note that hospitals are increasingly becoming places where acute, intensive, short-stay treatment is given while the community (including nursing homes) is now the preferred place for convalescence and long-term care.

One of the consequences of the implementation of the 1989 White Paper will be to continue the shift of long-term geriatric care out of general hospitals. This division between in-patient hospital care and care in the community has important consequences for the nursing care and management of a range of conditions and client groups, especially those of chronic disease and mental incapacity. The financial and emotional costs to lay carers, and the appropriateness of paid and professional help which lay carers receive can vary widely. These are matters which are now increasingly being raised for discussion and action.

Summary

This chapter has identified some of the important influences upon patterns of health and illness and the provision of health care in modern Britain. The predominance of chronic diseases, together with changes in family and household structures and in patterns of employment have placed pressures upon care for both the general population and the NHS. The NHS is under further pressure from developments in medical technology and practice, rising consumer expectations and demands, and the costs of its work force. Changes in the management and organizational structure of the NHS in the 1990s are partly a result of governmental attempts to respond to these pressures without simply increasing the funding of the NHS in real terms.

One of the consequences of these changes in the NHS is that the influence and control of the medical profession is being challenged by managers. Nurses may find that the medical supervision of their work is being supplemented or replaced by its managerial supervision. Nurses entering the NHS in the 1990s are thus joining an organization in a state of change. Indeed, in the future many more nurses may find themselves working outside the NHS in a range of privately run institutions. However, whatever the organizational context of their work, and despite the increased importance of health promotion activities, the core of nursing – caring for sick people – is unlikely to change.

References

Bhopal R.S. (1986) The inter-relationship of folk, traditional and Western medicine within an Asian community in Britain. *Social Science and Medicine*, **22**, 99–105.

Bone M. & Meltzer H. (1989) *The Prevalence of Disability among Children.* Office of Population Censuses and Surveys, HMSO, London.

Flynn N. (1990) *Public Sector Management.* Harvester Wheatsheaf, New York.

Fraser D. (1984) *The Evolution of the British Welfare State*, 2nd edn. Macmillan, London.

Fry J., Brooks D., & McColl I. (1984) *NHS Data Book.* MTP Press, Lancaster.

Ham C. (1992) *Health Policy in Britain: The Politics and Organisation of the National Health Service*, 3rd edn. Macmillan, London.

Higgins J. (1988) *The Business of Medicine.* Macmillan, London.

Illich I. (1990) *Limits to Medicine: Medical Nemesis: The Expropriation of Health.* Penguin, London.

Jefferys M. & Sachs H. (1983) *Rethinking General Practice: Dilemmas in Primary Care.* Tavistock, London.

Klein R. (1989) *The Politics of the NHS*, 2nd edn. Longman, London.

Martin J., Meltzer H. & Elliot D. (1988) *The Prevalence of Disability among Adults.* Office of Population Censuses and Surveys, HMSO, London.

Office of Health Economics (1989) *Compendium of Health Statistics*, 7th edn. Office of Health Economics, London.

Parker G. (1990) *With Due Care and Attention: A Review of Research on Informal Care*, 2nd edn. Policy Studies Centre, London.

Secretaries of State for Health, Social Security, Wales and Scotland (1989) *Caring for People: Community Care in the Next Decade and Beyond.* Cm 849. HMSO, London.

Sharma U. (1992) *Complementary Medicine Today: Practitioners and Patients.* Tavistock/Routledge, London.

Strauss A.L., Fagerhaugh S., Suczek B. & Weiner C. (1985) *Social Organisation of Medical Work.* University of Chicago Press, London.

Tinker A. (1992) *Elderly People in Modern Society*, 3rd edn. Longman, London.

Further reading

Abercrombie N., Warde A., Southill K., Urry J. & Walby S. (1988) *Contemporary British Society.* Blackwell, Oxford.

Part II
Health, Illness and Social Structure

Chapter 3
Approaches to Health and Health Care

For most people the idea of health care probably conjures up images of doctors and nurses working in surgeries, clinics, and hospitals, using a range of medical technology. It is hardly surprising that health and health care have been so positively associated with medicine. We have grown up with a health care system, the main part of which is devoted to trying to restore people to health through treatments of one sort or another. Not only do we pay a great deal for this service through taxes and, perhaps, private health insurance schemes, but we are also grateful for the service we receive and tend, on the whole, to be trusting and compliant patients. As far as most people are concerned one of the major obstacles to improving the nation's health is that we do not have enough doctors, nurses and hospitals. However, the influence of medicine is not confined to treating the sick. Not only are medical institutions becoming more interested in 'screening' people for signs of disease, or vulnerability to disease such as raised cholesterol levels, but health care experts have also become increasingly powerful in influencing how people should, or should not, behave.

It has been argued that in terms of social control, or regulating human behaviour, medicine is taking over some of the functions previously associated with established religion (Turner 1987). The religious distinction between good and evil is being replaced by the medical distinction between what is healthy and unhealthy. For example, exhortations to regulate sexual activity are based less on (spiritual) grounds of the 'sinfulness' of promiscuity and more on the (medical) grounds of the threat to physical health from sexually transmitted diseases such as AIDS. In this chapter we shall examine the bio-medical model of health, the contribution of clinical medicine to improving health and the more recent 'medicalization' of behaviour. We shall then look at sociological approaches to health and consider the implications for health care in general and nursing in particular.

The bio-medical model of health

The development of medical science is most often depicted in terms of a series of spectacular breakthroughs, such as Pasteur's discovery of vaccinations. Each new discovery is another rung on a ladder of progress by which people are steadily climbing away from a state of disease and early death towards longer and healthier lives. It is this 'heroic' and steadily progressing view of medicine that is normally given in the history books. Contemporary medicine and health care is presented in much the same way. The media tends to concentrate on the dramatic, for example, TV appeals for donors to save lives or items on communities clubbing together to send a child away somewhere for a 'last chance' operation. Similarly, television documentaries on health are usually about new insights in medical research, with new cures 'round the corner' or, more recently, about cuts in the health service disrupting vital life-saving work. Literary and dramatic fiction, even when located at the rough end of health work as in BBC's *Casualty*, also tends to reinforce the heroic aspects of personalized health care.

From this perspective, health work is seen as a war waged by doctors and nurses against an impersonal enemy called disease. The nature of this war is determined by the state of medical science and technology. The idea that people's health (at least in our relatively affluent society) is predominantly a reflection of science's understanding of the disease process and the development of effective treatments can be called a bio-medical model of health. In this model:

- health is the absence of biological abnormality
- the human body is likened to a machine to be restored to health through treatments of one sort or another which arrest, or reverse, the disease process, and
- the health of a society is seen as largely dependent on the state of medical knowledge and the availability of medical resources.

The bio-medical model of health underpins the organization and delivery of health care in the modern world. Medical research is predominantly based around understanding the underlying biochemical or genetic disease process with a view to discovering cures. Hospital based, high technology medicine receives the majority of health care budgets (about two thirds in the UK for example). The general education of most health care professionals revolves around understanding the body and intervening to restore health, and the most prestigious and highly paid members of the health care professions are the experts in curative medicine, the hospital consultants and the leaders of medical research teams.

The origin of this situation can be found in the late nineteenth and early twentieth centuries. During this period there were great advances in medical science, such as the discovery and treatment of bacterial infection, new safer surgical techniques and developments in pharmacology. It was optimistically expected in developed countries after the Second World War that a much greater investment in health care and medical research would quickly be reflected in improvements in health standards. The argument behind such optimism went something like this: scientific medicine has already conquered the diseases that were major killers in the past, such as TB and polio and given time and proper investment, it will overcome the diseases of modern society, such as cancer, heart diseases, arthritis and mental illness.

How valid is this claim and how true is the assertion about the past on which it rests? In the developed world life expectancy has increased significantly in the past two centuries. But what exactly was medicine's role? We consider this question in the following section.

Infectious disease: the role of medicine

The work of most doctors and nurses is a series of individual cases which present a succession of specific problems where 'success' is judged in terms of improvements in the individual patient's health. However, another way of looking at health is to examine rates of health and illness in populations. This 'epidemiological' approach tries to document the health of a society by looking at a range of 'health indicators' such as its rate of mortality (the proportion of people dying each year). In terms of this criterion Britain, like the rest of the western world, has become much 'healthier' over the past century and a half. In 1851 the annual death rate was 22.7 per 1000 and life expectancy at birth was around 40 years. By 1990 the death rate had dropped to 11.9, and average life expectancy had almost doubled (Table 3.1).

The dramatic decline in the death rate from the middle of the last century was largely due to a fall in deaths from infectious diseases (Table 3.2). It was generally believed that clinical intervention played a major part in this process and, therefore, new developments in treatment would provide further improvements in health. Although this remains the dominant view, it has been questioned by several authorities within medicine. The distinguished immunologist, Macfarlane Burnett (1971), acknowledged the importance of medical intervention in controlling

Table 3.1   Expectation of life from birth, United Kingdom.

	Males	Females
1901	48	52
1931	58	62
1951	66	71
1971	69	75
1991	73	79

Source   Adapted from Table 7.4 of Central Statistical Office (1992) *Social Trends 1992*. Central Statistical Office, HMSO, London. (Reproduced by permission of Central Statistical Office.)

Table 3.2   Reduction of mortality 1848–54 to 1971: England and Wales.

	Percentage of reduction
Conditions attributable to micro-organisms	
(1) Airborne diseases	40
(2) Water- and food-borne diseases	21
(3) Other conditions	13
Total	74
Conditions not attributable to micro-organisms	26
All diseases	100

Source   T. McKeown (1979) *The Role of Medicine*. Blackwell Publishers, Oxford. (Reproduced by permission of Blackwell Publishers.)

bacterial infection, but suggested that the contribution of laboratory science may have come to an end. He argued that the diseases of modern society are caused by genetic disorders or social problems, such as over-population or pollution, which impinge on health. In his view, laboratory research has little to contribute to either of these problems.

Other critics have even questioned the contribution of clinical medicine in the past. In a celebrated work, Dubos (1960) argued that patterns of health and disease result from difficulties in adapting to a changed environment. The infectious diseases of nineteenth century industrial societies were largely a product of urban poverty and filth, and subsequent improvements in health owed much more to public health reforms than to medical intervention. The fact that there were developments in clinical medicine at the same time was incidental. Regarding the weight commonly given to the medical contribution, Dubos writes that 'when the tide is receding it is so easy to have the illusion that one can empty the ocean by removing water with a pail' (p. 23).

The question of the role of medicine in the decline of the infectious diseases has been investigated most systematically by McKeown (1976; 1979). By tracing the history of specific infectious diseases and seeing how many people were dying from them each year, McKeown was able to show that, in most cases, deaths from infections were declining long before effective medical treatment was generally available. This can be illustrated by looking at the history of some of the major infectious diseases: TB, scarlet fever, whooping cough and measles (Fig. 3.1).

The same broad pattern, with immunization and treatment playing a relatively minor part in the falling death rate, can be seen in the history of almost all the infectious diseases. The only exceptions being smallpox, diphtheria and, more recently, polio where immunization was an important factor. Of course, McKeown's observations do not mean that the availability of medical remedies is not important. Programmes of immunization against infection are a safeguard against the spread of certain infections. However, the fact that medical intervention played little part in the decline of the infectious diseases means that it is necessary to look for other explanations.

The public health measures of the nineteenth century, particularly those leading to cleaner water supplies, had a major part to play in reducing exposure to water- and food-borne infections such as cholera. However, that does not explain the decline in deaths from airborne infections, such as TB, which accounted for 40% of the total decline (Table 3.2). According to McKeown, the major reason for the declining death rate was that the human organism became stronger and more resistant to disease due to improved living conditions. The reasons for this, in order of importance were:

- Improved nutrition, resulting from improvements in agricultural production due initially to the introduction of new crops such as potatoes and maize, and later to mechanization and chemical fertilizers.
- Improvements in hygiene, particularly purification of water and sewage disposal and, later, food hygiene. This played a major part in the decline of water- and food-borne infections, which accounted for about a fifth of the total decline.
- Behavioural change, especially contraception and personal hygiene. The reduction in the birth rate not only led to better living standards but also ensured that the benefits of increased agricultural production were not wiped out by excessive population increase.
- Immunization and therapy had little effect on the reduction of mortality until the introduction of sulphonamides in 1935. Since the 1930s immunization and therapy have been important influences.

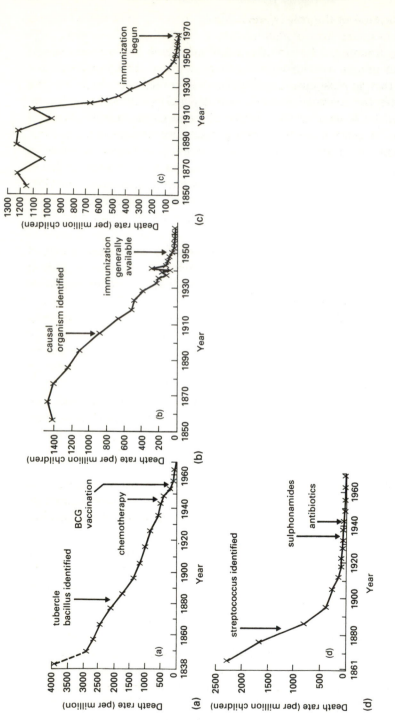

Fig. 3.1   The medical contribution to the decline in infectious diseases. (a) Respiratory tuberculosis: death rates, England and Wales. (b) Whooping cough: death rates of children under 15, England and Wales. (c) Measles: death rates of children under 15, England and Wales. (d) Scarlet fever: death rates of children under 15, England and Wales. (*Source*   T. McKeown (1976) *The Modern Rise of Population.* Arnold, London. © Thomas McKeown 1976. (Reproduced by permission of Edward Arnold (Publishers) Limited.))

Overmedication and iatrogenesis

As health in the past was influenced primarily by environmental change, McKeown argues that the best prospects for improving health in the future lie with changing, or at least moderating the effects of, the environmental factors associated with the diseases of modern society. He suggests that we are misusing our precious health care resources at present by directing most of them into high technology curative medical treatments which have a very limited power to influence patterns of health. Recently, Canada's health care has come under a scathing attack from a book which reached the bestseller lists (Rachlis & Kushner 1989). Developing the ideas of McKeown the authors show that the Canadian health care system, despite being acknowledged as one of the best in the world in terms of access and quality, has had relatively little impact on the health of the Canadian people. They argue that good health has been mistakenly equated with good medical care and advocate a shift in resources from curative to primary health care, with nurse practitioners playing a major role in 'well person' care.

Other critics go further than McKeown, arguing that modern medicine's obsession with technology and drug therapy is leading to an 'epidemic' of iatrogenic (i.e. doctor caused) disease. Adverse reactions to prescribed drugs, complications following surgery and the high rates of accidents in hospitals are all examples of iatrogenesis.

In a wide-ranging critique, Taylor (1979) claims that medicine has become a 'malignant' technology which is out of control. New technological procedures are now being applied without proper testing regarding both their value or their safety. Taylor cites evidence from university teaching hospitals showing that, excluding surgical complications and nursing errors, 20% of patients suffered some form of iatrogenic disease. There is also a 'multiplier' effect, with technology breeding technology. For example, induction of labour made premature birth more likely. This resulted in techniques such as ultrasound, x-ray and examination of amniotic fluid to determine foetal age and avoid some of the problems associated with prematurity. Hospitals are not the only source of iatrogenic disease; four out of five visits to a GP now result in the writing of a prescription. Melville and Johnson (1983) estimated that in Britain as many as 10 000 people die each year from (medical) drug-induced deaths, more than are killed on the roads.

Illich (1990) in what is probably the most radical critique, extends the concept of iatrogenesis and argues that the detrimental effects of medicine go beyond direct clinical harm. He accuses the 'medical establishment' – by which he means health care professionals, health administrators, pharmaceutical companies, the suppliers of medical equipment and other commercial institutions – of sponsoring sickness by creating unrealistic health demands which can then only be met by health care services and medical products (social iatrogenesis). Not only are more and more treatments being made available for long-recognized diseases, but more areas of life are being brought under the scrutiny and control of health care professionals. Experiences that were once seen as a normal part of the human condition, such as pregnancy, childbirth, childhood, unhappiness, ageing and dying have now been brought under the medical remit. Illich claims that the result of this increasing 'medicalization' of life is that health professionals have undermined people's ability to manage their own health and to cope with the pain and suffering that are an inevitable part of the human condition (cultural iatrogenesis). He argues that people 'unlearn the acceptance of suffering as an inevitable part of their conscious coping with reality and learn to interpret every ache as an indicator of their need for padding and pampering'. Similarly, as most people now die being treated in hospitals, death is seen less as an inevitability and more as a failure of treatment, something that ought not to have happened and which people find more difficult to accept and come to terms with (Chapter 9).

Illich argues that the professional dominance of medicine over healing should be broken and that people be encouraged to take more responsibility for their own health. This kind of critique is part of a much wider reaction against the dominance of scientific and technological expertise over ordinary people's lives and this, in turn, is seen as a consequence of the continuing process of industrialization.

Navarro (1975) offers an alternative interpretation. He locates the causes of overmedication and iatrogenesis in the capitalist political economy of modern western societies. Capitalist economies produce goods and services largely for profit and people are encouraged to consume and judge their 'success' in terms of what they have. Capitalist societies are thus geared around consumption, and the increasing consumption of health care services and medical goods has to be placed into this context. According to Navarro, health care professionals do not cause overmedication, they merely administer it on behalf of organizations such as private hospitals and pharmaceutical companies, who profit from it.

It is important to place these various critiques of bio-medicine into context. First, rates of medical cure have increased spectacularly in some areas (skin cancer and leukaemia for example). Second, by confining themselves to mortality rates as a 'measure' of health, McKeown and others have underestimated the contribution of clinical medicine to improving the quality of people's lives by, for example, controlling pain, restoring eyesight, improving mobility and so on. Third, critics of

McKeown have questioned the extent to which it is useful to speculate about the control of degenerative disease from a history of *infectious* diseases (Lever 1977). Finally, in respect of Illich's critique, there is no clear evidence that people necessarily give up responsibility for their health as a necessary consequence of medicalization. For example, middle-class Americans are probably the most highly medicalized people on earth. Yet many of them have not given up responsibility for their own health. On the contrary, they jog, work-out in gymnasiums, control their diet and show interest in a variety of forms of alternative healing.

However, the work of McKeown and others such as McKinlay and McKinlay (1977) – who came to the same conclusions about the effect of medicine on American health – has demonstrated the links between health and environmental factors beyond reasonable doubt. Most of the major diseases of modern society remain stubbornly resistant to medical cure while the resources for researching and treating them become squeezed in most developed societies (Chapter 2). In recent years attention, including the attention of governments and health professionals, is increasingly focusing on factors outside the health care system. An argument which is growing in influence in the present climate is that health depends less on what doctors and nurses do for patients and more on what people do for themselves.

The behavioural model of health

McKeown has argued that, while nutrition and hygiene were the major influences on health in the past, and remain so in the developing world, industrialization and affluence have brought a new set of health problems. There is growing evidence to suggest that the diseases of modern society are linked to 'behavioural' factors – such as sedentary life styles, refined diet and widespread use of drugs such as alcohol and tobacco – all of which are in principle preventable. Health professionals have become increasingly interested in the extent to which people, in part at least, 'bring about' their own health problems. For example, a report by the Medical Services Study Group of the Royal College of Physicians (1978) investigated 250 cases of people who had died before reaching the age of 50. They concluded that in 98 cases patients had contributed to their own deaths by behaviour such as overeating, drinking, smoking, or not complying with treatment.

In recent years doctors and, to a lesser degree, nurses have been at the forefront of campaigns to educate people into 'healthier' behaviour. There is something moralistic in the tone of many of these pronouncements. Whereas religious institutions once warned people of punishments waiting in the after-life for sinful behaviour, health professionals now warn of the dangers waiting in this life for those who engage in unhealthy behaviour. The Report of the Royal College of Physicians cited above states:

'Our initial finding will come as no surprise to the profession. Doctors have been saying for years that the causes of many of the diseases of middle life are not mysteries, but are contributed to by overeating, excess alcohol and tobacco.' (p. 1062)

On the other hand good, or healthy, behaviour has its rewards. McKeown cites research which assessed the effects on health of seven rules:

- don't smoke cigarettes
- sleep for seven hours
- eat breakfast
- keep weight down
- drink moderately
- exercise daily
- don't eat between meals.

The researchers concluded that health and longevity increased with the number of rules followed. Life expectancy at age 45 was 11 years longer for people following six or seven rules than for those following less than four (Belloc & Breslow 1972). As McKeown observed, 'virtue is not often so handsomely rewarded' (p. 87). More recently, the Government's strategy for health in England, *The Health of the Nation* (1992) stresses the importance of life style and behavioural factors. For example, the main 'strategies' for combating heart disease and stroke, which together accounted for 38% of deaths in England in 1991, were to encourage people to stop smoking, increase physical activity and reduce consumption of saturated fatty acids, sodium and alcohol (p. 47).

In recent years nurses have become increasingly involved with educating patients and promoting healthy life styles. Ewles and Simnet (1985) distinguish between primary, secondary and tertiary health education carried out by nurses. Primary health education is concerned with encouraging people to behave in ways that will help them to avoid disease or injury. This involves nurses not only helping to educate individual patients, but also working in schools, colleges and other community institutions developing programmes of education on things such as diet, misuse of drugs and generally encouraging young people to take more responsibility for their own health. Secondary health education is concerned with halting or reversing the development of an existing disease or condition. This may include the nurse encouraging high risk groups to make use of screening services or spotting signs of disability or developmental delay in children. In tertiary health education nurses aim at helping to prevent further complications where disease already exists so that the best possible level of health may be maintained; for example, giving guidance about diet to diabetic patients or helping patients adjust to irreversible disability.

Social aspects of health

Sociologists, while not necessarily disputing the importance of behavioural factors on health, nor the benefits of health education, have questioned over-simplified behavioural theories in a number of ways. Three main types of criticism have been made. First, that the social context of behaviour is ignored. Second, that many factors affecting health status lie outside the control of individuals. Third, that such programmes can become a form of social control.

The social context

Sociologists emphasize that human behaviour, including health behaviour, has to be understood in terms of the social context from which it emerges. When studied from the point of view of the people concerned, behaviour which may appear to be 'irrational' from a distance may actually have a 'rationality' of its own. Smoking behaviour among working class women provides a good example of this.

In the last two decades smoking has been identified as the major preventable cause of disease in the modern world. In general, people from the working classes have been less responsive to anti-smoking campaigns than the middle classes. Working-class women with children have become a priority target for health educationalists, not only for the damage they may be doing to their own health but also because their children are affected directly by 'passive smoking' and indirectly by 'socialization' into smoking behaviour. In a study of women in low income families caring for pre-school children, Graham (1987) argues that smoking must be set in the context of both poverty and motherhood. The women in her study who smoked exhibited more stress symptoms than those who did not and smoking was part of a central strategy by which they were able to maintain their caring role and protect their children when their calm broke down. For some women in the study smoking was associated with breaks from caring. As one woman put it, 'I smoke when I'm sitting down, having a cup of coffee. It's part and parcel of resting'. Graham argues that smoking, rather than being purely negative, has a paradoxical place in the lives of the women she studied. On the one hand, by helping women to cope with caring, it promotes family welfare; on the other hand it increases the risks of ill-health. This type of research shows that behavioural factors cannot easily be separated from the circumstances of people's everyday existence. Without such understanding, it is all too easy to blame individuals for unhealthy behaviour which has much deeper roots than their fecklessness or ignorance. Health education programmes, or the individual efforts of primary health workers such as community nurses, which fail to understand the meaning that behaviour has for individuals, are unlikely to be successful.

Social causes of ill-health

A second major criticism that sociologists make of behavioural theories is that many of the factors which influence health are outside the direct control of individuals. For example, poor health has been associated with material, or economic, factors such as poverty, poor housing, unemployment and manual work (Chapter 4). These 'deprivation' factors persist even after controlling for behavioural influences, such as smoking and alcohol consumption (Slater *et al.* 1985). Research has also consistently found links between emotionally stressful life events, the quality of people's social relationships and their health (Chapter 5).

The search for better health involves more than trying to change individual behaviour. The World Health Organization (1984) has recognized this by defining health promotion as, 'the process of enabling people to increase control over their health'. Ziglio (1992) argues that a 'structuralist', or social, approach to health promotion involves interventions in the form of the re-allocation of resources, community action, government legislation and, perhaps, more general social change to help produce safer and healthier environments. Tones *et al.* (1990) have examined some of the implications of this for nursing. They argue that nurses adopting this view can 'educate' patients not only about the health implications of their own behaviour but also about economic and social factors which can undermine health. They also suggest that the community nurse in particular can work with groups who have the power to bring about change.

Despite the rhetoric of social change contained in documents such as the Ottawa Charter for Health Promotion, most commentators acknowledge that, in practice, health promotion campaigns and policies still tend to be directed towards individual 'failings'. Critics such as Ziglio (1992) argue that health promotion policies which are focused too much on individual behaviour run the risk of blaming the victim, as our earlier example of smoking behaviour illustrates. They may serve to detract attention from the socio-economic influences on health and may also be used to legitimize rationing and cutting health services.

Social control

A third sociological approach suggests that health professionals some-times exercise a form of social control (Chapter 1) over patients that may have important ethical implications. This critique is most commonly applied to doctors, particularly when patients are institutionalized. For example, it has been widely argued that, by calling behaviour such as madness, alcoholism and anorexia 'diseases' and treating people (sometimes against their will) psychiatrists are controlling rather than caring for their patients (Chapter 8). However, some of these arguments can also be applied to 'community health care' and to nursing in parti-cular. For example, health visiting is a preventive service offering advice and support to families, especially to mothers of young children. The health visitor–client relationship is based on the trust and consent of the client. However, in certain cases, and without informing families, health visitors are expected to discover confidential information about families which is then routinely passed on to multi-disciplinary teams, including social services, probation service and the police (Taylor & Tilley 1989). What, in other circumstances, would be seen as an unacceptable viola-tion of families' civil liberties has been justified on the 'medical' and preventive grounds that, as experts in child care, health visitors can recognize the 'symptoms' that may lead to poor child health, or even to child abuse and neglect. In short family life and child care have been 'medicalized' and inadequate child care, child abuse and neglect likened to 'diseases'. This then legitimizes 'surveillance' by health care profes-sionals, including community nurses.

In recent years, health professionals, including nurses, have re-dis-covered prevention and in many ways this is a positive move. However, nurses (and other health professionals) should be aware that preventive work that goes beyond mere advice and education may have unintended consequences. For example, Taylor and Tilley (1989) have argued that involving health visitors more in the management of child protection, and asking them to monitor families without their knowledge or consent, is threatening the basis of trust on which health visiting rests and may in time undermine important general health and educational work.

Medicine and the care of the sick

In the previous sections we have observed how doctors and nurses are once more becoming more involved in the maintenance of health and the prevention of disease. Project 2000 has stressed the importance of thinking based on concepts of 'health'. However, 'prevention' is in some ways a misleading term in that sickness in individuals can never be prevented, only postponed. Everybody is going to fall ill at some time and the majority of health care professionals, including the majority of nurses, are going to be involved in one way or another in the care of sick and disabled people.

In the context of caring for the sick, critics such as McKeown (1979) have argued that the dominance of the bio-medical model means that the bulk of health care resources are devoted to the investigation and treatment of acute illness at the expense of other conditions, such as many forms of chronic illness and disability, where the scope for medical treatment is limited or non-existent. Such selectivity has been justified on the grounds that this represents the most effective use of resources as improvements in treatment, such as advances in surgery and diagnostic technology, are a major reason for improvements in health.

This argument can be questioned on at least three grounds. First, as we have seen, the major determinants of the health of *populations* lie outside the influence of medical science and technology. Second, while some medical treatments are clearly of great benefit to *individuals*, the value of many others is questionable. For example, it was widely believed in the health care professions that the value of expensive coronary care units (CCUs) in reducing mortality after heart attacks was obvious. Therefore, randomized clinical trials to 'test' their value would be unethical, as mortality would be far higher amongst the group not admitted to CCUs. However, when clinical trials were conducted in Britain, researchers found little difference in mortality rates between patients treated in CCUs and those cared for at home (Hill 1978). In fact, if anything there was a slight bias in favour of home care. In this context medical critics have argued there should be a much more rigorous evaluation of the effectiveness and efficiency of medical procedures.

Third, if the benefits of health care were evaluated in terms of improving the *quality* of patients' lives, rather than merely correcting biological abnormality, then the case for moving some resources from the treatment of acute illness (which sometimes gives the patient only an extra few weeks, or days, of life) to the care of the chronically sick becomes much stronger. A great deal more could be done to improve the lives of the long-term sick, disabled, mentally disordered and the dying. However, the dominance of the bio-medical model means that the services devoted to these groups tend to be seriously underfunded and are sometimes referred to as the 'Cinderella' services.

Summary

In this chapter we have looked at the bio-medical model of health and questioned its ability to improve significantly life expectancy and the general health of populations. Unfortunately, carefully argued critiques of the *limits* of medicine have been generalized by some sociologists and nurses into a crude rhetoric that all medicine is more or less useless and the dominance of medicine is some sort of 'conspiracy' on the part of doctors. Such overstated responses overlook the many contributions of clinical medicine, They also deny the simple fact that for many seriously ill people, medicine represents a last hope to live a normal lifespan. As long as medical treatment offers that hope, most sick people and their relatives will expect it to be used. It is likely, then, that bio-medicine will continue to exert a major influence on health services, and many nurses will continue to work with doctors to try to restore people to health. In this respect nurses require more, not less, training in the biological sciences to enable them to take more responsibility for the diagnosis and treatment of patients.

Second, we examined the importance of social and behavioural influences on health and the increasing nurse involvement with health promotion. In this context, sociological research can make an important contribution in uncovering relationships between the health of people and factors in their physical and psychological environments. Finally, we looked at the way in which care of the sick had become synonymous with treatment, and considered a powerful argument for giving more attention to the care of the long-term sick and disabled. In this context, sociological research has provided valuable insights into patient experiences of chronic illness, disability, mental disorder and death, dying and bereavement. We examine these issues in Part III.

References

Belloc N. & Breslow L. (1972) Relationship of physical health status and health practices. *Preventive Medicine*, 1, 409–15.

Burnett M. (1971) *Genes, Dreams and Realities*. Medical and Technical, Aylesbury.

Central Statistical Office (1992) *Social Trends 1992*. Central Statistical Office, HMSO, London.

Dubos R. (1960) *The Mirage of Health*. Allen and Unwin, London.

Ewles L. & Simnet E. (1985) *Promoting Health: A Practical Guide in Health Education.* Wiley, Chichester.

Graham H. (1987) Women's Smoking and Family Health. *Social Science and Medicine*, **25**, 47–57.

Hill J. (1978) A randomized trial of home versus hospital management for patients with suspected myocardial infarction. *Lancet*, **1**, 832–7.

Illich I. (1990) *Limits to Medicine: Medical Nemesis: The Expropriation of Health.* Penguin, London.

Lever A. (1977) Medicine under challenge. *Lancet*, **1**, 353–5.

McKeown T. (1976) *The Modern Rise of Population.* Arnold, London.

McKeown T. (1979) *The Role of Medicine.* Blackwell, Oxford.

McKinlay J. & McKinlay S. (1977) The questionable contribution of medical measures to the decline in mortality in the United States in the twentieth century. *Milbank Memorial Fund Quarterly*, **55**, 405–28.

Medical Services Study Group of the Royal College of Physicians of London (1978) Deaths under 50. *British Medical Journal*, **2**, 1061–62.

Melville A. & Johnson C. (1983) *Cured to Death.* New English Library, Sevenoaks.

Navarro V. (1975) The industrialisation of fetishism and the fetishism of industrialisation: a critique of Ivan Illich. *International Journal of the Health Services*, **5**, 351–71.

Rachlis M. & Kushner C. (1989) *Second Opinion: What's Wrong with Canada's Health Care System and How to Fix it.* Harper & Collins, Toronto.

Secretary of State for Health and Social Services (1992) *The Health of the Nation.* HMSO, London.

Slater C., Lorimer R. & Lairson D. (1985) The independent contributions of socio-economic status and health practices to health status. *Preventive Medicine*, **14**, 372–8.

Taylor R. (1979) *Medicine Out of Control.* Sun, Victoria.

Taylor S. & Tilley N.(1989) Health visitors and child protection: conflict, contradictions and ethical dilemmas. *Health Visitor*, **62**, 273–5.

Tones K., Tilford S. & Robinson Y. (1990) *Health Education: Effectiveness and Efficiency.* Chapman & Hall, London.

Turner B. (1987) *Medical Power and Social Knowledge.* Sage, London.

World Health Organisation (1984) *Health Promotion: A discussion document on the concept and principles.* Regional Office for Europe, Copenhagen.

Ziglio E. (1992) Indicators of health promotion policy: directions for research. In *Health Promotion Research* (Ed. by B. Badura & I. Kickbusch), World Health Organization.

Further reading

Black N., Boswell D., Gray A., Murphy S. & Popay J. (Eds) (1984) *Health and Disease: a Reader.* Open University, Milton Keynes.

Chapter 4
Inequalities and Differences in Health

In the previous chapter we saw that there have been great improvements in the health of the British population as a whole during the twentieth century. However, there remain significant differences and inequalities in health and health care particularly with respect to class, ethnicity and gender (MacIntyre 1986; Haynes 1991). In this chapter each of these will be analysed in turn, although it should be remembered that in practice they are inextricably intertwined giving rise to complex patterns of cross-cutting advantage and disadvantage. It should also be noted that health is but one aspect of a range of inequalities associated with these social divisions. Class, ethnicity and gender profoundly influence opportunities for education, housing, employment, leisure, welfare benefits, political influence, social prestige and much more besides. Hence, for some people illness and disease are part of a pattern of multiple deprivation that shapes their whole lives.

Class inequalities in health and health care

The concept of class

Class comprises the social relationships people make in earning a living. Two main aspects of these relationships can be distinguished: market situation and work situation. Market situation refers to relationships made in buying or selling labour, for example when the owner of a factory hires an operative to work on the assembly line in return for a wage. Work situation refers to all the social relationships people make in carrying out their occupational task; for example, in the course of a working day a nurse might interact with doctors, students, ward clerks, porters, administrators, and other nurses. For most people, market situation determines their income whilst work situation determines major aspects of their daily environment.

Groups of occupations tend to have similar market and work situations. Thus, most people in professional occupations (e.g. doctors, lawyers and accountants) tend to earn high salaries and exercise a good deal of authority in the workplace. In contrast, most members of unskilled manual occupations (such as porters and general labourers) tend to earn low incomes and have little control over their own work or that of others. Clusters of occupations with similar market and work situations can be ranked in a hierarchy of rewards. The distinction between non-manual ('middle-class') and manual ('working-class') occupations provides a very rough and ready division of advantage and opportunity. More sophisticated classifications typically identify a greater range of occupational groupings.

The Registrar General's Classification of Occupational Classes has been of great importance (see Table 4.1). With various amendments, this has been used to collect official statistics on health and health care since the early part of this century. It identifies six occupational groupings which reflect the market rewards each is able to command. It should be noted that there are various problems with this scheme. For example, men are allocated to a class position on the basis of their own occupations whilst married women are classified according to the occupation of their husbands. This is problematic for several reasons, not least because a great many married couples have jobs that are in different occupational categories. In the Registrar General's scheme social status or prestige, in addition to market factors, have influenced the placing of occupations in particular strata. Furthermore, little attempt is made to distinguish between people with the same occupational title but very different salaries or resources. For these reasons there is a degree of variation within, as well as between, bands. Despite these problems, however, the Registrar General's Classification is used very widely in research and in official statistics.

Table 4.1 The Registrar General's Classification of Occupational Classes.

Occupational class	Example
Social Class I Professional	doctors and lawyers
Social Class II Intermediate non-manual	teachers, nurses, most managers and senior administrators
Social Class IIIN Skilled non-manual	clerks and shop assistants
Social Class IIIM Skilled manual	bricklayers, underground coalminers and bus drivers
Social Class IV Semi-skilled manual	bus conductor and postman
Social Class V Unskilled manual	porters, cleaners and labourers

Evidence of class inequalities in health and health care

In the nineteenth century, class inequalities in life expectation and health were very marked. Rising standards of living, the introduction of the NHS and changes in patterns of disease might have been expected to lead to their disappearance. In fact, inequalities in health between the classes have remained substantial, and may even have increased, during the twentieth century (Townsend *et al.* 1988a).

Table 4.2 shows that men in Social Class V are 2.5 times more likely to die before retirement age than those in Social Class I. Death rates among women in Social Class V are nearly twice those of women in Social Class I. Class inequalities characterize over four-fifths of officially recorded causes of death. Some diseases popularly regarded as middle-class scourges, such as heart diseases, are actually more prevalent among low-skill manual workers. Measures of disability, long-standing chronic sickness and health-related absence from work show similar patterns of disadvantage.

Class inequalities also characterize infant mortality. Babies born to Class V parents are nearly twice as likely as those born into Social Class I homes to die before their first birthdays. Low birth-weight, often closely associated with infant mortality, is also more common in the lower social classes. Moreover, low birth-weight babies born into more affluent homes have better survival chances. Class inequalities are particularly sharp among those categories of infants known to be generally 'at risk', for example first babies of women aged 35 and over.

One way of estimating the significance of class inequalities in health is

Table 4.2 Occupational class and deaths of adults: standardized mortality ratios*, Great Britain, 1979–80 and 1982–83.

	Males (aged 20–64)	Females (aged 20–59)
Social Class I	66	69
Social Class II	76	78
Social Class IIIN	94	87
Social Class IIIM	106	100
Social Class IV	116	110
Social Class V	165	134
All classes	100	100
Ratio V/I	2.5	1.9

Source Office of Population Censuses and Surveys (1986) *Occupational Mortality: Decennial Supplement 1979–80, 1982–3.* Office of Population Censuses and Surveys, HMSO, London. (Reproduced by permission of Office of Population Censuses and Surveys.)

* Standardized mortality ratios represent the mortality of sub-groups within a population as a percentage of the mortality of the population as a whole.

to calculate so-called 'excess deaths': that is, the additional numbers of people who would survive if the more favourable health patterns of the professional and managerial classes applied more generally in the population. In the three year period 1970–72 alone, had Social Classes IV and V enjoyed the same mortality rates as Social Class I over 74 000 lives would have been saved.

The egalitarian principles of the NHS (Chapter 2, Chapter 11) ensure that class inequalities in health care in Britain are considerably less than in societies, such as the USA, where services are mainly provided in exchange for fees. Nevertheless, some class differences remain. People in manual occupations consult their GPs, and are admitted to hospital, more frequently than those in professional and white collar jobs. This would be expected, bearing in mind their greater medical needs. There are, however, geographical inequalities in the provision of services. Historically, NHS expenditure has been greatest in regions of the country with the highest proportion of middle-class people. Standards of premises, equipment and GP training are significantly worse in inner city areas and some local authority estates. In addition, middle-class patients appear to receive a better quality of service. Doctors tend to give longer consultations, more information and communicate more easily with their middle-class patients. Class inequalities are particularly marked in the use of preventive services. Many of these are intended to detect abnormalities at an early stage (e.g. cervical cytology screening, antenatal services, routine dental care). Others prevent illness by measures such as vaccination, immunization or health education. People in lower income groups make significantly less use of such facilities and appear to be less aware of health education programmes.

Explaining class divisions in health

The Black Report (Townsend *et al.* 1988a) has been very influential in shaping the debate about explanations for class inequalities in health and health care (Blane 1985, Carr-Hill 1987). This study, commissioned by the DHSS in the late 1970s, identified four different strategies for explaining class inequalities in health, commonly referred to as artefact, social selection, materialist, and cultural/behavioural theories.

Artefact theory

Artefact theory asserts that the apparent relationship between class and health is spurious, because various sources of distortion and bias have entered the calculation and interpretation of the statistics rendering them unreliable and invalid. Sociologists take the view that all bodies of statistics are social products, reflecting the methods and assumptions of those who devised them (Chapter 1). Thus, official mortality and morbidity statistics are shaped by the recording and classifying procedures adopted by doctors, nurses, coroners, statisticians and others. Errors and distortions can creep in at each stage of the compilation process. Where mistakes follow a pattern, sets of apparently objective statistics may foster quite false impressions. What is more, errors may be compounded when two different data sets (e.g. death certificate and census materials) are combined in order to calculate mortality rates for particular classes.

Artefact theorists also question the interpretation of evidence. Nowadays most deaths occur among retired people. Data about those in employment might, therefore, be a poor guide to the overall picture. There are also difficulties in applying the Registrar General's classificatory scheme to women, so in practice much of the focus is on males only. Furthermore, the Registrar General's classifications must be revised over the years as patterns of employment change. Some occupational groupings (such as professional, technical and managerial occupations) have rapidly expanded in size whilst others (such as unskilled manual workers) have shrunk considerably. This makes comparisons over time hazardous and raises doubts about the wisdom of focusing on Social Class V. Difficulties are also created by the internal diversity of the Registrar General's six occupational classifications, each of which includes a range of occupations with differing mortality rates.

Various ways have been found to rebut these technical criticisms. Corrections have been made to the statistics and more refined forms of analysis employed. New kinds of data have been generated, such as the Longitudinal Study, which avoid many sources of bias and provide evidence about the retired (Fox *et al.* 1985). Studies of specific groups of employees have provided valuable additional material. The outcome of all this has been to demonstrate a persistent and strong relationship between class and health. Moreover, it has been shown that the effect of some statistical errors has actually been to underestimate, rather than exaggerate, the extent of class inequalities in health (Bloor *et al.* 1987).

Artefact theorists alert us, then, to the social processes of production and interpretation of statistics. However, rigorous analysis of the data has reinforced rather than undermined the credibility of the relationship between class and health.

Social selection theory

This theory is based on the assumption that people in poor health are unlikely to hold on to well-paid jobs and are liable to move downward in the class hierarchy. Conversely, those with good health are said to be more likely to 'get on' (i.e. experience upward social mobility). Hence, it is argued, the higher social classes tend to collect the most healthy, and the lower classes the least healthy, members of each generation. These processes are said to account for class inequalities in health (West 1991).

Although some patients suffering from chronic illnesses (such as schizophrenia, bronchitis and epilepsy) do drift downwards in the occupational hierarchy, most sociologists are of the view that selection theories do not provide the main explanation for class inequalities in health. It is difficult to see how the specific risks associated with particular occupations can be explained in these terms. Thus, coal miners have high rates of respiratory diseases, such as pneumoconiosis and bronchitis, because of the exposure to hazards in work itself and not because of their social mobility prior to becoming colliers. Selection theory also has difficulty in accounting for class inequalities in infant deaths.

The most damaging criticisms of selection theory focus on the nature of social mobility itself. It is essential for the theory that health is a major determinant of the mobility chances of all individuals. In fact, however, educational achievement and family attitudes are far more important. Moreover, opportunities for mobility are heavily influenced by changes in the occupational structure itself, such as the expansion of professional, technical and managerial occupations during this century which provided many opportunities for the sons and daughters of manual workers to gain white collar jobs. Selection theory is based, then, on a mistaken analysis of the determinants of social mobility, and selection processes play only a marginal role in determining class inequalities in health.

Materialist theory

Materialist theories suggest that differences in the material circumstances of the social classes – such as income, housing, diet and working environment – are the key determinants of inequalities in health and the use of health care services. Both historical and contemporary evidence support this view (Blackburn 1991). As we saw in Chapter 3, increases in life expectation since the mid-nineteenth century are primarily due to improvements in material conditions. Increases in real wages led to improvements in diet and housing for the mass of the population. Public health measures, such as modern sanitation and clean water supplies, created safer urban environments. Measures such as these resulted in the decline of infectious diseases well before the advent of effective medical interventions and therapies (Chapter 3).

Townsend *et al.* (1988b) in a study of the North of England provide contemporary evidence of the close association between health and material deprivation. A detailed analysis of 678 electoral wards demonstrated close links between measures of material affluence (unemployment, car ownership, home ownership and household over-crowding) and measures of health (mortality, disability and low birth-weight). Direct measures of poverty and deprivation in a local area correlated more reliably with health than measures using the Registrar General's Classification of Occupational Classes. This probably reflects the diversity of occupations within each class grouping, referred to above. By focusing directly on poverty, wherever it is found, Townsend *et al.* identified a key determinant of health.

Links between low income and health are simple but devastating. Housing that is cold, damp, vermin-ridden or overcrowded creates well-known health hazards such as hypothermia, respiratory and parasitic diseases, rickets, stress-related diseases and depression. Low income families are more likely to face electrical and fire hazards in the home and risks from traffic and industrial plant in their neighbourhoods. Standards of diet are closely associated with income, with particular implications for levels of infant mortality. Opportunities for holidays, travel and leisure, which may relieve stress and facilitate recuperation, are similarly related to financial circumstances. Unemployment is associated with particular health risks, due to the emotional, social and economic problems that being out of work brings. It, too, is particularly prevalent among manual workers.

Groups particularly vulnerable to poverty include the retired, the unemployed, one parent families, large families and the low paid. About one-fifth of the British population receive incomes at or below Income Support levels. In addition, many of those who depend on welfare benefits find themselves caught in the 'poverty trap'. This means that even if they succeed in increasing their wages from employment they lose eligibility for means-tested benefits. As a result, their net incomes remain the same or may even decline marginally.

Work processes and working environments can pose very serious threats to health. The Health and Safety Executive estimates that some 2 million people in Britain suffer from work-related illness, resulting in the loss of 29 million working days each year. People in manual occupations are at far greater risk than others, particularly those involving contact with machinery, chemicals and industrial wastes. In the early 1990s, officially recorded occupational injuries were running at about 190 000 per annum, of which some 30 000 were major injuries. The HSE calculates, however, that only 30% of injuries at work are reported and appear in official statistics. Occupational diseases can be very insidious, developing gradually or lying dormant for decades. They include a range of cancers (largely due to contact with dangerous chemicals), respiratory diseases (as a result of breathing in various kinds of dusts), skin diseases, infectious diseases and poisoning. Wives and children of workers may be at risk from chemical traces inadvertently carried home on clothing or from pollution from local factories. Even the unborn may suffer as a result of genetic damage sustained by their parents. The stresses associated with low autonomy, repetitive tasks and close supervision at work can also cause health problems.

Access to services also reflects income levels. People who use private health care in Britain are overwhelmingly of white collar backgrounds. Many belong to private health insurance schemes that are a fringe benefit, or 'perk', attached to their job. Over the years charges have been introduced to the NHS for certain items, such as prescriptions, eye tests and dental work. Notwithstanding means-tested exemptions, charges are a disincentive for some patients. Moreover, even those services which are free may entail indirect costs that people on very low incomes may find hard to bear. Thus, a visit to a clinic might involve loss of pay or costs for transport and child minder.

An understanding of the effects of material deprivation and occupational hazards on health are of particular relevance for nursing practice and nursing models. Material factors can be of critical importance in determining the causes of disease and the progress of treatment. Occupational health nurses are particularly well placed to address the problems of injury and disease generated at the workplace. More generally, materialist theories question the wisdom of curing patients of their physical ills only to return them to the social conditions which caused their diseases in the first place. This perspective raises the issue of where the boundaries of professional concern and medical and nursing intervention should be drawn.

Most sociologists conclude, as did the authors of the Black Report, that differences in material circumstances are the main determinant of class inequalities in health. However, there are some aspects of the health behaviour of the poor that might seem difficult to explain in economic terms, for example high rates of cigarette smoking. These issues lead us to examine cultural and behavioural differences between the social classes.

Cultural/behavioural theories

These theories focus on class differences in health beliefs and health behaviour. These, in turn, are said to be derived from more general class based attitudes, values and life styles. Research evidence suggests that people in manual occupations are more likely than others to equate being healthy simply with an absence of disruptive symptoms (Chapter 6). Good health is more commonly regarded as a matter of luck or chance and health expectations are low. The onset of disease may be explained in terms of external factors outside individual control, such as heredity or environmental pollution. Moreover, when illness strikes a high value is placed on not 'giving in'. In contrast, people with professional and managerial backgrounds appear to have broader and more positive definitions of health. They have higher expectations and more commonly explain illness in terms of individual actions rather than external forces. They are more likely to anticipate future risks and to believe they personally can do something to reduce them. Less store is placed on 'soldiering on' when feeling ill. There is greater willingness to regard disease as a technical problem, to be dealt with by prompt or forward-looking action.

Middle-class health beliefs are more likely to result in early consultation and greater use of preventive services. Differences in beliefs may also influence aspects of health-related behaviour, such as smoking. Not only do men and women in Social Class V smoke more than those in Social Class I, they are also less likely to give up smoking. Life threatening behaviour of this kind is said, by cultural theorists, to be consistent with fatalistic attitudes, low expectations and failure to anticipate future risks. Similar points are made with respect to other class-related forms of behaviour, such as diet, exercise, consumption of alcohol and road accidents.

Cultural/behavioural theorists sometimes suggest that the poor are characterized by distinctive attitudes to life. Two rather different versions of this argument have gained currency. The 'culture of poverty thesis' argues that the poor are characterized by social disorganization. Family and community ties are said to be weak, as are ties with the wider society. As a result, it is suggested, individuals become undisciplined, impulsive and self-indulgent. In addition, dependence on welfare benefits is sometimes said to generate passivity and low expectations. In contrast, those who subscribe to the notion of 'class subcultures' argue that the poor live in cohesive and tightly knit communities, based around kinship and neighbourhood ties. These are said to support value systems at odds with those of the wider society, emphasizing physical toughness, suspicion of authority, a belief in fate and membership of collective entities such as families, gangs and communities.

Research has discredited the idea of a self-recruiting and closed underclass, dominated by a particular culture or set of values. Studies such as Blaxter and Patterson's (1982) portray poor people as resourcefully and actively responding to changing circumstances the best way they can. Their chief problems, with respect to health and life more generally, are lack of resources and of information. Moreover, many class differences with respect to life styles and attitudes can be explained in economic terms. Thus, attendance at preventive clinics, healthy eating and active leisure pursuits may involve additional expenditure. A further point to bear in mind is that life styles and behaviour make a bigger contribution to health for the affluent than for people on low incomes. For the well-off – enjoying good home and work environments – personal conduct becomes a major determinant of health chances. For the poor, personal conduct can rarely compensate for damp housing, pollution, low incomes and occupational hazards. Although everyone may benefit from a healthy life style, middle-class people are likely to gain significantly more (Blaxter 1990).

Cultural/behavioural explanations cannot be dismissed. There are differences in outlooks and behaviour between the social classes that are relevant to health and health care. However, there is a danger of stereotyping and stigmatizing the lives of the poor. This approach can lead to the belief that individuals simply have to 'change their attitudes' – and if they don't they are responsible for their own problems. The best way to avoid this 'blaming of the victim' is to integrate materialist and cultural explanations within a single analysis.

Synthesis of explanations

The ways in which people think and feel about themselves and others are profoundly influenced by their position in society. Equally, such 'world views' shape the ways in which people act, and hence their future lives. Explanations for health inequalities need, therefore, to take account of both material inequalities and cultural differences (Fig. 4.1).

Many of the matters raised by cultural/behavioral theories can be understood as issues of autonomy and control. People in low skill manual occupations have few opportunities to exercise choice or discretion. Their jobs offer little scope for exercising skills, making decisions or organizing others. Low wages give them little chance to make choices as consumers. They often depend on the local authority housing department for accommodation. They are subject to repeated periods of unemployment, making long-term financial planning very difficult. In all

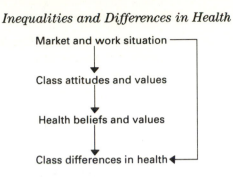

Fig. 4.1 Synthesis of materialist and cultural explanations.

these ways the poor experience a life which is routinely imposed from above and which is characterized by paucity of choices. Thus, poverty entails not only material deprivation but also emotional and psychological experiences. It may generate feelings of despair, anger or shame. The resulting stress, frustration or low self-esteem may have independent implications for health. It is not 'victim blaming' to recognize that, in these circumstances, such feelings may lead to actions that create new problems and humiliations.

Coping strategies are unlikely to enhance long-term optimism or planning. Acute shortages of resources creates a life style dominated by immediate crises and short-term responses. What to others might be modest extra costs, such as expenditure on a sick child, can devastate the family budget. Coping requires sacrifice, belt tightening and lowered expectations. 'Getting by' may demand a blend of dodging, scrimping and avoiding catastrophe which can be tense and exhausting. It may also involve behaviour, like smoking, which individuals know to be dangerous to long-term health but which help them withstand the stresses and demands of today (Graham 1987).

The beliefs and values of the poor may be regarded, then, not as irrational anachronisms but as reasoned assessments and responses to the threats and opportunities offered by the material circumstances of their lives. Such an understanding of the health cultures of different social classes may play an important role in informing the design and implementation of nursing plans for particular patients.

Ethnic divisions and health

Ethnic and 'racial' divisions

Ethnicity refers to an awareness among the members of a social group of shared origins or descent. Such an awareness may be based on physical features, such as skin colour, but may also be derived from other attri-

butes, including religion, language or nationality. Ethnic identities arise
in the context of social relations between groups and populations,
commonly giving rise to a sense of division or difference, of 'us' and
'them'. Ethnic minorities are thus formed in relationship with ethnic
majorities.

The term 'race' invokes supposed biological distinctions. It refers to
the attempt to identify natural sub-divisions within the human species,
based on bodily features or genetic differences. As such, 'race' is a failed
and discredited scientific concept. Biologists have abandoned it on the
grounds that no clear cut 'racial' categories have ever been scientifically
established and no biological basis for links between human behaviour
and so-called 'racial types' has been convincingly demonstrated.
Nevertheless the word remains in everyday use, often to refer to what
sociologists insist are ethnic divisions. There are grave dangers here of
importing the rhetoric of immutable biological divisions into debates
about the historically fluid and socially defined relations of ethnicity.

Cities such as Liverpool and Cardiff have long-standing ethnic minority populations stretching back generations. However, many of Brit-
ain's Asian and Afro-Caribbean communities came into existence after
the Second World War, as a result of migration from the New Com-
monwealth and Pakistan. Labour market shortages drew people to
Britain, sometimes aided by encouragement from potential employers.
Job opportunities concentrated local settlement patterns around parts of
London, the Midlands and the North of England. According to the 1991
Census 5.5% of the British population are members of ethnic minorities.
About a half are Asian, a quarter Afro-Caribbean and the remaining
quarter of other origins. In addition, some 2.25 million people living in
Britain are of Irish descent. An increasing proportion of Asian, Afro-
Caribbean and other ethnic minority people have been born in the UK
(currently estimated at over 50%) and are not, therefore, immigrants.
There are great differences in economic circumstances and cultural
traditions among ethnic minority communities in Britain, making generalizations hazardous. However, they tend to be located in deprived
inner city areas and poorer quality housing. Research shows that their
members experience discrimination and a range of disadvantages in the
labour market, including exceptionally high rates of unemployment
(Bhat *et al.* 1988).

Evidence of ethnic divisions in health

Much of the limited evidence concerning ethnic differences in health and
health care is less extensive than that with respect to class. Much of it
refers to immigrants only and is, therefore, an uncertain guide to the

health of ethnic minority people born in Britain. Older studies sometimes utilized very broad ethnic categories (such as 'Asian'), obscuring important differences between communities. Thus, for example, recent work, using more precise categories, has revealed a complex and shifting pattern of disadvantage with respect to infant mortality (Britton 1990). Mothers born in Bangladesh and in East Africa now have infant mortality rates below those of UK born mothers but babies born to mothers from Pakistan and the Caribbean still have significantly raised levels of infant deaths (Fig. 4.2).

New Commonwealth immigrants currently have overall mortality rates not dissimilar to those of the British-born population. Immigrants from Ireland, however, have been characterized by persistently raised death rates. Within this general picture, some diseases are prevalent within particular communities. Immigrants from the Caribbean have high death rates from TB, hypertension and cardiovascular diseases, diabetes, accidents and liver cancer. Asians have higher than average deaths from TB, liver cancer and ischaemic heart disease (Britton 1990). Eye diseases such as glaucoma are of concern among some Asian populations and sickle cell disease is found among Afro-Caribbean and other groups. Bone diseases, such as rickets and osteomalacia, and high blood lead levels have been found among adults and children in some Asian communities. A number of communities have comparatively high rates of diagnosis and hospitalization for mental illnesses, such as schizophrenia (Bhat *et al.* 1988) (Chapter 8).

Explaining ethnic divisions in health

It is usually the younger, fitter and more affluent members of any population who have sufficient energy and resources to negotiate the trials of long-distance migration. However, as the proportion of ethnic minority people born in Britain increases, these selection effects diminish in significance as a 'protection' against disease. This may be reflected in the increasing incidence of conditions such as coronary heart disease within Asian communities in the 1970s and 1980s. It is sometimes argued that the poor health of Irish immigrants reflects the relative ease of migration from Eire to the UK.

There are a few conditions, such as sickle cell disease, to which members of Afro-Caribbean, Asian and other ethnic minorities are particularly vulnerable for biological reasons. It has been suggested in some quarters that screening for, and treatment of, sickle cell disease has been neglected within the NHS. Because their communities are often located in inner city areas, ethnic minority people are more likely to encounter poorer quality NHS services and facilities. Some studies have drawn

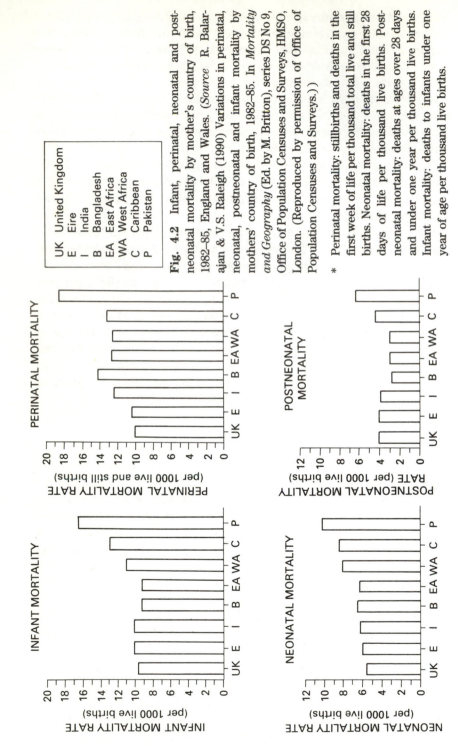

Fig. 4.2 Infant, perinatal, neonatal and postneonatal mortality by mother's country of birth, 1982–85, England and Wales. (*Source* R. Balarajan & V.S. Raleigh (1990) Variations in perinatal, neonatal, postneonatal and infant mortality by mothers' country of birth, 1982–85. In *Mortality and Geography* (Ed. by M. Britton), series DS No 9, Office of Population Censuses and Surveys, HMSO, London. (Reproduced by permission of Office of Population Censuses and Surveys.))

* Perinatal mortality: stillbirths and deaths in the first week of life per thousand total live and still births. Neonatal mortality: deaths in the first 28 days of life per thousand live births. Postneonatal mortality: deaths at ages over 28 days and under one year per thousand live births. Infant mortality: deaths to infants under one year of age per thousand live births.

UK United Kingdom
E   Eire
I   India
B   Bangladesh
EA East Africa
WA West Africa
C   Caribbean
P   Pakistan

connections between raised levels of infant mortality among Asian babies and poor quality of obstetric advice given to Asian mothers. There is also growing concern that some ethnic minority people encounter prejudice and stereotyping with respect to mental health at the hands of police, social services and health professionals.

A great deal of attention has been focused on cultural and behavioural explanations for ethnic inequalities in health. Research suggests that some ethnic minority communities in Britain sustain distinctive definitions of illness and traditions of health care (Bhopal 1986; Krause 1989). Moreover older American studies support the view that ethnically based health cultures are associated with contrasting ways of experiencing pain, interpreting symptoms and relating to the medical profession (Chapter 6). Nurses need to be aware of, and show respect for, the values, beliefs and traditions of ethnic minority patients (Henley 1979). Language difficulties, religious differences and family customs may generate or exacerbate misunderstandings.

On occasion, the life styles of ethnic minority communities have been portrayed as irrational, 'exotic' or inferior. The implication is that minority communities should solve their problems by adopting 'western' modes of behaviour. Indeed, a number of health education campaigns have been launched along just these lines (Pearson 1986). This view fails to recognize the racist stereotypes sometimes incorporated in health services and neglects material deprivation as a source of health problems. The cultural approach is also very unrealistic, grossly underestimating the difficulties of changing a whole community's way of life. It can, therefore, become patronizing and unintentionally racist.

Materialist explanations can account for many health problems of minority communities. For example, high blood lead levels among Asian children have been attributed to cultural factors such as the use of eye make up ('surma') with a lead content; this neglects the risks associated with paintwork and plumbing in old houses and traffic congestion in inner city areas. Similarly, TB, rickets and high rates of infant mortality are known as classic indicators of poverty. This is widely accepted with respect to class inequalities in health but less often recognized in discussions about deprived ethnic minority communities. Neglect of materialist explanations has meant that important aspects of ethnic minority ill-health, such as occupationally related diseases, are only just beginning to be researched.

Gender divisions and health

Sex concerns biological or anatomical differences that are universal and unchanging. Gender, on the other hand, refers to the culturally-specific ways in which men and women behave within any particular society or group that are learnt in the course of childhood and adult socialization. Sex, then, refers to the differences between male and female, gender to masculinity and femininity. During human history there have been many variations in gender relationships. The extent and form of social inequalities between men and women have also changed greatly. However, there are no known societies in which women have enjoyed greater economic and political power than men. Sociologists refer to this pattern of male dominance as patriarchy.

Evidence of gender divisions in health

In Britain, as in many western societies, life expectation for women is several years longer than that of men (see Table 3.1). Gender differences in life expectation are found at every stage of the life cycle. However, women also have consistently higher levels of recorded chronic and acute illness. As a result, it appears that women are more likely than men to adopt the sick role and make use of health services (e.g. women consult their GPs more often than men). Women are also more likely to be diagnosed as suffering from depressive illnesses, more likely to be admitted to a mental hospital and more likely to be prescribed psychotropic drugs such as tranquillizers. This evidence points to an apparent paradox: at its simplest, women live longer but seem to get sick more often than men (Verbrugge 1985).

Explaining gender differences in health and health care

Some differences in service use can be accounted for by the additional needs of women in respect of pregnancy and confinement. In addition, there may be sources of bias in the way in which evidence is compiled and interpreted. Thus, interviewing and other procedures used to collect statistical evidence may under-report male illnesses and consultations. However, most commentators conclude that, even after taking these factors into account, gender differences in health and health care remain to be explained.

Gender differences with respect to employment, income and work conditions have complex implications for health. Although there has been an enormous increase in female employment in recent years, women are still less likely than men to be in continuous employment throughout their lives. Moreover, women are concentrated in a relatively narrow band of routine white collar and semi-skilled manual occupations. As a result, women are less at risk from traditional occupational injuries and diseases, although some 'feminized' occupations (such as nursing) are subject to widespread and persistent occupational hazards, such as back injuries. Some women, however, encounter new kinds of occupational hazards, such as repetitive strain injury, that have only recently gained recognition and are particularly associated with female employment (Reid *et al.* 1991). Housework remains predominantly the responsibility of women, even in those homes where couples share chores. Despite its similarities with many forms of manual employment, little research has been done on the health risks entailed in domestic labour. Within poor households women may be particularly at risk. Wives and mothers have traditionally managed on low incomes by putting their own welfare second to that of their husbands and children. Moreover, massive increases in divorce and female-headed one parent families (Chapter 10) have left many women in poverty.

Gender based attitudes and values may account for differences in health and illness behaviour. 'Macho' lifestyles can involve activities such as excessive drinking, smoking, dangerous sports, fast driving or physical violence. More generally, masculine attitudes often entail an emphasis on aggression, competition and achievement in leisure and work. Such pressures may generate high levels of stress and frustration, with implications for the incidence of heart diseases, cancers and other conditions. It is noticeable that as women adopt behaviours that once were largely male preserves, such as smoking, so their health profiles have changed (Waldron 1991). In this context, it is interesting to note the high incidence of smoking among nurses (Jacobson, 1981).

Feminine roles may entail different stress patterns to those of men. Thus, women may encounter discouragement and disadvantage in the labour market, restricting career opportunities. As a result, even when in employment, many may look to family life as a primary source of gratification. Here they may encounter the emotional pressures of personal relationships and the relatively low prestige accorded to their domestic responsibilities. As they grow older, wives and mothers may find themselves occupying an 'empty nest' whilst other family members make lives of their own. This description is over-simplified but it highlights that unhappiness, or 'dis-ease', may be built into feminine roles and gender stereotypes. Such feelings may be difficult to articulate and may be interpreted as a personal failure of some kind. They may give rise to physical distress, chronic illness and resorting to the sick role. It should further be noted that gender differences may be cut across by other social divisions, such as class. Working-class women are particularly vulnerable to depressive illnesses. This, in turn, is related to aspects of their family lives, particularly the extent to which they lack confiding and affectionate relationships with their partners (Chapter 8).

Culturally defined gender roles may also be implicated in the willingness of men and women to admit to health problems, both physical and emotional. It may be that traditional feminine identities are less threatened by open expressions of pain or vulnerability. The sick role and illness behaviour may be less stigmatizing for women than men. This may also be the (possibly unspoken) view of doctors and medical staff, reflected in their willingness to diagnose and treat male and female patients. This is not to suggest that it is easier to relinquish feminine than masculine social obligations. Indeed, the emotional and practical difficulties involved in rescheduling responsibilities for care of children and other household members are arguably greater than those of temporarily relinquishing the commitments of work and public life that figure prominently in male identities. It might, however, be that men and women use the sick role in different ways, reflecting their gender identities. Women may more commonly employ the sick role as a coping strategy, enabling them not to escape from social obligations but to fulfil them. Cultural stereotypes may enable women more commonly to seek, and receive, medical support in managing their lives. This may be reflected in different usage of psychotropic, or mood changing drugs by men and women.

The broadest and most sweeping perspective on gender differences in health focuses on patriarchy, that is inequalities in opportunities and resources enjoyed by men and women. As patients, women have experienced the rapid growth of medical control and medical management of key aspects of their personal lives, such as childbirth and menopause. In the process, unsubstantiated assumptions about 'naturally' female ways of acting, thinking and feeling have been embodied in medical knowledge (Oakley 1984) (Chapter 12). This 'medicalization' process (Chapter 3) is said to have subjected female patients to the authority of a largely male-dominated medical profession. Feminists argue that gender differences in health and health care reflect these wider inequalities in power and control.

Summary

This chapter has reviewed the well-established patterns of inequality and difference in health and health care which exist in modern Britain. Inequalities of the kind discussed in this chapter deserve to be high on the professional agendas of those concerned with health care, although this is not always the case. Materialist perspectives point to the importance for health of tackling poverty; for example, by upgrading welfare benefits or by public health measures aimed at improving housing standards, pollution emissions and employment conditions. It may be that, if they are fully to benefit their most deprived patients, nurses need to be familiar with the entitlements and operations of the social security system and other aspects of the welfare state. Analysis of health cultures indicates that policies which rely on individual use of preventive services and individual responses to health education programmes are in danger of increasing rather than diminishing inequalities in health. Cultural theories imply that the institutions of the health care system need to be adapted to complement the life styles of patients in greatest need. This might take the form of 'outreach' services; that is, services which go into the most deprived communities to seek out need rather than waiting for patients to come to the surgery in an advanced state of illness. Community based nurses are well placed to play a prominent and effective role in such programmes (e.g. mobile health clinics, needle exchange schemes, and 'on-the-street' care of the homeless). Workplaces may be an effective setting for the delivery of such care, although the needs of the unemployed must not be neglected. The long-standing presence of nurses in places of employment provides them with a firm foundation for such initiatives. The patterns of inequality described here will also be of critical importance to the delivery of community care. All this requires nurses who are familiar with the social dimensions of health inequalities.

References

Balarajan R. & Raleigh V.S. (1990) Variations in perinatal, neonatal, postneonatal and infant mortality by mothers' country of birth, 1982–85. In *Mortality and Geography* (Ed. by M. Britton), series DS No 9, Office of Population Censuses and Surveys, HMSO, London.

Bhat A., Carr-Hill R. & Ohris S. (Eds) (1988) *Britain's Black Population*, 2nd edn. Gower, Aldershot.

Bhopal R.S. (1986) The interrelationship of folk, traditional and western medicine within an Asian community in Britain. *Social Science and Medicine*, **22**, 99–105.

Blackburn C. (1991) *Poverty and Health*. Open University Press, Milton Keynes.

Blane D. (1985) An assessment of the Black Report's explanations of health inequalities. *Sociology of Health and Illness*, **7**, 432–45.

Blaxter M. (1990) *Health and Life Styles*. Tavistock/Routledge, London & New York.

Blaxter M. & Patterson E. (1982) *Mothers and Daughters: A Three Generation Study of Health Attitudes and Behaviour*. Heinemann, London.

Bloor M., Samphier M. & Prior L. (1987) Artefact explanations of inequalities in health: an assessment of the evidence. *Sociology of Health and Illness*, **9**, 231–64.

Britton M. (1990) (Ed.) *Mortality and Geography*, series DS No 9, OPCS. HMSO, London.

Carr-Hill R. (1987) Inequalities in health debate: a critical review of the issues. *Journal of Social Policy*, **16**, 509–542.

Fox A. J., Goldblatt P.O. & Jones D.R. (1985) Social class mortality differentials: artefact, selection or life circumstances. *Journal of Epidemiology and Community Health*, **39**, 1–8.

Graham H. (1987) Women's smoking and family health. *Social Science and Medicine*, **25**, 47–56.

Haynes R. (1991) Inequalities in health and health service use: evidence from the General Household Survey. *Social Science and Medicine*, **33**, 361–8.

Henley A. (1979) *Asian Patients in Hospital and Home*. Pitman Medical Library, London.

Jacobson B. (1981) *The Ladykillers*. Pluto Press, London.

Krause I. (1989) Sinking heart: a Punjabi communication of distress. *Social Science and Medicine*, **29**, 563–75.

MacIntyre S. (1986) The patterning of health by social position in contemporary Britain: directions for sociological research. *Social Science and Medicine*, **23**, 393–415.

Oakley A. (1984) *The Captured Womb*. Blackwell, Oxford.

Office of Population Censuses and Surveys (1986) *Occupational Mortality: Decennial Supplement 1979–80, 1982–3*. Office of Population Censuses and Surveys, HMSO, London.

Pearson M. (1986) Racist notions of ethnicity and culture in health education. In *The Politics of Health Education* (Ed. by S. Rodmell & A. Watt). Routledge & Kegan Paul, London.

Reid J. *et al.* (1991), Pilgrimage of pain: the illness experiences of women with repetition strain injury and the search for credibility. *Social Science and Medicine*, **32**, 601–612.

Townsend P., Davidson N. & Whitehead M. (1988a) *Inequalities in Health: The Black Report/The Health Divide*. Penguin, Harmondsworth.

Townsend P., Phillimore P. & Beattie A. (1988b) *Health and Deprivation: Inequality and the North*. Croom Helm, London.

Verbrugge L. M. (1985) Gender and health. *Journal of Health and Social Behaviour*, **26**, 156–82.

Waldron I. (1991) Patterns and causes of gender differences in smoking. *Social Science and Medicine*, **32**, 989–1005.

West P. (1991) Rethinking the health selection explanation for health inequalities. *Social Science and Medicine*, **32**, 373–84.

Further Reading

Townsend P., Davidson, N. & Whitehead M. (1988) *Inequalities in Health: The Black Report/The Health Divide*. Penguin, Harmondsworth.

Social Science and Medicine (1991) Special edition on 'Health Inequalities', Volume **32**(4), part 1.

Chapter 5
Social Integration, Social Support and Health

Gerhardt (1985) has written that, 'since its beginnings during the fifties in the United States, medical sociology has been greatly concerned with attempts to supplement or substitute medical explanations of illness by sociological ones' (p. 161). As we have already seen, one line of sociological inquiry has examined the social context of behaviour that is either beneficial or detrimental to health (Chapter 3), while another has considered the relation between structural factors and health (Chapter 4). In this chapter we look at a third approach which explores the relationship between social influences and positive or negative *emotions* and health. First, we shall explain the concept of stress and the relationship between stressful life experiences and health. We shall then show how this relationship is shaped by broader social processes by examining the key sociological concepts of social integration and social support. Finally, we consider some of the implications of this work for health care in general and for nursing in particular.

Stress and health

Lay concepts

The idea that the sources of good and bad health have their origins in social life and social relationships is not new. In traditional or tribal societies, dominated by magical and spiritual thought, illnesses were often attributed to the actions of others. These might be supernatural beings, such as gods or invading spirits, or an enemy using sorcery or witchcraft. In such cases the sufferer might employ a witchdoctor, or shaman, to counter the magic. In contemporary industrial societies, as Herzlich (1973) has shown, people are more likely to see their inner reserves of strength being 'attacked' by the stress arising from strained relationships, problems at work, or the 'pace' of modern urban life. Ideas of being 'stressed out', suffering from 'burn out' and so on have entered everyday language. There is now an enormous popular literature on the subject which sees stress as a condition of modern life and offers all sorts of advice on avoiding and coping with it. Although there is little scientific evidence to support its claims, the multi-million pound 'stress industry' offers various techniques to ward off the effects of stress, ranging from expert 'stress counselling' to tapes telling people 'to lie back and concentrate on the orange liquid filling their veins'. Helman (1990) has suggested that such healing rituals have 'become a secular version of more traditional concepts of sorcery and other forms of impersonal malevolence, and of divine punishment, fate and possession by malign spirits' (p. 265). While an understanding of 'lay theories' of health and illness have implications for health professionals (Chapter 6), it is also important to distinguish between 'lay' and 'scientific' uses of the concept of stress.

The stress process

In scientific terms, stress is a *theoretical concept* used to describe the relationship of an organism to its environment. It is neither a peculiarly modern relationship, nor is it avoidable. It is common to all living organisms. *Stressors* are stimuli (e.g. physical danger) requiring an adaptive response from an organism. *Stress reactions* are inherent physiological mechanisms (such as the secretion of adrenalin) which prepare an organism for action when demands are placed on it. Most stress reactions are brief and have no long-term health implications. However, physiological changes resulting from long-term exposure to stressors – such as excessive secretion of hormones and build up of corticosteroids in humans – can weaken the body's defences and make it more vulnerable to disease (Fig. 5.1). *Mediators* are factors influencing the adaptive capabilities of the organism.

Stressors which tax the adaptive capabilities of an organism threaten its survival and may, ultimately, threaten the survival of the species. Selye, who first described the concept in 1936, argued that stress plays a part in all diseases. However, stressors should not be seen only in negative terms. Adaptation to stressors is also the process by which species evolve and develop. Health, or more simply the successful functioning of an organism, is not due to an absence of stressors but to a *balance* between stressors and adaptive capabilities or, put another way, a harmony between organism and environment.

Psychosomatic disease

Like all creatures, human beings are potentially vulnerable to stressors in their physical environments but, due to their capacity to use language

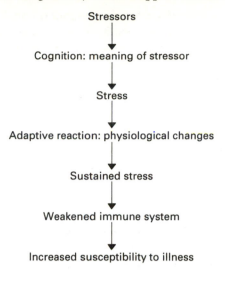

Fig. 5.1 Stress and illness.

and interpret things in a *meaningful* way, they are also more vulnerable to emotional and psychological stressors. Freud was one of the first people to posit the notion of psychosomatic disease when he argued that certain physical conditions, such as asthma and peptic ulcers, may be caused by unresolved psychological conflicts. As more evidence from individual biographies on the coincidence between disease and periods of undesirable life experiences began to accumulate, the scope of the concept of psychosomatic disease became widened.

Pioneering research by Cannon, Wolffe and Selye suggested that stimuli perceived as threatening, whether physical or psychological, were capable of producing broadly similar physiological reactions in people. Selye (1956) argued that what he called a 'general adaptation syndrome' has three stages:

- *alarm*   where the organism becomes aware of a threat
- *resistance or adaptation*   where the organism recovers to a higher functional level
- *exhaustion or fatigue*   where recovery fails, or is impeded, due to the continuing assault of stressors.

The discovery of links between life experiences and physiological adaptation means that the list of potential stressors for humans is very wide, and includes things such as natural disasters, violence and interpersonal conflict, illness in self or others, bereavement, overwork, unemployment, social change and migration. Such events are not necessarily stressful in themselves. Stress is set in motion by the ways in which individuals interpret and respond to them. Thus, the anticipation of problems – such as fear of unemployment, worry over the possible breakdown of a cherished relationship or the realization that some long-desired goal will not be achieved – can also be a source of stress.

Knowledge of the biological mechanisms that may intervene between a psychological reaction to a stressor and possible damage to health is beginning to increase. Developments in immunology and endocrinology have led to research which has demonstrated that emotional stress can exert an immunosuppressive effect on the body, making people potentially more vulnerable to infections, malignancy and auto-immune disease. Clinical studies have revealed positive links between impaired immune function, such as lower killer cell activity and, for example, bereavement, anticipation of bereavement, separation and divorce and major life changes (Kaplan 1991).

It is important to put research on psychosomatic disease into perspective. The relationship between stressors, mediators and disease is clearly very complex and, at present, research findings are expressed in very general terms. First, exposure to stressors and evidence of biological change are not necessarily predictors of disease. Second, unlike germ theory where a particular agent (e.g. TB bacillus) is associated with a specific disease, the relationship between stress and disease is *non-specific*. That is, exposure to a particular stressor (e.g. unemployment) does not determine a specific disease outcome. Rather, it appears to be a factor influencing the *general susceptibility* of individuals and social groups to a variety of diseases (Najman 1980). Nevertheless, the study of the relationship between life experiences and disease is developing into one of the most exciting and potentially fruitful areas of research in both behavioural and biological sciences. In this general context, sociological research has examined the ways in which social factors may influence both exposure to stressors and people's abilities to adapt to them.

Life change and anomie

People's behaviour, their perceptions of the world and of themselves are shaped by the cultural values into which they are socialized (Chapter 1). These values define what is appropriate and inappropriate behaviour, good and bad, success and failure and so on. Social norms and values also regulate and help to channel individuals' behaviour by defining certain goals and means of attaining them. Sociologists use the term *anomie* to describe situations where people find that the norms and values around which their lives had been structured are no longer applicable to their current conditions. *Acute anomie* is caused by sudden change, or crisis, which places the individual into an unfamiliar situation. *Chronic anomie* refers to circumstances where the rules of a social group have become unclear to individuals or do not provide a means of meeting their aspirations. In this section we shall use these ideas to examine some sources of stress and place them in wider social contexts.

Life events and acute anomie

Over the past three decades many research studies have focused on the impact on health of major life changes requiring adaptation from individuals, such as migration, marriage and divorce, bereavement, occupational change and unemployment. This relationship has been studied in a number of ways. Some researchers have examined the effect on health of a *particular* life event commonly associated with stress. For example Rees and Lutkins (1967) compared the health of a group of widowed men in the year following bereavement with that of a control (i.e. matched) group of men. They found that the widowed group had a 40% higher mortality rate. Similarly, Parkes *et al.* (1969) in a study titled 'Broken Heart', examined the death rates of over 4000 widowers for nine years following the death of their wives. In the six months following bereavement, the death rate of the widowed men was 40% above the average for married men of the same age. Research has also found rates of mortality and morbidity positively linked to a number of other specific life changes, including unemployment (Arber 1987), retirement (Kasl 1980) and migration and cultural change (Marmot *et al.* 1975).

Other approaches have used an inventory of a combination of life events. The best known of these is the Social Readjustment Rating Scale developed by Holmes and his associates (Holmes and Rahe 1967). Four hundred healthy adults were asked to rank a list of potentially disruptive events, not all of them negative, in order of the amount of life change they thought would be involved. There was a consistency in the respondents' answers. Death of a spouse was ranked highest in terms of adjustment needed with 100 points, divorce scored 73, marriage 50, change of residence 20, minor infringements of the law, holidays and Christmas scored least with 12 points. The Holmes–Rahe Scale hypothesizes that the more life change 'points' people accumulate over a given time, the more they are likely to suffer a decline in health. For example, a score of 150 points or below suggests a one in three chance of a serious health change over a two year period, while a score of 300 points or more suggests a 90% chance.

A major limitation of this approach, and one which critics feel diminishes both its predictive and explanatory power, is that the *meaning* of 'life events' varies between cultures, sub-cultures and individuals. For example, the life event of divorce may be traumatic and stigmatizing for a devout Catholic living in a rural area, but for some Hollywood film stars divorce and re-marriage is simply something that happens every few years. The issue of the different meanings events may have for different individuals illustrates a recurring problem in the social sciences of attempting to produce 'objective' data and yet take into account people's subjective perceptions of their experiences (Chapter 1). In attempting to resolve this dilemma in their research on life events and depression in women, Brown and Harris (1978) developed an approach that was more context sensitive. Subjects were interviewed in order to ascertain their own views of difficult and potentially stressful events, then researchers ranked their seriousness in terms of an established set of criteria. Brown and Harris found links between depression and life events which were seen as having long-term and threatening implications. However, events which were seen as having only short-term implications, even if they were traumatic at the time, were not associated with depression.

Severe life events, especially those involving loss, and having long-term implications, are 'psychosocial transitions' which can disrupt the pattern of people's lives and place them in states of anomie. First, they can change in what Parkes (1971), in his classic formulation of the problem, calls the 'life space'. That is, the areas in which the individual interacts, such as the familiar worlds of home and work, and around which most behaviour is organized. Second, they may challenge the taken-for-granted assumptions people hold about the world and through which they make sense of their past and present experiences. For example, the cruel death of a loved one could undermine an individual's religious faith. Third, psychosocial transitions may involve shifts in a person's status and identity. For example, people who have become divorced, unemployed or disabled may find themselves being defined differently by others and this may affect the view they have of themselves (Chapter 6).

Stress is the result of an individual's inability to adapt to these psychosocial changes. As we shall see in the following sections, people's capacity to adapt to, or cope with, stressors is influenced by the support they are able to draw from others. The causal mechanisms linking such stresses to disease remain unclear, but many researchers believe that it usually involves some form of psychiatric disturbance (Murphy & Brown 1980). From the sociological point of view, it is important to realize that potential stressors are not random events, but tend to be related to other regularities in social life (Chapter 1). For example, rates of mortality, divorce, unemployment, and exposure to violence vary between societies and between different groups within a society.

Social norms and chronic stress

While the cultural norms of a society can protect against stress, in some circumstances they can make it more likely. This can be illustrated by looking at coronary heart disease (CHD). This condition is the largest cause of premature death in the developed world and is believed to be associated with a number of risk factors ranging from genetic predisposition to diet and life style. In a famous paper, Friedman and Rosenman (1959) suggested that CHD was also influenced by psychosocial factors. They showed that individuals with what they called 'Type A behaviour patterns', characterized by aggression, ambition, competitive drive and impatience, were twice as likely to develop CHD as people of the same age without these traits. Friedman and Rosenman go on to argue that, in some respects, the values of western industrial societies encourage and reward Type A behaviour patterns. People in executive, managerial and professional occupations, in particular, are expected to strive for promotion and material success. Movement up and down the occupational ladder, as well as the inevitable failure of many to achieve the 'success' they crave, is conducive to the development of chronic anomie and stress. Developing this line of argument, Waldron (1978) has examined the relationship between Type A behaviour and gender. CHD is twice as common in men as it is in women. Waldron argues this is due, in part, to the socialization of boys into 'masculine' roles (Chapter 1), where more of the characteristics of Type A behaviour are expected and encouraged.

Social integration

Despite the accumulating evidence of links between stress and health, the majority of people exposed to threatening stressors do not suddenly become ill or die. This gives rise to consideration of the factors that might *mediate* between exposure to stressors and an illness outcome. Psychological theories, many stimulated by the work of Lazarus (1966), have focused on personality and cognitive factors that influence individuals' differing abilities to cope with stress. The distinctive sociological contribution to this problem has been to explore the relationship between broad processes of social order and change, individuals' interpersonal social relations, and their health.

Individualism and integration

One of the major characteristics of modern and modernizing societies is
a trend towards increasing 'individualism'. That is, people have become
more aware of themselves as separate, autonomous units and the relationship of individuals to society has changed its form. In modern
societies social order is based less on custom, tradition and the
unquestioning acceptance of certain authorities and more on people
exercizing choices and preferences and calculating what actions serve
their individual interests. Durkheim described this as a transition from
'mechanical' to 'organic' solidarity. For example, in modern western
societies marriage is less of a commitment to a formal institution where
things are arranged for the marriage partners, and more an expression of
an individual commitment to another person. The strength and duration
of the marriage, or partnership, is dependent on a continuing interpersonal commitment.

Classical social theorists, such as Durkheim and Weber, recognized
the benefits of such change in terms of giving people more freedom,
autonomy and choice and in helping to liberate many from the stresses
of having to toil merely to survive. However, they also recognized that
such changes had their costs, one of the most significant of which was
that the relationship of the individual to the group was becoming
increasingly tenuous or diluted. In times of personal crisis, individuals
were more likely to lack the support and help of a number of others and
to be thrown back onto their own resources. It seems that modernization
and individualization have brought a new set of stressors, the results of
which can be seen, for example, in the form of the enforced idleness of
many young and the widespread loneliness of many elderly people.

Integration and health

In his classic study of suicide, Durkheim (1952) attempted to explain the
seemingly 'individual' act of suicide sociologically. He observed that
there were significant differences in the suicide rates of various social
groups and that these differences remained remarkably stable over time.
According to Durkheim, differences in suicide rates were products of
different types of social life. For example, the statistics showed that
Catholic areas had lower suicide rates than Protestant ones, that people
who were married with children had lower suicide rates than the
unmarried and childless, and that the suicide rate of a society fell in
times of political upheaval or war.

In observing the relationship between religious, domestic and political
differences and suicide, Durkheim was not arguing that these factors are

themselves causes of suicide. Rather, he was arguing that these correlations reveal a common underlying *social* cause of suicide which was
the extent to which individuals were *integrated*, or bonded, into the
social groups around them. In modern industrial societies, which tend to
be increasingly 'individualized', the more people are integrated into
society the more they are 'protected' from suicide. Durkheim went on to
advance the proposition that: 'suicide varies inversely with the degree of
integration of the social group of which the individual forms a part'.
Durkheim's study has been criticized for its over-simplified view of
suicide (Chapter 8) and its acceptance of the reliability of offical suicide
statistics (Taylor 1982). However, his concept of integration remains one
of the central ideas in sociology and subsequent studies have confirmed
many of his original findings.

With developments in the stress hypothesis, sociologists have become
increasingly interested in relationships between social integration and
health. Much of this work has tended to confirm Durkheim's original
hypothesis of the protective influence on individuals of close social ties.
This can be illustrated by looking at the effects on health of two
apparently integrating institutions, the family and religion.

Although family relationships can be a great source of stress (and
violence) for individuals and certain types of family life have been cited
by some as a major source of mental illness (Chapter 8), in general
terms, family life appears to have a positive effect on health. Epidemiological studies have consistently shown that the married have lower
mortality rates than the unmarried and that men appear to benefit from
this source more than women (Trovato & Lauris 1989). Religion also
seems to offer an important source of support for some although, following Durkheim, it appears that the support comes less from the belief
itself and more from the integrating effect of religious ritual and involvement in tightly knit religious communities. Several studies in the
United States have drawn attention to the comparatively low mortality
rates of Seventh Day Adventists and Mormons. Another study found that
a population attending Church regularly had death rates almost half
those attending Church infrequently (Comstock & Partridge 1972).

Marriage and religious practices, along with other integrating institutions such as employment, voluntary organizations and political groups,
bind individuals into wider social relationships that offer a sense of
belonging, purpose, meaning and value to life. They help protect individuals from anomie by structuring personal timetables and providing
publicly recognized social status. Many of the life events most commonly
associated with stress, such as unemployment and divorce, are psychosocial transitions and tend to reduce the ties that the individual
experiencing them has with others (Taylor & Ashworth 1987).

Social support

While studies of social integration suggest that institutions which bind individuals together in modern societies have a positive effect on health, there remains the problem of explaining how more or less integrating social contexts are related to health. In the last two decades a great deal of sociological research has examined the relationship between social support and health. 'Measures' of social support relate to the existence and quality of a person's social relationships. Thus, social integration is a characteristic of *populations*, or institutions, and social support is a property of *individuals*. Although the two are clearly related (Fig. 5.2), methodologically, studies of social support tend to adopt the longitudinal approach of studying individuals over time.

Social support and health

In a well known study, Berkman and Syme (1979) studied a group of nearly 5000 adults over a nine year period. A social network score was calculated for each person in terms of four 'integrating' criteria: marriage, regular contact with friends and relations, church membership and membership of informal associations. After controlling for health status and for health practices (e.g. diet, smoking), at the start of the study, the authors were then able to show a positive relationship over time between high levels of social support and good health. Mortality rates for the most poorly supported individuals were between two and three times higher than those who were well supported. Similarly, House *et al.* (1988), after controlling for health status, health practices and other socio-demographic variables, showed that high indices of social relationships were associated with lower mortality rates. Gore (1978) interviewed a group of men who had just experienced involuntary redundancy, calculated their level of support by means of a 13 item index and divided them into 'supported' and 'unsupported'. Over a two year period, he found that the unsupported group reported more physical illnesses and scored higher on an index of depression.

While there is some evidence that social support is of general benefit in promoting health, most researchers have suggested that its main impact is as a 'buffer' in helping people adapt to stressful life events. Social support can mediate the effects of stressors in a number of ways through physiological and cognitive channels.

First, research in biology and socio-biology has shown that the mere physical presence of a familiar member of the same species can buffer some of the effects of experimentally induced stress in animals and

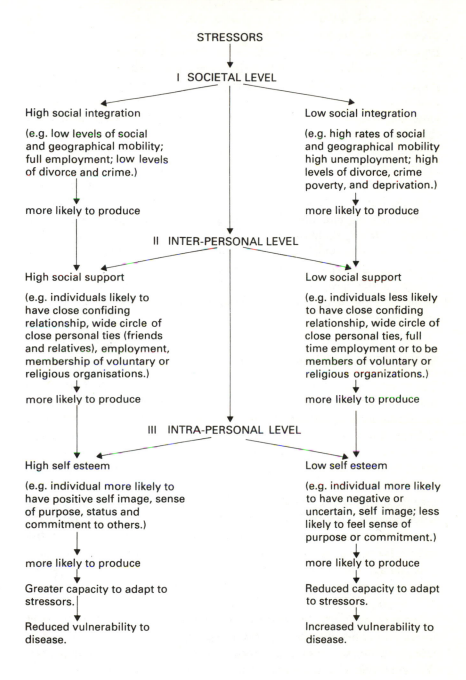

STRESSORS

I SOCIETAL LEVEL

High social integration

(e.g. low levels of social
and geographical mobility;
full employment; low levels
of divorce and crime.)

more likely to produce

Low social integration

(e.g. high rates of social
and geographical mobility
high unemployment; high
levels of divorce, crime
poverty, and deprivation.)

more likely to produce

II INTER-PERSONAL LEVEL

High social support

(e.g. individuals likely to
have close confiding
relationship, wide circle of
close personal ties (friends
and relatives), employment,
membership of voluntary or
religious organisations.)

more likely to produce

Low social support

(e.g. individuals less likely
to have close confiding
relationship, wide circle of
close personal ties, full
time employment or to be
members of voluntary or
religious organizations.)

more likely to produce

III INTRA-PERSONAL LEVEL

High self esteem

(e.g. individual more likely to
have positive self image, sense
of purpose, status and
commitment to others.)

more likely to produce

Greater capacity to adapt to
stressors.

Reduced vulnerability to
disease.

Low self esteem

(e.g. individual more likely
to have negative or
uncertain, self image; less
likely to feel sense of
purpose or commitment.)

more likely to produce

Reduced capacity to adapt
to stressors.

Increased vulnerability to
disease.

Fig. 5.2   The social context of stress and health.

humans. Clinical data has also shown that contact with, or even the presence of, another person can modulate human cardiovascular activity in stressful settings such as intensive care units.

Second, social support can help individuals make a psychological adjustment to stressful life experiences. Emotional support can reassure individuals that they are still cared for and give them the opportunity to vent negative feelings. Instrumental support, such as physical care, financial assistance or help with responsibilities like child care or shopping, is often essential in helping individuals get through day-to-day living after a stressful experience. Both emotional and, to a lesser extent, instrumental support also have the effect of showing the individual that he or she is worthy of the concern of others, and thus help to maintain, or re-establish, the individual's sense of self-esteem and worth. Finally, as stressful life events like bereavement or sudden sickness, are psycho-social transitions which place people in unfamiliar or anomic situations, informational support is often crucial. For example, if a person has become ill then properly administered information about diet, exercise, medication and so on is often an essential part of successful adaptation and coping.

Sickness, disability and social support

While social support is a significant factor in the origins of disease, it also has implications for patterns of patient recovery from illness. Serious illness and its aftermath is obviously a psychosocial transition requiring considerable adaptation. For example, loss of speech or a part of the body from radical surgery may produce a 'grief' reaction, while a tran-sition from independence to dependence on others may undermine an individual's identity, autonomy or sense of worth. Survey research has suggested that the kind of care an individual receives, particularly in terms of social support in the community, can have an important effect on recovery. High levels of social support from people close to the patient, friendship ties and, to an extent, community carers and self-help groups, have been found in research studies to have a beneficial effect on patterns of recovery from, for example, breast cancer, heart attack and stroke.

In this context, researchers have been interested in the relative impact of different types of social support. Glass and Maddox (1992) studied 44 patients in the six months following a first stroke. While the impact of different levels of social support had little effect in the first month, by the end of six months there were positive correlations between high levels of social support and patient recovery. Patients reporting high levels of emotional support showed the most dramatic improvements. The authors argue that emotional support is particularly important in helping patients adjust to the disfiguring consequences of paralysis by making them feel accepted despite their altered body image.

The relationship of instrumental and informational support to recovery was more complex and problematic. While it was generally beneficial, there was the danger of too much instrumental support from nurses and relatives leading patients into overdependence and learned helplessness. Informational support was beneficial, providing it was consistent with patients' capacity to understand. Information patients cannot understand can add to their sense of confusion and increase feelings of helplessness. Glass and Maddox conclude that the rule of thumb with emotional support is simply the more the better, while instrumental and informational support have to be used in moderation and tailored to the needs and capacities of the patient.

Physical disability represents a major challenge to modern societies (Chapter 7). Most disabled people cannot 'recover' in the sense of being made physically well. However, a number of research studies have shown that, in addition to the severity of the condition, the quality of life and perceived health of chronically disabled people is influenced by a variety of social and psychological factors, one of the most important of which is social support.

People with physical disabilities have two sources of handicap. The first stems from the restrictions imposed by their condition. The second comes from reactions of others which, research has suggested, play an important part in shaping the meaning of the disability for the disabled person (Chapter 7). As we have suggested, close and supportive social ties and involvement in social activities can enhance feelings of self-esteem and autonomy. Patrick *et al.* (1986), in a two year follow-up study of people with disabilities, found that those with few contacts showed more signs of physical and mental deterioration than those with higher levels of contact. In another follow-up study, 149 rheumatoid arthritis patients were asked questions about their health status, patterns of social interaction and sense of well-being (Fitzpatrick *et al.* 1991). The researchers found that the patients' psychological state was influenced as much by social relationships as it was by physical condition. They concluded that lack of social support may be a key indicator of people who may be at risk of poor health status.

Structural factors and social support

While the processes of social integration and social support outlined above potentially affect all members of modern societies, some groups are more vulnerable to stressors, low integration and lack of social support than others. In particular, there are significant links between stress and support and some of the 'structural' factors considered in Chapter 4. Stressful life events, such as unemployment, marital diffi- culties and adult and infant mortality, are more common amongst the lower socio-economic groups. Research in the United States has sug- gested that blacks are more prone to stress than whites as they are doubly disadvantaged. First, they are more likely to have low socio- economic status and secondly, they are more likely to be the victims of discrimination.

Low socio-economic status is also related to lower levels of social support. Oakley and Rajan (1991), studying a sample of pregnant women in England, found that very weak social networks were associated with material deprivation, while Whelan (1993) showed that people enduring the chronic stress of poverty and 'primary life style deprivation' had comparatively low levels of emotional, instrumental and informational support. The interaction between class, gender, stress and support is illustrated by the work of Brown and Harris cited above. They attempted to identify the differing life situations and associated stress factors which led to higher rates of depression amongst working-class women than middle-class women. Working-class women were doubly dis- advantaged. First, they were more likely to experience long-term major life difficulties (such as poor housing or financial problems) and major stressful life events (such as death of a family member or job loss). Second, they were more vulnerable to the effects of stress. This was because certain key 'vulnerability factors' – the presence of three or more dependent children at home, the loss of their mother before the age of 11, lack of paid employment and absence of a close confiding rela- tionship – were all more common amongst working-class women. These were factors which had the effect of lowering self-esteem and making women more vulnerable to the effects of stressful life events. As these factors arose from the social situations, Brown and Harris argued that although depressive illness was a biological condition, its origins lay in society and social factors.

Summary

This chapter has examined the relationship between social stress and health. There is now a growing body of research evidence suggesting that events which disrupt the pattern and organization of people's lives can create psychological distress and physiological reactions which, in some circumstances, may undermine individuals' immune systems and make them more susceptible to disease. A proper understanding of this process will only come about through multi-disciplinary research in the biological, behavioural and social sciences. One of the most important sociological contributions in this area has been to show the extent to which the effect of stressors can be mediated by social support. In hospital care it is now beginning to be appreciated that the emotional, instrumental and informational support traditionally given to patients by nurses, is not simply to 'service' bio-medical intervention, but is itself a crucial part of the healing process and should be valued as such (Chapter 12). In community settings, the research considered in this chapter suggests that an important aspect of health promotion and care of the chronically sick and disabled involves attempting to extend social support through, for example, community action, mobilizing friendship networks, developing self-help groups. There is also scope to make creative use of lay care.

While most research into stress, social support and health has inevitably focused on groups of individuals, it is important to remember that people do not live in a social vacuum and their experiences are shaped by broader social processes. Sociological research has shown that exposure to stressors and people's abilities to adapt to them are clearly related to the material inequalities of society, thus adding another dimension to the study of health inequalities. Sociologists have also drawn attention to social changes, such as individualism and lack of integration, which are reducing people's scope for social support at the inter-personal level. It is perhaps ironic that so many people seem to be abandoning traditional sources of social support just when sociologists are discovering how important they are for people's health. Nurses and other health workers cannot change societies, they simply have to mitigate the consequences as best they can.

References

Arber S. (1987) Social class, non-employment and chronic illness: continuing the inequalities in health debate. *British Medical Journal*, **294**, 1069–73.

Berkman L. & Syme S. (1979) Social networks and host resistance and mortality: a nine year follow-up of Alameda County residents. *American Journal of Epidemiology*, **109**, 186–204.

Brown G. & Harris T. (1978) *The Social Origins of Depression.* Tavistock, London.

Comstock G. & Partridge K. (1972) Church attendance and health. *Journal of Chronic Disease*, **25**, 665–9.

Durkheim E. (1952) *Suicide: a sociological study.* Routledge, London.

Fitzpatrick R., Newman S., Archer R. & Shipley M. (1991) Social Support, disability and depression: a longitudinal study of rheumatoid arthritis. *Social Science and Medicine*, **33**, 605–11.

Friedman M. & Rosenman R. (1959) Association of specific overt behavior pattern with blood and cardiovascular findings. *Journal of American Medical Association*, **169**, 1286–96.

Gerhardt U. (1985) Stress and Stigma Explanations of Illness. In *Stress and Stigma* (Ed. by U. Gerhart and M. Wadsworth). Macmillan, Basingstoke.

Glass T. & Maddox G. (1992) The quality and quantity of social support: stroke recovery as a psycho-social transition. *Social Science and Medicine*, **34**, 1249–61.

Gore S. (1978) The effect of social support in moderating the health consequences of unemployment. *Journal of Health and Social Behaviour*, **19**, 157–65.

Helman C. (1990) *Culture, Health and Illness*, 2nd edn. Wright, London.

Herzlich C. (1973) *Health and Illness*. Academic Press, London.

Holmes T. & Rahe R. (1967) The social readjustment rating scale. *Journal of Psychosomatic Research* 11, 213–18.

House J. (1988) Social Relationships and Health. *Science*, **27**, 540–45.

Kaplan H. (1991) Social psychology of the immune system: a conceptual framework and review of the literature. *Social Science and Medicine*, **33**, 909–23.

Kasl S. (1980) The impact of retirement. In *Current Concerns in Occupational Stress* (Ed. by C. Cooper & R. Payne). Wiley, New York.

Lazarus R. (1966) *Psychological Stress and the Coping Process*. McGraw Hill, New York.

Marmot M., Syme L. & Kagan A. (1975) Epidemiological studies of heart disease and stroke of Japanese men living in Japan, Hawaii and California. Prevalence of coronary and hypertensive disease and associated risk factors. *American Journal of Epidemiology*, **102**, 514–25.

Murphy F. & Brown G. (1980) Life events, psychiatric disturbance and physical illness. *British Journal of Psychiatry*, **136**, 326–38.

Najman J. (1980) Theories of disease causation and the concept of general susceptibility. *Social Science and Medicine*, **14A**, 231–7.

Oakley A. & Rajan L. (1991) Social class and social support: the same or different? *Sociology*, **12**, 31–59.

Parkes C. (1971) Psycho-social transitions: a field of study. *Social Science and Medicine*, **5**, 101–115.

Parkes C., Benjamin B. & Fitzgerald R. (1969) Broken heart: A statistical study of increased mortality among widowers. *British Medical Journal*, i, 740–43.

Patrick D., Morgan M. & Charlton J. (1986) Psychosocial support and change in the health status of physically disabled people. *Social Science and Medicine*, **22**, 1347–54.

Rees W. & Lutkins S. (1967) Mortality and Bereavement. *British Medical Journal*, **4**, 13–16.

Selye H. (1956) *The Stress of Life*. McGraw Hill, New York.

Taylor S. (1982) *Durkheim and the Study of Suicide*. Macmillan, London.

Taylor S. & Ashworth C. (1987) Durkheim and social realism: an approach to health and illness. In *Sociological Theory and Medical Sociology* (Ed. by G. Scambler). Tavistock, London.

Trovato F. & Lauris G. (1989) Marital Status and Mortality in Canada. *Journal of Marriage and the Family.* **51**, 907–22.

Waldron I. (1978) Type A behaviour pattern and coronary heart disease in men and women. *Social Science and Medicine*, **12B**, 167–70.

Whelan C. (1993) The role of social support in mediating the psychological consequences of economic stress. *Sociology of Health and Illness*, **15.1**, 86–101.

Further reading

Helman C.G. (1990) *Culture, Health and Illness*, 2nd edn. Chapter 11, Culture and Stress. Wright, London.

Morgan M. Calnan M. & Manning N. (1985) *Sociological Approaches to Health and Medicine*, Chapter 8, Social support. Croom Helm, Beckenham.

Part III
Experiences of Health and Illness

Chapter 6
Social Definitions of Health and Illness

This chapter introduces some of the important concepts and problems associated with understanding how people come to see themselves as ill and how their experience of being ill is influenced by nurses and other professionals. These concepts and problems are relevant to understanding the issues addressed in the remaining chapters in this section. We start by examining the apparently straightforward issue of defining health, disease, and illness and understanding their relationship. Next, we briefly review the salient features of 'interactionist' approach in sociology, as much of the research cited in this section comes from this source. Most episodes of disease are never brought to the attention of formal health care workers, so we consider why this should be so, and look for explanations of how people come to seek help for their illness. Once people enter the health care system they give up a certain amount of control over their lives to doctors, nurses and other health workers. In the second half of the chapter we look at doctor–patient and nurse–patient relationships, and provide two examples to illustrate the power of professionals in defining and influencing the experiences of their clients.

Health, disease and illness

Health

We all think we know what 'health' is, but it is actually very difficult to define. When discussing health care it is important to realize that what people think of as health or illness can vary quite widely. Health can be defined as the absence of disease (i.e. negatively), or it can be seen simply as physical fitness. Another way to define health is in terms of what people are able to do (i.e. functionally), thus health may be seen as 'optimal functioning' or the ability to do things. The World Health

Organization uses a much wider definition of health as a positive state of physical, psychological and social well-being.

All of these definitions of health were found in a 1987 survey of health and life style (Blaxter 1990). In this survey the definitions of health used by respondents varied with their social status and their illness situation (as measured by a range of physiological, psychological and social measures of health). There was an association between how the respondents assessed their overall health, e.g. as good or poor, and health status as defined by the physiological check list of symptoms. The adults surveyed saw health as having a number of dimensions. The most common definition of health was as a state of psychological and social well-being. This was chosen mainly by those respondents who saw their own health as good and by those who distinguished between their own physical and mental health. Those who saw health primarily in terms of the presence or absence of disease were mainly healthy and disease free themselves, as defined by the physiological measures. The definition of health as 'fitness' was mainly used by young adults, but also by those respondents who felt guilty about their health behaviour and those in poor health. Older respondents and those in poor health were most likely to see health in terms of their adaptation to everyday life or their functional ability to perform normal social and work roles. The survey also found a social class gradient in both the objective and subjective ranking of health status, with worse health among the lower classes. Respondents from the lower social classes were also more likely to see their health as poor whether or not it was defined as poor by the physiological check list. Other British studies have shown that there are a range of ideas about health, disease, and illness which people draw upon to make sense of their symptoms and feelings of being unwell (Blaxter & Patterson 1982; Calnan 1987; Williams 1990).

It is important to be aware of the differing definitions of health and the associated attitudes towards healthy behaviour which individuals and groups hold. For example, in Britain during the 1980s a lot of effort was directed to health promotion and health education strategies aimed at changing individuals' health behaviour (Chapter 3). These campaigns were based upon an acceptance of the positive and all inclusive WHO definition of health rather than upon the 'functional' definition of health as the ability to do things, or the negative conceptions of health as the absence of disease, which are found in many of the groups the campaigns were aimed at. The approach further assumes that people are in control of and can change their general behaviour.

In poor and working-class groups where financial constraints and employment prospects are restricted, individuals are unlikely to believe they have 'free choice' or a substantial amount of control over their lives.

Negative or 'functional' definitions of health prevail (Chapter 4). Where group members do not believe they can materially affect their health, such campaigns are unlikely to succeed (Cornwall 1984). This is confirmed by the generally poor success of health education and health promotion campaigns among working-class sectors of British society. Even in middle-class groups who are receptive to the messages of health promotion, and who may feel guilty about non-healthy activities, discrepancies can be found between their belief in the importance of 'healthy living' and the pragmatic choices and decisions which they make in their everyday life. For example, they may drive to the shops because it is quicker rather than walking, which they believe to be healthier (Backett 1992).

Disease

Disease is a condition defined by doctors and based upon the observation of biological pathology. The conception of disease is 'objective', 'scientific' and based on the bio-medical model of pathology which is the basis of modern medical thought (Chapter 3). The bio-medical model of pathology is a relatively recent way of viewing illness. In the period prior to modern medical thought and practice doctors and other healers mainly dealt with the verbally expressed concerns of the sick person (which included the physical treatment of conditions). Modern medicine is more concerned with diagnosing and treating 'objective' and scientifically defined disease processes occurring within their patients' bodies than with dealing with the 'whole person'. Although the starting point of diagnosis may be the patient's verbal report, this must be substantiated by other evidence, and may even be discounted or ignored in the treatment of the patient.

The main focus of nursing work is disease, especially in acute hospital settings, but nurses must be aware of and respond to the patient's subjective feelings and interpretations. Given their central role in patient care, nurses often find themselves in the role of 'mediator' or 'translator' between doctors (using the language of disease) and patients (using the language of illness) (Chapter 12). As Littlewood (1989) puts it, nurses are ideally placed 'to negotiate between the goals of the doctor and the goals of the patient'. The awareness that nurses must respond to the patient's illness, and not simply attend to their disease is at the centre of a number of developments within nursing. For example, the use of the 'nursing process' which requires nurses to identify *patient* problems rather than disease treatments is one way in which this may be achieved. 'Primary nursing' and the attempts to develop 'therapeutic nursing' further extend the philosophy and practice of 'patient-centred' nursing, and are thought by many to be beneficial and effective (Pearson *et al.* 1992; Salvage 1992) (Chapter 12).

Illness

In contrast to the 'objective' view of disease, the concept of illness refers to the person's subjective experience of ill-health. It goes beyond the biological and physical consequences of disease, affecting the person's subjective well-being and their social functioning. Illness is recognized by departures from the person's normal state of being and by altered feelings which may be diffuse. To be ill, then, is not simply to be in a physically altered state, but also to be in a socially altered condition which is normally disruptive of everyday life and is undesired.

Illness is both personal and social. The individuals who feel ill are likely to talk to others in their attempts to make sense of their physical symptoms and feelings of 'dis-ease' and departure from normal functioning. While they may draw upon bio-medical ideas and knowledge to make sense of their illness, people also use other ideas which are current in their social groups both to make sense of their illness and to decide what action, if any, they should take. For example, ideas of what constitutes 'flu', how to recognize it, and how to treat it ('feed a cold, starve a fever'). Such 'lay theories' of illness may be complex and detailed, and provide explanations which link the experiences of illness to the personal and social circumstances of the ill person in ways which may be more consistent and believable to them than professional medical explanations.

Cornwall's qualitative study of East Londoners (1984) shows the way in which general perceptions of health and illness as matters that are largely beyond the control of the individual reflect ideas and experiences in other areas such as paid work. These general perceptions are broadly based upon medical ideas, and in everyday life are modified by taking account of the individual circumstances (e.g. the nature of their work) and characteristics (e.g. the 'weak constitution') of individuals. People also differentiated between whether illnesses were 'normal' (infectious diseases), 'real' (disabling and life-threatening diseases) or 'health problems which are not illness' but which are linked to natural processes such as ageing or reproduction. It was also recognized that not all illness was treatable.

Donovan (1986) similarly shows how the health beliefs of Afro-Caribbeans and Asians linked their health behaviour to their life situations and cultural beliefs. For example, in both groups of respondents diet was seen as linked to health and illness, and the use of remedies such as herbal teas or 'hot' and 'cold' foods was part of their cultural beliefs and

DISEASE

		Present	Absent
	Yes	Acute infection	'Hypochondria'
FEEL ILL			
	No	Early stages of cancers	Health

Fig. 6.1 Possible relationships between health and disease.

world view. Among Asians, dietary practices were also linked to religious beliefs and practices.

Disease and illness

There is a relationship between disease and illness, but it is not as clear cut and simple as one might first think (Fig. 6.1). Having the symptoms of disease does not necessarily lead to someone defining themself as ill. One reason for this is the changing pattern of disease in modern society. The acute infectious diseases typical of earlier times were relatively easy for both practitioners and lay people to recognize, being signalled by clear and visible departures from normal states of being. They were also of relatively short duration. The chronic diseases of the present day are harder to notice, having slow, insidious and sometimes asymptomatic onset. They are harder for both practitioners and lay people to recognize, and a long period of gradual accommodation to symptomatology may occur prior to their recognition and definition as illness. Thus, people may be diseased but feel well – as in the early stages of a disease of the circulatory system. They may also see themselves as 'healthy' or 'well within themselves' despite having a long-standing condition such as diabetes.

Illness and identity

Much of the work on social definitions of illness comes from the qualitative (or interpretive) approach within sociology known as symbolic interactionism, or more simply 'interactionism' (Hewitt 1991). The central idea of the approach is that social action is based on shared meanings and negotiations between people. Language is central to this process because it provides common definitions and meanings which allow individuals to see their behaviour in the same ways as others do. Social life is possible because people talk with each other, can agree upon the values, rules and meanings of activities, and can control their behaviour self-consciously. That is, they can treat themselves as 'an object' and reflect upon both their past behaviour and what they intend to do in the future. They can also compare themselves and their actions to what other people think about them and expect from them.

Self-conceptions, that is the ideas we have of ourselves, are important for the way we behave. An important source of our self-conceptions, especially in infancy and childhood, is the way other people react to us. For example, we may believe we are good nurses because patients, peers and senior colleagues behave in ways which tell us this is true. Because we see ourselves as good nurses and take pride in this identity, we arrive for work on time, participate in ward meetings, and sometimes work on after our shift to finish care work with patients. Because we act like this, people identify us as good nurses. Similar examples of the reciprocal influence of the attitudes of others, self-conceptions, and behaviour will be found elsewhere in this section.

The starting point in extending these ideas to the analysis of illness is that we interpret and give meanings to the signs and symptoms of disease. It is these interpretations which are central to the understanding of illness behaviour. As we will see, not all disease is defined as illness. Lemert (1972) emphasizes that it is not the change or difference in a person's feelings or behaviour itself which is crucial, but the reactions of individuals to it. He distinguishes between 'primary' and 'secondary' deviance. That is, departures from normal states which are interpreted and dealt with as part of normal social behaviour (primary deviance), and those which are interpreted in a way which leads to changes in normal social behaviour (secondary deviance). In the context of illness, it appears that the primary deviance of disease symptomatology is frequently disregarded or 'normalized'. For example, tiredness is sometimes defined as an inevitable consequence of physical activity (primary deviance), and at other times it is seen as a sign of illness (secondary deviance).

A particularly striking development of Lemert's approach which has been influential within the sociology of health and illness is 'labelling theory' (Schur 1979). Labelling theory emphasizes the powerful influence of social definitions upon the behaviour of health professionals and ordinary people, paying particular attention to possibly negative consequences. Two examples of labelling theory will be considered at the end of this chapter, and in Chapter 8 we discuss the labelling theory of mental illness.

Illness behaviour

When we think about illness and the way people come to use the NHS a number of common-sense assumptions may be made which when investigated further prove to be untrue. The basic assumption might be that illness behaviour is a direct result of the appearance of symptoms: we start in a condition of health, become ill, recognize that we are ill by the appearance of symptoms, and then decide to seek professional help, usually by visiting a medical general practitioner. However, on closer inspection this straightforward account does not describe illness behaviour very well. As we shall see, the majority of symptoms are not referred to a doctor, and the seriousness or perceived seriousness of the symptoms is merely one element influencing decisions about illness behaviour.

Symptoms and help-seeking

A number of studies have demonstrated that most episodes of illness are either ignored or self-treated, with only a minority of cases being taken to the doctor for attention. For example, a study by Scambler and colleagues (1981) found that for the ten most frequently recorded symptoms the ratio of consultations per symptom ranged from 1:74 (for nerves, depression or irritability) to 1:9 (sore throat). Overall the ratio was one consultation for every 18 symptoms. Wadsworth *et al.* (1971) in their classic study in South London found that although 91% of their sample reported having symptoms of disease just over a quarter of these said they were taking no action with respect to their symptoms, and just over half were taking action without reference to the professional health system (e.g. self-medicating). Less than a fifth of the sample were seeing their GP (16%) or visiting a hospital as an in- or out-patient.

This and other studies show that the majority of 'health care' takes place within the community or what Kleinman (1985) has referred to as the 'popular' sector of health care. The 'professional' sector of health care – where most nurses work – is a second source of health care. There is also a third source of help, which Kleinman calls the 'folk' sector, comprising non-professional specialists offering alternative, complementary or non-orthodox care which is also widely used in Britain (Chapter 2). People may use both orthodox and alternative healers to treat their illness, especially in the case of chronic illness.

Factors influencing help-seeking

Another common-sense assumption which is made to account for the fact that not all episodes of disease are taken to the doctor is that people distinguish between 'serious' and 'non-serious' conditions. Hence, the reasoning goes, serious conditions are more likely to be brought to professional attention than those which are mild. Unfortunately, although people do make active decisions about which illnesses to take to the doctor, this assumption is also untrue. Research has consistently shown that serious conditions are not necessarily brought to the attention of GPs, and that for every serious condition which is being treated in the NHS there are more, sometimes many more, untreated cases in the community.

How do we explain these apparent anomalies? A number of factors can be readily identified. The recognition of symptomatology is important – not all signs of disease are recognized as such, and in some social groups recognition is better than in others. Similarly, the interpretation of the severity of the illness may vary, and the shift from acute infectious diseases to chronic degenerative diseases as the major causes of morbidity in our society may partly explain difficulty in recognizing and interpreting severity. Judgements about the appropriate form of treatment or action to be taken also vary, and depend upon the nature and availability of help and advice, access to help, and often the particular circumstances of the individual.

Symptoms may be recognized as requiring help and attention, but professional help may not be sought. Sometimes the embarrassment caused by them or their perceived threat is an important barrier to help-seeking. For example, women may delay checking out a potentially cancerous lump in their breast because of their fears of mastectomy and its consequences for their attractiveness to their partners. Another factor which may be important is the assessment of the comparative costs and benefits of seeking medical help. Although the logic and values which inform a person's illness behaviour may not be those of doctors or nurses, it has its own rationality based in the beliefs, values and relationships within the individual's social world (Chapter 4). Many women, for example, place their duties to their family before seeking advice about their ill-health.

Lay referral

The ideas which people hold about health, disease and illness are culturally transmitted, and depend upon the social groups to which they belong. In his influential analysis of the effects of social factors upon illness behaviour, Freidson (1972) looks at the importance of 'lay referral' within social groups. He identifies two main dimensions of social networks which influence illness behaviour: the social cohesion or inter-connection of the network, and the nature of the beliefs which are held by its members (Fig. 6.2). In terms of cohesiveness, social networks can be tightly integrated and inter-connected groups or communities where everybody knows everybody else and where most, if not all, social activity takes place with other group members (e.g. a mining community). At the other extreme are those which are characterized by very limited and intermittent contacts between members (e.g. professionals).

Health beliefs and attitudes can conform closely to the latest medical ideas – as in professional groups. Alternatively, they may be firmly based upon folk beliefs and remedies passed down from one generation to the next, and which may differ significantly from current medical thought – as in 'traditional' white working-class communities and some ethnic minority communities. In modern Britain differing attitudes towards health and illness, and differing patterns of illness behaviour can be found between different social classes and different ethnic groups, while gender and age differences are also to be found.

Decision making

Having considered the social factors which influence an individual's illness behaviour, we still need to understand how people decide to seek professional advice. One way of approaching this has been to emphasize the role of health beliefs by examining the role of individual motivations,

	LAY CULTURE	
	Cosmopolitan	Parochial
Loose and truncated	Medium/high use	Medium/low use
	Professional and managerial	Working class in new towns
Cohesive and extended	High use	Low use
	?	Traditional working class

SOCIAL NETWORKS

Fig. 6.2 Lay culture, social networks and utilization of services.
(*Source*   Adapted from E. Freidson (1972) *Profession of Medicine: A Study of the Sociology of Applied Knowledge*. Dodd Mead, New York.)

beliefs and perceptions (Eraker *et al.* 1984). However, although this approach has the virtue of taking the role of individual choice seriously it suffers from an over-rationalistic emphasis. Decisions about health and illness cannot usefully be seen as single, once and for all choices. There are many factors influencing illness behaviour and decision making (such as work and family commitments) which vary through time. Rather than looking at entry into the formal health care system in terms of individual rational decision making at a particular point in time, it is more useful to think of such decisions as the result of a social process stretching over a period of time. Such a model is proposed by Zola (1973).

Zola suggests that the presence of symptoms is not in itself sufficient to lead to help-seeking behaviour. Rather, symptoms may form a constant backdrop to life and must be interpreted as interfering with normal life before medical help is sought. People develop a range of adjustments or accommodations to their symptoms, which may 'normalize' them and, to use Lemert's terms, maintain them in the state of 'primary deviance'. It is not necessarily when people become sicker that they seek help, but when the accommodations made to the symptoms by individuals (or their family) break down – the help which is sought may only partly be for the physical relief of symptoms.

Zola identified five 'triggers' which activated the decision making process (Fig. 6.3). An interpersonal 'crisis' could lead to a person seeking medical treatment. Such crises need not be severe, nor even directly connected to the symptom, but the adverse change in the person's social circumstances draws attention to them, and leads to action being taken about them partly to solve the crisis. Secondly, the symptom(s) may come to be perceived as interfering with the person's social or personal relations, e.g. a peptic ulcer interfering with socializing and drinking with friends. Both of these were important triggers for Italian Americans attending the out-patient clinic Zola studied.

Americans from an Anglo-Saxon background were more likely to be prompted by the symptoms' interference of their work or physical activities. They were also more likely to use temporal markers to decide whether or not to seek help – 'If it's not better by Thursday I'll see the doctor'. This seems to be a common decision-making strategy, and given the ebb and flow of symptoms in the early stages of chronic disease it may not always be effective. The most common trigger for the Irish Americans in the study was pressure from others to seek help. This is a typical pattern for children, whose parents often take them to a doctor because of changes in their normal behaviour.

Fig. 6.3 summarizes the main points of the chapter so far by combining Zola's model of how people come to seek medical help with the survey evidence about illness behaviour.

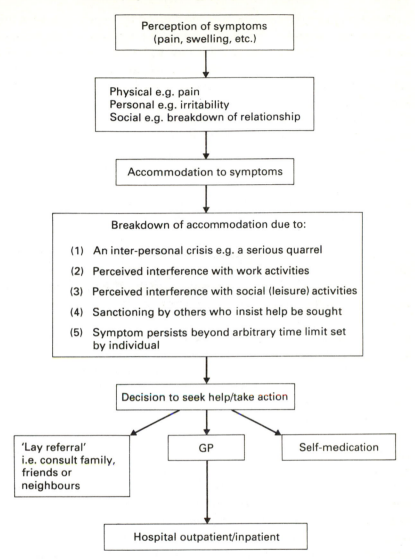

Fig. 6.3 A model of the help-seeking process. (*Source* Adapted from I.K. Zola (1973) Pathways to the doctor – From person to patient. *Social Science and Medicine,* **7**, 677–89.)

The sick role

This chapter has concentrated upon the definitions of health and illness among the general population. It is now time to consider the role of health care workers, especially the relationships between nurses and their patients.

The concept of the sick role was introduced by Parsons, and his formulation has proved to be very influential (Freidson 1972). Parsons suggested that illness posed problems for both the sick person and for social order, and that as a recurring social problem it becomes regularized and transformed into a social role. He identified four main aspects of this sick role:

- sick persons are released from their normal obligations, such as going to work
- they are seen as unable to recover by their own efforts
- they must wish to recover as quickly as possible
- they must seek professional medical advice and co-operate with the physician in the treatment of their illness.

The sick role is seen as complementary to that of the physician. If physicians are to have intimate access to patients, what protection is there for patients to ensure that this is not abused? Parsons identifies a number of mechanisms which serve to protect the patient:

- the formal education and training of physicians
- the disease focus of physician behaviour
- the emphasis on objectivity and emotional detachment
- the commitment to acting in the interests of the patient rather than the self-interests of the physician
- the rules of professional conduct and collegial control.

Although Parsons developed his analysis of the sick role to explain doctor–patient relations, his analysis can be used to make sense of nurse-client relations. Although nurses are less powerful than doctors, their work is with people who have entered the 'sick role' and, like doctors, they have privileged and often intimate access to patients. Their training, the definition of their work as 'patient-centred', and their rules of conduct similarly function to protect patients from exploitation.

There have been a number of criticisms of Parsons' analysis, the most important being those by Freidson (1972) and by Szasz and Hollander (1956). Freidson emphasizes that there are differences between the knowledge, interests and expectations of doctors and their patients which may lead to tension and conflict, and criticizes Parsons for presenting an unduly consensual model of doctor–patient relationships. In everyday life, matters are not as free from tension or disagreement as Parsons suggests. This is equally true for nurse–patient relationships, with the additional complication that these are influenced by the relationships between nurses and doctors, which have their own tensions and conflicts (Chapter 12). Szasz and Hollander criticize Parsons for not analysing the whole range of possible doctor–client relationships, and for not recognizing that doctors and patients may be more or less active in controlling the encounter.

The power of expert definitions

We have already discussed the importance of self-conceptions for behaviour and the influence of other people upon our self-conceptions and upon illness behaviour leading to professional help. Similar considerations apply once people have entered health (or other) systems of care. Once people have entered the sick role and become patients they surrender a certain amount of control over their lives. The decisions made for and about them by health professionals can profoundly influence their lives for better or for worse. This is illustrated by two studies which demonstrate the power of 'expert' definitions, and the importance of recognizing the influence of them.

Mild mental retardation

Mercer's analysis of the consequences of applying the definitions of mild mental retardation used by different groups of experts dealing with schoolchildren in Los Angeles provides our first example. (Current practice is to refer to people with learning difficulties.) Table 6.1 compares two of the 'expert' models she identifies, the medical or 'pathological' model and the sociological or 'social system' model. While the pathological model sees mental retardation as an intrinsic property of the individual, the social system model emphasizes the relativity of definitions of mental retardation, and highlights both the influence of social definitions or labels upon treatment and the importance of being aware of the consequences of such labelling. Mercer's conclusion is that the different definitions used by experts to identify mental retardation resulted in different children being labelled as mentally retarded. An unintended consequence of applying the medical model of pathology was that Mexican-American and black children were disproportionately identified as being mentally retarded.

Blindness

Perhaps the most dramatic example of 'labelling theory' is Scott's study of how the definitions of blindness used by experts working with the newly blind in New York shaped the meaning, experience and abilities of

Table 6.1 Contrasting models of mental retardation.

Aspect	Pathological model	Social system model
1. Definition of mental retardation	Emphasis on defining the characteristics of abnormality with a tendency to neglect examination of 'normal' more positive aspects of behaviour.	Focus on the social processes leading to definition of abnormality: abnormality is relative.
2. Focus of attention	Focus on the individual being assessed – the pathology is *in* the individual.	Expands focus to social factors – greater flexibility in thinking about the abnormal.
3. Practical consequences for action	(a) Search for cause as route to treatment. (b) Bias towards biological explanations. (c) Search for unrecognized cases of pathology.	(a) Search for aspects of differential socialization leading to 'abnormality'. (b) Removes sub-cultural bias in measurement and evaluation. (c) Highlights significance of types of social system which assume responsibility and care.
4. Underlying assumption	Biological findings can be applied across social and cultural boundaries.	Effective action requires system changes rather than/as well as changing individuals.

Source J. Mercer (1972) Who is normal? Two perspectives on mild mental retardation. In *Patients, Physicians and Illness* (2nd edn). (Ed. by E.G. Jaco), pp. 66–85. The Free Press, New York. (Reproduced by permission of J. Mercer.)

the blind person. The absence or severe impairment of vision prevents blind people from relating to the distant environment, meaning that they will be unable to find their way around an unfamiliar place without mechanical aids or help from other people. Total blindness (and not all those defined as blind suffer from complete loss of vision) prevents direct access to the printed word, and to objects too large to apprehend by touch. Blindness can thus be viewed as a technical problem for navigation and apprehension of the physical world.

The professionals working with blind people studied by Scott saw becoming blind primarily as a major psychological event which was a basic blow to self-conception and personality. They stressed the need for the newly blind person to accept and adjust to their profound loss psychologically and to cope with the presumed anger, grief and depression it caused. Their main goal was the psychological adjustment of the client to the fact of blindness, rather than their mastery of new technical skills to compensate for the loss of vision. There was strong pressure upon their clients to redefine themselves from a person who had a serious visual problem requiring technical solutions to someone who was psychologically damaged and in need of psychological support. 'Uninsightful' clients who persisted in their 'simplistic' demands for technical solutions were defined as uncooperative, and denied restorative services until they had come to appreciate the 'true' (i.e. psychological) nature of their problem. Scott suggests that 'gradually, over time, the behaviour of blind men [and women] comes to correspond with the assumptions and beliefs that blindness workers hold about blindness' (1969, p. 119).

Nurse–patient relationships

We can apply the insights from the studies of other health professionals to nursing. Following Szasz and Hollander, we can identify a continuum in the relative control exercised by nurses and patients over their interactions (Table 6.2). At one extreme, epitomized by intensive care settings, nurses are dominant and active while patients are passive and compliant. At the other extreme, found where nurses are employed to care for rich clients in their own home, the patient is dominant and the nurse responsive to their requirements. In between these extremes are situations where nurses guide alert and co-operative patients, for

Table 6.2 Variations in nurse–patient relationships.

Nurse–patient	Nurse's role	Patient's role	Example
Active – Passive	Does something to the patient	Does what is told (may be hospital in-patient)	Coronary care nursing
Guidance – Co-operation	Tells patient what to do	Co-operates (obeys)	Acute infections
Mutual participation	Helps patients to help themselves	Negotiates treatment and other decisions with nurse	Most chronic illness, in the community
Co-operation – Guidance	Co-operates with patient in reaching the patient's goal(s)	Advises nurse what to do	Stable complex chronic disease managed at home
Passive – Active	Is told what to do by patient	Directs nurse	Rich patient receiving private nursing care

Source Adapted from T.S. Szasz & M. Hollander (1956) A contribution to the philosophy of medicine, *AMA Archives of Internal Medicine*, **xcvii**, 585–92.

example in the treatment of infectious diseases or accidental injuries, more equal relationships where nurse and patient help each other in the management of relatively stable long-term conditions, and even cases where knowledgeable patients guide nurses in the management of their condition. The introduction of primary nursing aims to move nurse–patient relationships to these more equal and co-operative patterns.

Disease conditions and places of care

The nature of the patient's disease condition has an important effect upon nurse-patient relationships. Where it develops slowly over a period of time patients may have already made some adjustments to it, or mentally rehearsed possible outcomes of seeking professional help for it. With a sudden onset, particularly if it is as a result of an accident, there is no such preparation time, and the patient may be more dependent upon professional definitions. Where a condition is chronic but stable, the patient may become more expert than the nurse in both its technical management and in recognizing signs of deterioration or danger, and hence take the lead role in its management.

The place where nurses and patients meet is another important factor influencing the relative power and control exercised by each party. Patients are likely to have the most control and influence in their own home (where the nurse is in some sense a guest) and least power and control as in-patients in an NHS hospital.

The nature of the condition and the places where nurses and patients meet seem the most powerful factors in producing the variations in 'activity' and 'passivity' suggested by Szasz and Hollander: nurses (and other health professionals) are most powerful, active and controlling in hospital situations where the patient is critically ill and literally dependent upon their actions, whereas patients are most powerful, active and in control when the consultation is in their own homes and is about a long-standing, well-managed physical condition. However, nurse-patient relationships are also influenced by a number of other factors, such as the personal characteristics of the patient and the nurse, the relative knowledge each has about the condition and its treatment, and the social status and cultural background of patient and nurse.

'Good' and 'bad' patients

The ideas that nurses have about diseases and about patients influence their relationships with patients. Although the personal characteristics of patients and practitioners are not supposed to intrude into or influence treatment, the evidence is that they do have some effect upon relationships (for both doctors and nurses), and that they may influence patient care (Jeffery 1979; Smith 1992; Stockwell 1972). We can summarize the extensive (but scattered) evidence about how the attitudes of nurses to their patients are influenced by social factors as follows:

- *age*   older people are more likely to be ignored or overlooked than younger people
- *status*   people from lower social classes, especially the 'rough' and homeless receive less sympathy, attention or consideration
- *gender*   adult males, especially of working age, are more likely to receive information and to get preferential treatment
- *ethnic background*   Afro-Caribbean and Asian people are more likely to be discriminated against than whites.

Kelly's review (1982) suggests that 'good' patients (those whose conditions challenge and expand nursing skills) receive more care and attention than 'bad' patients (those with 'trivial' conditions or who are mutilated, incontinent or chronically or terminally ill). Patient behaviour is also influential, with co-operative, responsive patients who follow the rules being seen as 'good', while non-compliant, demanding, aggressive, complaining and manipulative patients are liable to be seen as 'bad'. Thus, in a general medical ward a complaining old woman suffering from a broken hip is likely to receive less care and attention than an affable young businessman with a kidney infection.

Information and communication

What people know and understand about their condition is important, both for their well-being and for nurse-patient relationships. A recurrent finding in surveys of patient satisfaction with care is the dissatisfaction of patients with the information and communication they receive from health staff. To the extent that nurses and patients share the same views about the condition and its treatment, communication between them will be facilitated. However, where patients hold widely different views from nurses this may introduce conflict and tension into their relationship. It is in the latter situation that mis-communication and withholding of information from patients are most likely to be found.

Nurses (and doctors) may try to maintain their control over patients by limiting or concealing information, especially in situations where there is 'bad news' for the patient. Research in the area of terminal care suggests that it is very difficult for nurses to conceal bad news from patients over any length of time, and that attempts to do so not only typically result in failure, but may also generate suspicion, mistrust, anger and hostility among patients. This has negative consequences for relationships between nurses and their patients (Chapter 9). With patient-centred nursing it is difficult to see how nurses' control of information in this manner can be justified. Where communication is free and open more trusting relationships are likely to be the norm, to the benefit of all concerned.

Summary

One of the paradoxes of health care in modern Britain is that although the use of health care is thought to be high (and possibly inappropriate at times), many treatable diseases are not seen by health workers. Disease is ubiquitous in human groups, and normally remains at the level of primary deviance. People adjust or accommodate to their symptoms and seek help only when such accommodation breaks down. The meanings of illness are socially constructed and transmitted within the social groups to which people belong, and may be discordant, or even opposed, to professional definitions. The adequate treatment of disease requires nurses (and doctors) to pay serious attention to the health and illness beliefs of their patients, and to respond to their feelings and expectations. The development of 'patient-centred' nursing has come about partly in recognition of this (Salvage 1992, Chapter 12).

References

Backett K. (1992) Taboos and excesses: Lay health moralities in middle class families. *Sociology of Health and Illness*, **14**, 255–74.
Blaxter M. (1990) *Health and Lifestyles*. Tavistock/Routledge, London.
Blaxter M. & Patterson E. (1982) *Mothers and Daughters*. Heinemann, London.
Calnan M. (1987) *Health and Illness: The Lay Perspective*. Tavistock, London.
Cornwall J. (1984) *Hard Earned Lives*. London, Tavistock.
Donovan J. (1986) *We Don't Buy Sickness, It Just Comes*. Gower, London.
Eraker S. A., Kirscht J. P. & Becker M. (1984) Understanding and improving patient compliance. *Annals of Internal Medicine*, **100**, 258–68.
Freidson E. (1972) *Profession of Medicine: A Study of the Sociology of Applied Knowledge*. Dodd Mead, New York.
Hewitt J.P. (1991) *Self and Society: A Symbolic Interactionist Social Psychology*, 5th edn. Allyn & Bacon, Boston.
Jeffery R. (1979) Normal rubbish: Deviant Patients in Casualty Departments. *Sociology of Health and Illness*, **1**, 90–108.
Kelly M. (1982) Good and bad patients: A review of the literature and theoretical critique. *Journal of Advanced Nursing*, **7**, 147–56.

Kleinman A. (1985) Indigenous systems of healing: Questions for professional, popular and folk care. In *Alternative Medicine: Popular and Policy Perspectives* (ed. by J. Salmon), Tavistock, London.

Lemert E. M. (1972) *Human Deviance, Social Problems and Social Control*, 2nd edn. Prentice Hall, Englewood Cliffs, NJ.

Littlewood J. (1989) A model for nursing using anthropological literature. *International Journal of Nursing Studies*, **26**, 21–9.

Mercer J. (1972) Who is normal? Two perspectives on mild mental retardation. In *Patients, Physicians and Illness* (Ed. by E.G. Jaco), 2nd edn, pp. 66–85. Free Press, New York.

Pearson, A., Ponton S. & Durant I. (1992) *Nursing Beds: An Evaluation of the Effects of Therapeutic Nursing*. Scutari, Harrow.

Salvage J. (1992) The new nursing: Empowering patients or empowering nurses? In *Policy Issues in Nursing* (Ed. by J. Robinson, A. Gray & R. Elkan), Open University, Milton Keynes.

Scambler A., Scambler G. & Craig D. (1981) Kinship and friendship networks and women's demand for primary care. *Journal of the Royal College of General Practitioners*, **26**, 746–50.

Schur E. M. (1979) *Interpreting Deviance: A Sociological Perspective*. Harper & Row, New York.

Scott R. (1969) *The Making of Blind Men: A Study in Adult Socialisation*. Russell Sage Foundation, New York.

Sharma U. (1992) *Complementary Medicine Today*. Tavistock/Routledge, London.

Smith P. (1992) *The Emotional Labour of Nurses: How Nurses Care*. Macmillan, London.

Stockwell F. (1972) *The Unpopular Patient*. Royal College of Nurses, London.

Szasz T.S. & Hollander M. (1956) A contribution to the philosophy of medicine. *AMA Archives of Internal Medicine*, **xcvii**, 585–92.

Wadsworth M., Butterfield W. & Blaney R. (1971) *Health and Sickness: The Choice of Treatment*. Tavistock, London.

Williams R. (1990) *A Protestant Legacy: Attitudes towards Death and Illness among Older Aberdonians*. Oxford University Press, Oxford.

Zola I. K. (1973) Pathways to the doctor: From person to patient. *Social Science and Medicine*, **7**, 677–89.

Further reading

Black, N., Boswell, D., Gray, A., Murphy, S. & Popay, J. (eds) (1984) *Health and Disease: a Reader*. Open University Press, Milton Keynes and London.

Chapter 7
Chronic Illness and Physical Disability

Throughout this text it has been noted that the burden of disease in modern Britain has shifted very markedly from the acute infectious diseases characteristic of the nineteenth and early twentieth centuries to long-term, chronic diseases. There are also many members of our society, especially among the elderly, who have long-standing disabilities. Most nursing work, both in hospitals and in the community, involves working with people who are chronically ill and who may have physical disabilities. Chronic illness and physical disability are major sources of difficulty and suffering for individuals and families, and may present health care workers with significant problems in their treatment and appropriate management. Most people who have a chronic illness and/or a disability manage their conditions primarily in their own homes (although with some use of hospital services), often with the aid of a variety of statutory services, including community nurses.

In this chapter we look at the distribution of chronic illness and disability in modern Britain, and review common social accompaniments of disability. We identify some general coping tasks, before looking at the ways in which people experience their chronic disease and disability. The influence of the severity, onset, stability and visibility of the disabling condition are discussed. Negative, stigmatizing, attitudes are then examined. Finally, we consider the role of other people in shaping these experiences including an examination of the part which nurses may play.

Impairment, disability and handicap

It is now recognized to be useful to distinguish between impairment, disability and handicap, so we begin by briefly considering these terms. The relationships between them are illustrated in Fig. 7.1.

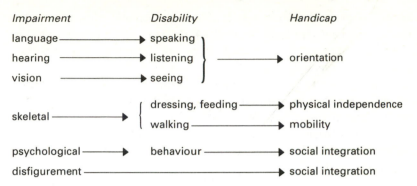

Fig. 7.1 The relationship between impairment, disability and handicap. (*Source* Based on J. Martin, H. Meltzer & D. Elliot (1988) *The Prevalence of Disability among Adults.* Office of Population Censuses and Surveys, HMSO, London. (Reproduced by permission of Office of Population Censuses and Surveys.))

Impairment

Impairment refers to any disturbance or interference with the normal structure and functioning of the body. Impairment may be mild (an ingrowing toenail) or severe (a collapsed lung), transitory (a gashed hand) or long-lasting (eczema). It does not inevitably lead to disability and/or handicap.

Disability

Disability refers to the loss or reduction of functional ability and activity. For most practical purposes it is defined in terms of activity restriction, especially mobility and dexterity, and there are a number of scales for measuring disability in terms of restriction of 'activities of daily living' which nurses use on a regular basis (Henderson 1979).

Handicap

Handicap refers to the social disadvantages which result from impairment and/or disability and which prevent individuals from performing normal roles (e.g. work or leisure activities). Handicap is a common partner to disability. It may result from the ways in which the restrictions of physical disability affect a person's participation in everyday life (e.g. architectural barriers preventing access to buildings by people in wheelchairs). Handicap may also result directly from people's attitudes towards people with disabilities (e.g. embarrassment about the trembling hand of a sufferer from Parkinson's disease). Impairment may lead directly to handicap even though it is not disabling (e.g. avoiding someone who is facially scarred).

Nursing work with people who have disabilities is primarily focused upon managing their impairments and disabilities but nurses, especially those working in the community, need to be aware of the dimension of handicap since their activities and attitudes may be important contributory factors to the handicapping of people who are chronically ill and/or have a disability.

Chronic illness and disability in British society

Estimates of the number of people with a disability in Great Britain vary according to the criteria used in defining disability and the research methods used (see Chapter 1). In 1988 the Office of Population Censuses and Surveys estimated that there were more than 6 million disabled adults in Great Britain – 3.5 million women and 2.5 million men (Martin *et al.* 1988). At all levels of disability except the most severe the great majority of people with disabilities were living in private households. Almost 14% of people living in private households had at least one disability, and the majority of disabled adults had more than one type of disability. The most common types of disability were difficulties in movement (often caused by arthritis), followed by disabilities in hearing, sight and personal care (Fig. 7.2). In communal institutions mental complaints, particularly senile dementia, were most common.

There are around 360 000 disabled children (Bone & Meltzer 1989). Among children with disabilities there were more boys than girls, and the commonest types of disability were behavioural, followed by disabilities in communication, locomotion and intellectual functioning (Fig. 7.2). The rates decline with increasing age, especially in the area of behaviour, which suggests that 'it is likely that the very different questions asked about behaviour in children and adults are responsible for at least part of the difference' (Bone & Meltzer 1989, p. 24).

Common features of chronic illness and disability

It is difficult to generalize meaningfully about the experience of chronic illness and disability given the wide range of conditions and people who are affected, but a number of commonalities can be identified.

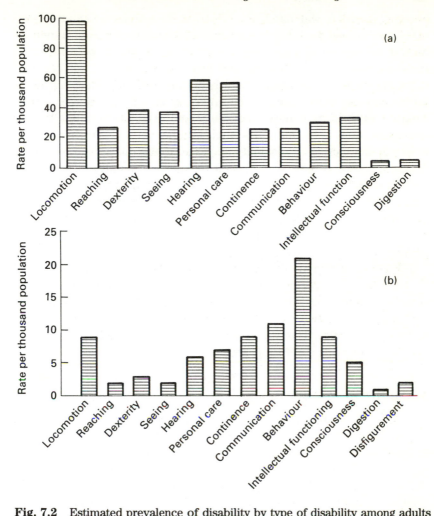

Fig. 7.2   Estimated prevalence of disability by type of disability among adults and children in Great Britain. (a) Adults and (b) Children. (*Sources*   J. Martin, H. Meltzer & D. Elliot (1988) *The Prevalence of Disability among Adults* and M. Bone & H. Meltzer (1989) *The Prevalence of Disability among Children*. Office of Population Censuses and Surveys, HMSO, London. (Reproduced by permission of Office of Population Censuses and Surveys.)

Age

As age rises, so do levels of chronic illness and disability. Although many old people remain fit and active until very late in their lives, chronic illness and disability are common experiences for old people, especially those over the age of 75. While people who are elderly may not consider themselves as disabled, it is clear that old people are more likely to become disabled and handicapped as their activities become more restricted. Indeed disability, in the sense of some restriction of activity, is normal among the elderly. A typical progression would be for the old person to experience a background level of impairment, e.g. reduced mobility, vision and hearing, which is neither seriously disabling nor a threat to their independence. This may gradually deteriorate into a situation marked by multiple pathology and disability which, although restricting, does not compromise their independence. A further decline in health and increasing disability may lead to the old person becoming dependent upon others (usually their partner and family) for help with basic activities of living if they are to remain living in their own home. Finally, this situation may break down, perhaps as a result of an episode of acute illness or an accident (such as a fall resulting in a fractured femur) which leads to hospitalization and the long-term loss of independence.

The effect of chronic illness and disability is mediated by the social support old people receive. Those who are isolated are likely to be more adversely affected by the same level of sickness or disability than those with supportive networks, and are more likely to be admitted to nursing homes or hospitals. The most frequent causes of disability among old people are arthritis, confusion, senile dementia and strokes.

Social class and income

Chronic illness and disability are strongly class-related. The general pattern of disadvantage by social class has been discussed in Chapter 4. People from lower social classes as compared to people from middle and higher social classes are more likely to experience chronic illness and disability, are more likely to experience financial, domestic, and work-related difficulties as a result of their condition, and are less likely to be able to solve such difficulties adequately (Blaxter 1976). This greater ability to resolve problems among higher social classes is related to their higher level of material resources and their greater ability to control events. However, for some people from higher social classes one of the consequences of chronic illness or disability may be a decline in their wealth and social status as a result of their inability to remain in work.

One important consequence of chronic illness and disability is that it is more costly to be ill or disabled than to be in normal health. Direct costs may be incurred through the alteration of the home to accommodate disability, more frequent laundry, special dietary requirements, additional heating costs, and the employment of additional help in the home. Indirect costs may also be significant as activity restriction may affect access to large (and cheaper) supermarkets and require the use of taxis.

Not only may people with disabilities suffer loss of income through restriction or loss of paid employment, but their partner or other main 'lay carer' may have to give up their paid employment in order to look after the person. Loss of income and the increased costs of being ill or disabled are unlikely to be adequately compensated for by the range of financial arrangements available through the welfare state systems (Dalley 1991).

Gender

Gender relates to the experience of chronic illness and disability in two ways. First, women are more likely to act as unpaid 'lay carers' for people with a chronic illness and/or a disability in the community than are men. The main source of such care is the person's spouse or partner, with daughters and the wives or partners of sons also providing such 'lay care'. Male carers are more likely to receive help in their caring activities from other paid and lay carers than are female carers (Ungerson 1987; Parker 1990). Second, old women are more likely to experience chronic illness and disability and to live longer. Above the age of 75 women are much more likely to become chronically ill and disabled. Those over 85 are particularly vulnerable to social handicapping as they are the most likely to be bereaved, isolated and lacking social and financial support (at this age women outnumber men by 4:1). Old women may be doubly disadvantaged – caring for their disabled partner at home, and then being left to cope with their own disabilities alone after his death.

Negative attitudes

The experience of overprotection and other negative attitudes is another common feature of chronic illness and disability, which we will consider in more detail later in this chapter. People who are ill or who have a disability may be prevented from doing things which they are capable of because other people exaggerate the difficulties and limitations involved. Further, people with a chronic illness or disability may be discouraged or even prevented from taking the sorts of risks which 'normal' people routinely take, e.g. travelling alone, getting married, participating in sport. One of the main ways in which handicap occurs is through the negative attitudes of other people. If they focus upon what the person is unable to do (their dis-abilities) rather what they can do (their abilities) the chronic illness or disability may become the person's dominant status, with all of their life becoming focused around it and its disadvantages. It is sometimes a short step from such unthinking handicapping to more active discrimination against people with a chronic illness and/or disability.

Coping with chronic illness and disability

A number of 'tasks' or problems in coping with chronic illness and disability can be identified. Kelly (1992) suggests that these can be considered at four levels:

- the technical and practical management of the condition
- the management of thoughts and feelings
- the management of interpersonal relations
- interpreting and making sense of the condition.

Nurses have an important technical and/or supportive role to play at each of these levels.

The technical tasks of coping with chronic illness and disability involve both the learning and mastery of new skills (e.g. using an artificial limb, changing colostomy bags) and gaining useful information (e.g. about how to manage special diets). These technical tasks of body management may be overlaid and infused with cognitive and emotional meaning. Changes in the appearance of the body and in its functioning may profoundly affect the way people think about themselves and their levels of self-esteem.

Charmaz (1983) suggests that chronically ill people face a constant struggle to maintain a positive feeling of worth and sees the 'loss of self' as a fundamental form of suffering for them. Strong feelings and emotions may be aroused as people try to come to terms with the loss of previous abilities and social roles. The technical tasks of recovery and rehabilitation may be adversely affected until these psychological, cognitive and emotional tasks have been managed.

The meanings of chronic illness and disability are not merely personal, but are the result of shared experiences and interactions with other people, and another important level is that of relating to others. This may involve establishing new types of relationships with people (e.g. those involving greater dependency) and the re-negotiation of existing relationships, especially within the household. Finally, the sick or disabled person needs to be able to make some sort of sense of their condition before they can fully adjust to it. Until they can do this they may be unable to develop stable and predictable ways of managing their disability or illness. Among other things this may involve redefining ideas of what is 'good' and 'bad' in such a way as to emphasize the positive aspects of life (e.g. 'I can still get out and about', 'our marriage is stronger'), and to diminish the negative consequences of illness and disability.

Chronically ill and disabled people accommodate and adjust to their illness and disabilities in a variety of ways. The most common strategy is that of 'normalization', that is to attempt to act as normally as possible, and to minimize as far as possible the significance of those activities associated with the technical management or adjustment to the disability. Other strategies, which may be used alongside normalization, are denial of the disease or disability (e.g. doing what one always did, despite the difficulties and consequences), and avoidance of other people. All of these strategies may be compromised by the level of disability and the reactions of other people.

Factors influencing the experience of physical disability

There are a number of aspects of impairment which influence a person's response to and experience of chronic illness and disability. The severity, patterns of onset and the stability of the condition, are firmly grounded in the impairing and disabling consequences of the condition. The visibility and intrusiveness of the condition refer more directly to the social and potentially handicapping consequences of impairment and disability.

Severity of the condition

The common-sense assumption that severity is the most important influence on adjustment is not supported by research or clinical experience. People with similarly severe conditions may show markedly different levels of recovery, disability and handicap. This is illustrated by the example of the 'cardiac invalids' – people who (according to medical definitions of what is possible) unnecessarily restrict their activities following a heart attack. The impact of severity is mediated by a range of psychological and social factors. What doctors and nurses tell patients about the severity of their conditions and its likely consequences is crucial in shaping their expectations of what is possible. Similarly, the expectations and attitudes of their family and friends will be important in encouraging or restricting their activities.

Onset of condition

The way in which chronic illness and disability appears has a profound influence upon identity and coping. Three main patterns may be identified: the acquisition of disability at birth or in infancy, suddenly (perhaps as a result of an accident), or as a result of a lengthy period of chronic illness (Table 7.1).

A certain number of people are born with their disease or disabling condition either as a result of a genetic condition (e.g. cystic fibrosis, Down's syndrome) or due to something going wrong during pregnancy or at birth (e.g. a neural tube defect leading to cystic fibrosis). Infants may acquire a disability through infections, for example deafness resulting from bacterial meningitis or measles. The main initial problems associated with such disabling conditions concern the adjustment of the parents (Darling 1979, Voysey 1975), whose reactions have been described in terms of coping with loss and grief (loss and grief are discussed in Chapter 9). Nurses and other health workers may also experience emotional difficulties, and be particularly upset if an infant is impaired as a result of a technical failing during or shortly after delivery.

Problems for the disabled individual concern both the technical consequences of learning to live with their illness and disability and in learning and adjusting to the fact that they are different from other people. Critical stages in coming to terms with their identity occur when the child first leaves the shelter of its family on entry to school, and at the time of transition from full-time education at school. The latter infrequently leads on to further or higher education, and may not result in entry to full-time paid work. Finally, for those individuals who are severely disabled and living in their parental home, the death of their parents may lead to institutional care.

The acquisition of a disability as a result of sudden trauma is most likely to occur among teenagers and young adults, usually as a result of accidents. These young people are confronted with the dual problem of coping with the physical losses and restrictions of their disabilities and with coming to terms with the social handicaps which ensue. For those with a severe disability there may be major problems in coming to terms with their new identities as the disruption of life plans at this stage of life may be particularly difficult to cope with. Not only are there physical losses, but life plans and goals in the central areas of marriage, children and career may come into question or become impossible to achieve. It is in understanding this category of disabled people that the idea of disability as 'loss' is particularly useful.

Other relatively common causes of sudden disability are stroke and heart attack, conditions which mainly affect middle-aged and elderly

Table 7.1   Three patterns of physical disability.

Type of onset	Age at onset	Typical conditions	Main typical problems and difficulties
At birth or infancy	0–5	Cystic fibrosis Spina bifida Down's syndrome	*For parents* Shock Loss of a 'normal child' Interpreting developmental delays
			For children Mastering normal developmental tasks Learning they are different Living a normal social life despite obstacles to education, work and sexual relations
Sudden and unexpected	Teenage and young adult	Spinal cord injury	Shock and loss Impact on identity and self-image Rehabilitation Reconstructing their lives despite difficulties for work, leisure and sexual relations
	Middle age	Coronary heart attack	Shock Changing pattern of work and family roles and responsibilities
	Old age	Stroke	Shock Rehabilitation Dependence upon others
Slow and gradually worsening	Middle and old age	Arthritis Respiratory diseases Parkinson's disease	Maintaining a balance between normal social activities and the demands and restrictions of the condition Increasing dependence upon others For some conditions, uncertainty over stability and deterioration of condition

people. Although older people will experience similar difficulties of coping and adjustment to the young people we have just been discussing, they may have fewer difficulties in adjusting to their losses and changed identities. This is because they will largely have achieved (or failed to achieve) their life plans and goals. For example, they are more likely to be in paid employment and to have children.

The most common source of disability is a long term disease. In such circumstances the onset of disease may be slow and insidious, with a gradual process of accommodation and adjustment to increasing levels of impairment and activity restriction. This pattern is typically found in middle and, especially, old age. Increasing levels of disability as a result of the progression of a chronic illness may be one of the factors leading to retirement from paid work. At this stage of life, illness and disability may be accepted as a normal part of ageing, and psychological adjustment to them may in some respects be easier. However, as we have already suggested there may be a greater likelihood of social isolation, and people in old age may have fewer physical and financial resources to call upon in coping with their condition.

Stability of the condition

The stability of a condition is a critical variable as it affects predictability, planning and control. Generally speaking a stable condition is much easier to come to terms with than one which varies in its effects. For example, rheumatoid arthritis is characterized by high levels of uncertainty about both the extent to which activities may be restricted and the amount of pain. It affects joints of the body, and the amount of pain and joint stiffness fluctuates over both the long term (months or years) and the short term (hours or days). Although both pain and activity restriction are present to some extent for most of the time, sufferers have to balance the expectations and demands of their social life with the management of unpredictable pain. What could be done easily and with no pain in the morning (e.g. using a vacuum cleaner) may be both difficult and painful in the afternoon (Locker 1983).

Multiple sclerosis, Parkinson's and other diseases of the neurological system are other conditions which are characterized by continuing uncertainty about functional ability (Pinder 1990; Robinson 1988). With such conditions it is difficult for the person to plan ahead, to make social or work commitments, or to be reliable in interactions with others. This unpredictability means that it is difficult for individuals to exercise much control over their environment. By contrast, a fixed disability (e.g. an amputation) allows the development of routines and coping strategies, giving some control and dependability. They also allow people to plan ahead and to co-ordinate their social life with others, and to exercise reliable control over their environment.

Visibility of the condition

The visibility of a condition (e.g. facial burns, constant hand tremors) is important because people who are different in appearance or behaviour from normal expectations are most likely to be noticed. They are also prone to stigmatization.

Stigmatization

The most influential analysis of stigmatization is that of Goffman (1990). He defines a stigma as an attribute which is deeply discrediting:

'An individual who might have been received easily in ordinary social intercourse possesses a trait that can intrude itself upon attention and turn those of us whom he [or she] meets away from him [or her], breaking the claim that his [or her] other attributes have on us. [S]He possesses a stigma, an undesired differentness from what we had anticipated.'

He identifies three main sources of stigma: 'abominations of the body' such as visible physical disabilities, 'blemishes of individual character' such as homosexuality and mental illness and 'the tribal stigma of race, nation, and religion'.

Stigmatization is based upon the use of relatively simple and over-simplified ideas about people, that is stereotypical thinking. It involves the generally unreflective application of labels to people on the basis of their perceived negative attributes leading, as Goffman suggests, to their exclusion from a range of social life. Stereotyped ideas are resistant to change, and may be very coercive. For example, ideas of disability may prevent people from recognizing what people with disabilites are still capable of doing.

Stigmatized ideas about physical disabilities and mental illness are widespread, are learnt in early childhood, and are transmitted and reinforced through the mass media and in everyday conversations. For example, in modern Britain deaf people may be stereotyped as slow and stupid, blind people as particularly perceptive, and those with Down's syndrome as especially affectionate and happy. Similarly, parents of children with a disability may be stereotyped as heroic, saintly and better than normal.

These stereotyped ideas serve both to make sense of potentially problematic encounters and to legitimate the avoidance of encounters with those who are stigmatized. Research by Albrecht *et al.* (1982) in the US suggests that while people may be willing to work beside physically disabled and mentally ill people, they are unwilling to form regular friendships with them. The main reason they gave for distancing themselves socially from physically disabled people was the ambiguity they posed to normal interaction.

Stigmatization poses two inter-related problems for people with a chronic illness or disability: managing the impact of stigma upon their self-conceptions and identity and managing their social interaction with other people. Looking at the problem for self-conception, Goffman makes the distinction between 'virtual identities' which are attributed on the basis of stigmatized ideas, e.g. deaf people are stupid, and the person's actual social identities (she is a successful business woman). Where the stigmatized condition is very visible or intrusive it may be difficult for people to escape the coercive power of attributed virtual identities, and it may be very difficult for them to have any control in managing their interactions with others. They are, to use Goffman's terms, 'discredited'. In many cases a negative spiral of exclusion from meaningful interaction, self-withdrawal, and diminished self-esteem may result (Fig. 7.3).

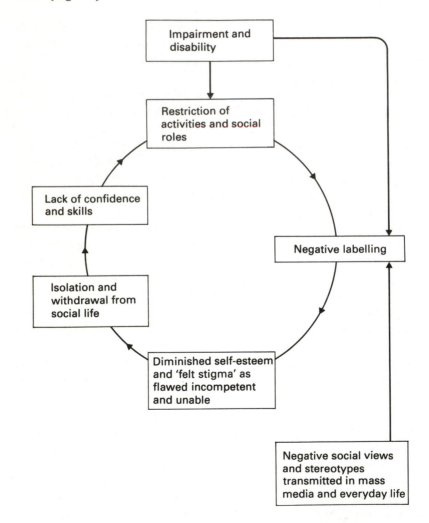

Fig. 7.3 Negative feedback between stigmatization, self-esteem and participation in social activities.

Where the potentially stigmatizing condition is not visible, e.g. epilepsy, the person is potentially 'discreditable', but is in a position to conceal the condition or to 'manage' the amount of information revealed about it. This does not mean that people fully avoid the damaging consequences of stigma to self-esteem. Scambler (1989) suggests that for people with epilepsy their sense of 'felt stigma' was so strong that they tried to keep it secret. The 'felt stigma' which they experienced caused them more anxiety and distress than their actual experiences of stigmatization, which were rare. The progress of some disease conditions, e.g. diabetes or the HIV/AIDS syndrome, may lead people from a situation where their condition (HIV) is invisible and unknown to others (i.e. discreditable) to one where the onset and development of the disease (AIDS) may so alter their appearance and/or behaviour that it becomes known, and they come to occupy a 'discredited' and stigmatized status.

Public and professional reactions to AIDS illustrate very clearly the effects of stigmatization and its basis in stereotypical thinking. The deadly nature of the disease, its close association with marginal and stigmatized groups such as drug addicts, homosexuals and prostitutes, and its mode of transmission through sexual contact have combined to make it a feared disease. Reactions to people with AIDS, especially in the USA, have been extreme (Conrad 1986), and have been amplified by the continuing high media profile about the dangers of AIDS to society. Weeks (1989) characterized the early reactions to AIDS as a 'moral panic'. Despite a clearer knowledge and understanding about HIV/AIDS in the 1990s stigmatization of AIDS sufferers persists among both the general public and health workers. As Conrad (1986) commented: 'While AIDS is contagious, so is the fear and stigma. The fear of AIDS has outstripped the actual social impact of the disease.'

The role of others

In a very real sense the experiences of chronic illness and disability are socially defined in interaction with other people. People with disabilities may challenge our ideas about what is 'normal' behaviour, possibly making us uncomfortable about the range of activities and capacities we take for granted. They may take longer over mundane tasks such as eating or dressing, may only be able to perform them in unusual ways, or require assistance with them. Not only do illness and disability affect the individuals' own activities and abilities but they may also limit the lives of other people by restricting their activities and requiring the reorganization of their previous routines, roles and ways of viewing the world. In the short term, such disruption may be acceptable and – as with infants – even welcomed. However, over the long term it is likely to be disvalued and to create some difficulties for 'lay carers' and others closely associated with people with disabilities.

We can identify five different types of people with whom people who are chronically ill and disabled have dealings.

Normal people

The first category are those people with whom they have only casual or passing contact. 'Normals', as Goffman (1990) calls them, are likely to know very little about the condition. At this level, avoidance and stigmatization may occur because people are ignorant, embarrassed or frightened. They may also simply be unwilling to deal with the perceived restrictions of interacting with people who have a disability.

Family and close friends

Close others, such as family and friends, make up one category of what Goffman refers to as 'wise' people. They have insight into the experiences of people who are chronically ill or have a disability because of their close association with them. The impact of chronic illness and disability upon family and friends can be profound, with their work and social life being disrupted by the needs of care and the restrictions on activity which arise from living with someone who has a disability. Close associates may themselves become stigmatized ('courtesy stigma') because of their relation to the ill or disabled person. Although strong emotional strains may arise, for example as a result of the burden of care or the difficulties of giving non-disabled children the care and attention they deserve, there is no evidence of higher than average marital breakup or difficulties.

Professionals

Professional health and social workers are another important category of 'wise' people. They are in a position to shape the experience of illness and disability through the help and support they provide, and by the way they define such illness and disability (Chapter 6). Because of their central role in the care of people who have a chronic illness and/or disability, nurses are a particularly important group of 'wise' people. In many cases their attitudes towards the illness or disability (as well as to the person who has it) may be critical in shaping the response of patients towards it.

Chronic illness and disability may be difficult for nurses to deal with because they may find it difficult to accept that people won't get better.

In particular they may experience difficulties when they are unable to provide adequate relief of symptoms. Another difficult situation is when they are required to give 'bad news'. A number of strategies aimed at avoiding openness and honesty can be identified here. Nurses (and doctors) may pretend that there is still uncertainty about the prognosis even though they know that there is nothing they can do or that the patient will get worse. They may only disclose some of the bad information initially, hoping that the patient will come to realize that all is not well. Another strategy is to reveal bad news to relatives, and to use them as agents to give the bad news to the patient. Finally, they may engage in purely symbolic or 'placebo' activities which have no direct value for the management or palliation of the patient's condition but which give the impression that something useful is being done.

On the basis of their knowledge, nurses can answer many questions which patients and their lay carers have about:

- the nature of their condition ('Will it get worse?' 'Why is the skin like that?')
- probable activity restrictions ('Will I be able to go back to work?' 'How long before we can resume sexual relations?')
- how to manage the condition ('When is the best time to do the injections?' 'I'm having difficulty stopping my colostomy bag leaking').

They may also be able to point out the unanticipated potential for activity which may remain ('you may find that you can continue with your gardening provided that directly you feel breathless you take deep breaths and don't become anxious').

There are, however, a number of potential pitfalls. Nurses may be unresponsive to the wishes of patients and their carers. This may occur because they apply their own (professionally based) judgements of need and value rather than those of the patient. Thus, they may misdefine or ignore what patients feel they need, while giving care and treatment which patients see as inappropriate or unnecessary. What may be trivial to the nurse may be central to the patient, and vice versa.

Nurses may ignore, or fail to recognize, the knowledge which sick and disabled people and their families have about their condition and its consequences for everyday life. Unless nurses (and other professionals) pay sufficient attention to the knowledge and abilities of people who have a chronic illness or disability they are in danger of underestimating their abilities. Individually and collectively people with disabilities are being prevented from using their abilities. Oliver (1990) claims that the various health and welfare institutions of British society which are intended to help them are in fact sources of their handicap and oppression.

Nurses, especially community nurses may become caught up in problems associated with the frequent lack of co-ordination among care givers, and may even become caught in the cross-fire of competition between different professional experts involved with a case (rarely a person!). Unless these various pitfalls are avoided the nurse may deliver non-responsive and even coercive advice, 'help' and care.

Alternative healers

The use of alternative healers (i.e those with non-medical training or qualifications) by chronically ill people may in part be related to the better communication and information they are thought to provide (Sharma 1992). The main reason why people use alternative therapies is the failure of medicine to deal with chronic illness, especially musculoskeletal conditions, in a satisfactory way (Sharma 1992). Modern medicine may not only be unable to cure chronic disease, but it may also be unable to palliate symptoms such as chronic back pain adequately. Further, many sufferers find their drug therapy undesirable or the medical regimes over-invasive. The impersonality and lack of adequate information characteristic of much modern medical and nursing practice (especially in hospitals) is in sharp contrast to the time, information and personal attention received from alternative therapists. Sharma suggests that patients feel empowered and informed by alternative therapists, with greater control over the choice of treatment. Referring back to Table 6.2, we could characterize such client-practitioner relationships as those involving guidance and co-operation and mutual participation.

Self-help groups

The last category of people who may be important are those with similar or the same conditions as the chronically ill or disabled person. Goffman (1990) calls these the 'own'. The 'own' can provide invaluable psychological support, insight into the person's problems and difficulties, and relevant and practical information and help. The important role of self-help organizations and informal contact with fellow sufferers cannot be underestimated.

Summary

Chronic illness and physical disability affect substantial numbers of the British population. Sociological studies have demonstrated that people's experience of chronic disease and disablity cannot be reduced to their physical aspects. The physical restrictions of their impairments or disabilities are accompanied by social handicaps which may prove to be more restricting and damaging. In particular, over-simplified and limiting views of disability may damage the self-esteem of people who are chronically ill or disabled and restrict their activities. In some cases they and their intimates may suffer from stigmatization. Nurses play a key role in helping people with chronic illnesses and disabilities to cope with their condition. They also play a key role in aiding unpaid lay carers to support and care for such people in their own homes.

References

Albrecht G., Walker V. & Levy J. (1982) Social Distance from the stigmatised: A test of two theories. *Social Science and Medicine*, **16**, 1319–27.

Blaxter M. (1976) *The Meaning of Disability: A Sociological Study of Impairment.* Heinemann, London.

Bone M. & Meltzer H. (1989) *The Prevalence of Disability among Children.* Office of Population Censuses and Surveys, HMSO, London.

Charmaz K. (1983) Loss of self: A fundamental form in suffering of the chronically ill. *Sociology of Health and Illness*, **5**, 168-95.

Conrad P. (1986) The social meaning of AIDS. *Social Policy*, **17**, 51–6.

Dalley G. (Ed.) (1991) *Disability and Social Policy.* Policy Studies Institute, London.

Darling R. (1979) *Families Against Society: A Study of Reactions to Children with Birth Defects.* Sage, New York and London.

Goffman E. (1990) *Stigma: Notes on the Management of Spoiled Identity.* Penguin, Harmondsworth, Middlesex.

Henderson V. (1979) *Basic Principles of Nursing Care*, Revised edn., International Council of Nurses, Geneva.

Kelly M. P. (1992) *Colitis.* Tavistock/Routledge, London.

Locker D. (1983) *Disability and Disadvantage: The Experience of Chronic Illness.* Tavistock, London.

Martin J., Meltzer H. & Elliot D. (1988) *The Prevalence of Disability among Adults.* Office of Population Censuses and Surveys, HMSO, London.

Oliver M. (1990) *The Politics of Disablement.* Macmillan, London.

Parker G. (1990) *With Due Care and Attention: A Review of Research on Informal Care*, 2nd edn. Policy Studies Centre, London.

Pinder R. (1990) *The Management of Chronic Disease: Patient and Doctor Perspectives on Parkinson's Disease.* Macmillan Press, London.

Robinson I. (1988) *Multiple Sclerosis.* Tavistock/Routledge, London.

Scambler G. (1989) *Epilepsy.* Tavistock/Routledge, London.

Sharma U. (1992) *Complementary Medicine Today: Practitioners and Patients.* Tavistock/Routledge, London.

Ungerson C. (1987) *Policy is Personal: Sex , Gender and Informal Care.* Tavistock, London

Voysey M. (1975) *A Constant Burden: The Reconstitution of Family Life.* Routledge & Kegan Paul, London.
Weeks J. (1989) AIDS: The intellectual agenda. In *AIDS: Social Representations, Social Practices* (Ed. by P. Aggleton, G. Hart & P. Davies). Falmer, London.

Further Reading

Anderson R. & Bury M. (Eds) (1988) *Living with Chronic Illness: The Experience of Patients and their Families.* Unwin Hyman, London.

Chapter 8
Mental Disorders

Mental disorders present additional problems to those discussed in Chapter 7 both for those affected by them and for health care professionals. Within nursing this is reflected in the specialities of psychiatric and mental handicap nursing. In this chapter we first look at theories of mental disorder and its distribution. Next, we examine the experiences of mental illness, and the specific problem of suicide and self-harm. We then look at the shift from institutional to community care of the mentally disordered. Finally, we consider the issue of psychiatric care and social control.

Disease or behaviour?

As we saw in Chapter 1, in any social situation there are expectations as to how people should normally behave. Sociologists use the term *deviance* to describe behaviour that radically departs from what most people in a social group consider normal or acceptable. Those who deliberately break the rules of a group may be seen as immoral, delinquent, or criminal and would probably be punished in one way or another. At one time those who appeared unable to conform to behavioural norms through no fault of their own were seen as 'idiots', 'lunatics' or, in some cases, as being possessed by demons or evil spirits. However, it is now generally accepted that such people are suffering from mental disorders and are in need of care and treatment from health professionals. In recent years many types of deviant behaviour once seen as strange, immoral, or even criminal, have become 'medicalized' and brought within the realm of treatment. To many people this trend is an indication of a more humane and compassionate society. However, others argue that it may be counterproductive, restricting the opportunities of the mentally disordered to live comparatively normal lives and sometimes legitimizing an oppressive form of social control over them.

Mental disorder is a wide and ill-defined area but we can distinguish between three overlapping populations. First, there are those suffering from impaired bodily function such as people with learning disabilities or senile dementia. Paradoxically, although this is the group where there is the clearest evidence of physical disease, it is also the category of disorders least responsive to medical treatment. Second, there are people with behavioural problems, such as eating disorders or alcohol abuse, who are now often treated by health care professionals *as if* they had diseases. Third, there are people who have what are called mental illnesses, such as schizophrenia or depression. Here there is considerable debate about whether such conditions are diseases or behavioural problems.

A distinction can be made between biological and psychological theories of mental disorder (Table 8.1). Biological theories argue that all,

Table 8.1   Models of mental illness.

	Medical	Psychological	Social
Definition/ diagnosis	Mental illnesses are diagnosed by doctors in terms of clearly defined criteria and are symptoms of underlying *bodily* disease.	Mental illnesses are diagnosed by doctors or therapists. Precise diagnosis difficult. Mental illnesses are diseases of the *mind* which may, or may not, have an organic basis.	Diagnosis of mental illness problematic. Often owes more to social factors than clinical evidence. Behaviour 'labelled' as 'illness' may be response to difficult, or oppressive situation.
Causes	Uncertain, but growing evidence of genetic predisposition and biochemical causes.	Often caused by experiences in patients' past, especially in early childhood.	Triggered by social circumstances that create stress, lower self-esteem and sense of control.
Treatment	Medical, surgical and nursing care.	Psycho-analysis to help reveal subconscious conflicts or cognitive disorder. Behaviour modification.	Individuals may require help and treatment in short run, but condition will not improve if changes are not also made in their life situation.
Goal	To restore patient to health through treatment, or at least control symptoms and prevent condition getting worse.	To give patient insight into origins of problems and help develop strategies for combating them.	To help reduce rates of mental illness by revealing social influences.

or most, mental disorders are symptomatic of an underlying *bodily* malfunction and offer, or sometimes impose, medical treatments of one sort or another. Psychological theories suggest that some mental illnesses and behavioural disorders may be a product of personal experiences which distort thought processes and are thus 'diseases' of the *mind* rather than the body. Psychological theories do not necessarily reject biological influences or medical treatments, but argue that they should be accompanied, or replaced, by various therapies which may help to give patients insight into the psychological sources of their mental distress or behavioural disorder.

Biological theories

As we suggested above, conditions of mental handicap (such as Down's syndrome) or dementia (such as Alzheimer's disease) are now known to have organic bases. However, in the case of the mental illnesses, evidence of biological causation is far less conclusive. Mental illnesses are typically divided into psychoses and neuroses although, in practice, it is sometimes difficult to distinguish between them. In general terms, psychotic states involve a distorted perception of reality and can sometimes be very frightening for the sufferer, relatives and nurses. In contrast, sufferers from neurotic disorders, such as some obsessional behaviour, usually have insight into their problem and seek treatment.

Schizophrenia is a generic name for a group of psychotic disorders which tend to manifest themselves in early adulthood. Schizophrenic behaviour is characterized by disordered thought patterns, a loss of touch with reality, hallucinations, and may include trances and rigid body postures (catatonic schizophrenia) and fears of persecution (paranoid schizophrenia). Schizophrenia tends to run in families, which suggests a genetic predisposition to the disease, but in practice it is difficult to isolate genetic influences from environmental ones (Wender *et al.* 1974). More recently, biological theories have focused on chemicals in the body called neurotransmitters. There is some evidence that schizophrenia may be the result of over-activity of the neurotransmitter called dopamine. However, there are difficulties with this hypothesis. Even if a consistent association was found between dopamine activity (or any other biological indicators) and schizophrenic behaviour, it would be difficult for researchers to be sure if they were discovering cause or effect. In general terms, while the evidence for an organic basis to psychotic diseases has been accumulating in recent years, it is far from being conclusive and the importance of external events in 'triggering' the process cannot be ruled out.

Psychological theories

Most psychological theories focus on neurosis and behavioural disorders, and attempt to locate the sources of mental disorder in the patient's personal experiences. A number of theories have examined the relationship between the 'formative' experiences of early childhood – especially traumatic experiences – and mental disorder in later life. Psycho-analytical theory argues that there are crucial stages in the *emotional* development of the child, such as separation from the mother and the recognition of sexual identity. Unresolved conflicts at this stage remain in the person's unconscious mind and can produce anxieties and neuroses in later life. One of the tasks of psycho-analytic therapy is to help to provide insights into the childhood origins of the patient's present distress.

Cognitive psychology focuses on thought processes in the conscious mind and argues that there are distinct stages in the child's *intellectual* development by which it comes to think rationally about itself and the world. From this perspective, it is argued that factors (such as traumatic childhood experiences) can impede this process and lead to distorted cognitive perceptions in later life. For example, that part of cognitive development where the child starts to appreciate the effect of its actions on others may fail to materialize, leading to a 'psychopathic' personality where acts of gross cruelty occur without any apparent remorse. In cognitive psychology thought processes are seen as causal influences in their own right and not mere reflections of biochemical changes or unconscious impulses. Cognitive therapy therefore focuses directly on the patient's 'irrational' or 'distorted' beliefs, testing them against reality and trying to establish more rational perceptions (Dryden & Golden 1987).

Family theories

A third approach attempts to locate the sources of mental disorder in later childhood and adolescence. For example, in a seminal paper the Bateson group (1956) suggested that some forms of schizophrenia may result from patterns of family interaction where a child is placed in a no win, or 'double-bind', situation usually by a parent. They describe the case of a boy whose expressions of affection towards his mother were unwelcome, but when he was not affectionate was accused of not loving her any more. Developing this 'family model' Laing and Esterson (1964) attempted to show that 'schizophrenic' behaviours were in fact unconscious 'strategies' to cope with unliveable family situations. From this point of view, the source of mental illness is the *interaction* between the

patient and other family members. Schizophrenia is evidence of a disordered family rather than a disordered individual. This approach has
been widely criticized as 'unscientific' and impressionistic, as well as
failing to explain why people exposed to more or less similar experiences do not also become schizophrenic. However, it has had some
influence and followers argue that therapy should involve families rather
than individuals.

Despite the important differences between, and within, biological and
psychological theories, there are also similarities. Both tend to work
within established medical definitions of mental disorder and both
attempt to locate its causes within the bodies, or minds (or both) of
individuals. In contrast, sociological research has suggested that mental
illnesses have also to be understood in terms of wider social influences
(Table 8.1).

Patterns of mental disorder

Age

High rates of mental disorder are found among old people and, as
with physical disorders, the symptoms of mental disorder increase
sharply with age. Age differences are in part due to biological
processes of maturation and ageing, but social aspects are also important. For example, while there is an organic basis to senile dementia
(Alzheimer's disease), a feared mental disorder associated with old age,
this diagnosis is often mistakenly applied to old people who are confused. Confusion among old people may result from a number of sources
such as social isolation, inadequate diet, drug interactions in the treatment of chronic illness and the negative effects of hospitalization. Once a
confused old person has been diagnosed as demented the reactions of
nursing and other staff may serve to maintain them in a state of confusion and indeed to enhance the confusion of genuinely demented old
people further. Nurses may believe that it is futile to try to talk normally
with demented persons, but by failing to do so they may reinforce their
isolation and deny them important social orienting cues about time and
place.

Gender

There are clear differences in reported rates of mental disorder between
males and females in modern Britain. Females are more likely to be
diagnosed as suffering from neurotic disorders while males are more

likely to be diagnosed as suffering from personality disorders. The differing experiences of males and females at work, in the family and in their leisure activities may generate different levels and types of mental disorder. For example, the greater prevalence of alcoholism amongst males than females seems to be directly related to male patterns of sociability and leisure. Most cases of mental disorder are treated at the primary care level, where females are twice as likely to be diagnosed by their general practitioners as having psychiatric disorders than males. Gender differences are least marked between single males and females and most marked between married men (who are least likely to show signs of mental disorder) and married women (who are most likely to do so). The patterning of gender roles in our society seems to be directly implicated in these differing rates of mental disorder between the sexes (see Chapter 4). Help seeking and 'emotionality' are part of conventional ideas about female roles, whereas males are expected to restrain their expression of emotion, to deny illness, and to be more reluctant to seek help from others. It may be that women are more likely than men to see their problems as some type of mental disorder and are more willing to seek professional help for them. It is also probable that GPs and psychiatrists, influenced by cultural expectations of gender, are more willing to diagnose women as mentally disordered (Miles 1987).

Social class

Diagnosed mental disorders are highest among the lower social classes and lowest among the upper echelons of society. While downward social mobility may be the result of mental disorder, it is thought that the adverse life situations of lower class members generate higher levels of stress than in other social classes, thereby causing higher rates of disorder (Miles 1987). For example, the work of Brown *et al.* (1978) reviewed in Chapter 5, suggested that working-class women were more likely to experience stressful life events (such as financial difficulty or marital breakdown) than middle-class women, and to be more vulnerable to them.

Types of treatment are also related to social class. Lower social classes are more likely to receive institutional and physical forms of care whilst upper classes are most likely to receive non-institutional treatment such as psychotherapy. It may well be that psychiatrists use different criteria to define people from different social classes as mentally disordered and that they are more inclined to define members of lower social classes as psychotically disordered than members of other social classes.

Ethnicity

Overall rates of recorded mental disorder for Afro-Caribbeans and for some groups of Asians from the Indian subcontinent and East Africa are higher than for the general population, as are their rates of compulsory admission to mental hospitals. Once admitted they are more likely to be diagnosed as psychotic and to receive more physical forms of treatment than the general population. Rates of admission to psychiatric hospitals among Afro-Caribbeans (but not Asians) are also higher than for the general population (Fernando 1988). It is hard to discuss these striking patterns of mental disorder among these ethnic minority groups without over-simplifying or misrepresenting the complexities involved (see Chapter 4). Two main types of explanation have been suggested: those which attempt to identify causal factors leading to higher rates of mental disorder, and those which argue that social and cultural factors influence the definition and distort the diagnosis of mental disorders.

Causal influences have been sought in the stresses of migration, the effects of racism and discrimination, and the social class position of ethnic minority groups. Mass immigration into Britain ceased in the mid 1970s, and the initial migrants and their families are now well established in Britain (see Chapter 4), so migration is no longer a major factor. The effects of racism and discrimination are hard to prove, although the anxiety and stress they cause may well contribute to mental disorder. Social class position appears to be a factor only for Afro-Caribbeans, whose higher rates are partly explained by their over-representation among the lower classes.

There may be difficulties for psychiatrists and psychiatric nurses in dealing with members of ethnic groups other than their own. The ideas of psychiatry are firmly rooted in modern western thought, and may thus lead to difficulty in adequately understanding the cultural beliefs of ethnic minority groups holding dissimilar world views. Krause's discussion of the 'sinking heart' syndrome found among the Punjabi population illustrates this point well (1989). The syndrome involves both physical and emotional aspects, and has clear parallels to depression, being linked to worry, anxiety, unhappiness and loss of control. To a psychiatrist or psychiatric nurse it may appear that a Punjabi with 'sinking heart' is 'somatizing' their presentation of depression as a way to avoid facing its emotional aspects. However, a diagnosis of depression may be unhelpful because it implies self-centredness which is associated with negative social and cultural values by Punjabis. Also, some degree of helplessness is seen as an inevitable, God-given, part of life and not as the result of individual failing or responsibility. Finally, the Punjabi explanation of 'sinking heart' is similar in some ways to the western explanation of coronary heart disease in terms of 'Type A' personality responses to stressful situations. Given the sharp distinction between 'body' and 'mind' underpinning most modern health care, it may be difficult for nurses and doctors to understand expressions of mental disorder by people whose culture and beliefs affirm their inseparability.

Experiences of mental illness

Recalling the distinction made in Chapter 6 between 'disease' and 'illness' we can characterize the contributions of sociological research to the understanding of the experiences of mental disorders as stemming from their focus upon the social definitions and meanings of mental illness. Similar processes of recognition, definition and accommodation occur with the symptoms of 'mental illness', as were described for physical symptoms. However, the negative attitudes held towards mental disorders make both lay people and general practitioners less likely to define problems in terms of mental illness. As with physical illnesses, there are more cases of unreported mental disorders in the community than are being treated within the NHS or in private practice.

Societal reaction

Scheff (1966) argues that mental illness is not a disease, but a label applied to people displaying a wide variety of behaviours. The single most important factor leading to entry to the role of the mentally ill is not the symptoms but the reaction of others to them. Most aberrant behaviour is denied or of passing significance, especially where it can be explained by reference to 'everyday' explanations such as being tired or having had too much to drink. It is people whose behaviour *regularly* fails to meet our expectations, *and* where other explanations of their behaviour fail, who are likely to become labelled as 'mentally ill' (Fig. 8.1).

Labelling is influenced by factors such as the amount, visibility and intrusiveness of the symptoms. Family and friends will accommodate to and deny very strange behaviour for long periods before they reluctantly resort to defining their partners or relatives as mentally ill (Miles 1987). Thus, the tolerance of other people to the behaviour is important. Different types of behaviour seem to be tolerated more readily in some groups than in others (e.g. schizophrenic behaviour in manual groups). People also respond differently to the same behaviour in different types of people (depression seems less likely to be recognized among women). Other relevant factors are the relative power and status of the person

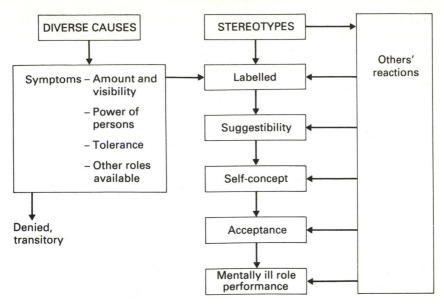

Fig. 8.1 The labelling theory of mental illness. (*Source* D. Field & S. Taylor (1992) The Contribution of Sociology. In *A Textbook of Psychiatric and Mental Health Nursing* (Ed. by J.I. Brooking, S.A.H. Ritter and B.L. Thomas) p. 151, Churchill Livingstone, Edinburgh. (Reproduced by permission of Churchill Livingstone.))

(more powerful and high status persons are more able to resist the label), and whether other roles are available, such as the witch doctor or shaman in some pre-industrial societies, or the eccentric in our own.

A key role is played by stereotypes of madness. Scheff proposes that such stereotypes are learned in early childhood and reinforced by the mass media and in ordinary social activities. In the crisis surrounding labelling, the stereotypes of madness clarify and make sense of the strange and unpredictable behaviour. In this process the person's past behaviour may be selectively reconstructed, and signs of individuality and previously acceptable idiosyncrasy become reinterpreted as signs of incipient madness. Research has suggested that professional health workers, including psychiatric nurses, are also prone to reinterpret a person's behaviour in terms of their label of mental illness (Rosenhan 1973). People who become labelled as mentally ill also know the common stereotypes, may come to accept their applicability to themselves, and to incorporate them into their self-conceptions and behaviour. Once they have been defined as mentally ill they are 'rewarded' for playing the role of the mentally ill (that is, doing what the doctors and nurses want them to do) and 'sanctioned' for not doing so. Treatment regimes may lead to a great loss of independence and individuality, especially in hospital settings, and non-compliance may lead to a range of 'punishments' in the form of further curtailments of activity.

Scheff's arguments have been criticized as being more applicable to psychotic than to neurotic disorders. First, it appears that stereotypes of the mentally ill as bizarre, dangerous and unpredictable, are being complemented by more accepting and less stigmatizing ideas about less severe mental disorders (Miles 1987). Secondly, Scheff underplays the extent to which individuals may willingly embrace the sick role, allowing them legitimately to give up the struggle to live a normal life. Finally, Scheff's approach does not explain the origins of mental disorder only the reactions to it (Gove 1975).

Hospitalization

Once defined as mentally ill a person may be treated by their GP or as an out-patient at a psychiatric unit attached to a general hospital. In extreme circumstances the person may be admitted to a psychiatric unit in a general hospital or become a long-term patient in a mental hospital. Sociological studies of mental hospitals (e.g. Goffman 1991) have shown the possibly negative consequences of admission to them. The restrictions on movement, the need to fit into the ongoing routines of hospital or institutional life, having to ask permission for, or help with, things previously taken for granted, all promote dependency by eroding self-esteem and undermining the patient's sense of autonomy and identity. In extreme cases a state of childlike dependency may develop, which may be interpreted by nurses as further evidence of mental illness and deterioration. Long-term residents may become unable to function effectively in the community because they have become 'institutionalized'.

Within psychiatric hospitals, nurses exert great influence upon patient behaviour and recovery prospects both through the way in which they interact with patients and through their definition of patients (Towell 1975). In wards and institutions characterized by low staffing levels, high levels of physical care and many confused residents a vicious circle of neglect, lack of stimulation, and low staff morale may be found. Indeed, the confusion and apathy among residents in many residential and nursing homes may be as much a result of poor institutional care as they are of mental disorder.

The community

Entry to hospital may assume great significance for the future life of the mentally disordered, whereas treatment from a GP in the community may not. Discharge from hospital is often accompanied by feelings of stigma, and by often justifiable fears about negative attitudes, and discrimination in the community. Such attitudes contribute to the difficulty of setting up 'half-way houses' and other community based treatment schemes for mentally disordered and mentally handicapped people. Despite the apparently greater recognition and acceptance of mental disorders as part of everyday life, mentally ill and mentally handicapped people still suffer from discrimination and stigmatization at work and in the community. The idea that such conditions are essentially incurable persists, and so ex-mental patients may be avoided and find it difficult to resume their previous work and family roles. They are more likely to be living in group accommodation or on their own, to be without work, and to be homeless than the general population (Brandon 1991). It is thus not surprising that a common strategy followed by ex-mental patients is that of 'passing' for normal by hiding the fact of their hospitalization and diagnosis from others.

Family members play a key role in the community care of those with mental disorders and people with learning difficulties. Typically they accept and underplay their substantial and unpaid 'labours of love'. However, they may have difficulty in coping with the disturbed person's distress, and may themselves be distressed by this. Manifestations of disorder such as confused speech, muteness or unpredictability may also be upsetting and difficult to cope with. Their lives may be directly disrupted by the burden of care and the strain which this causes, and by the changes in relationships which unpaid care may entail. They may be more indirectly affected by the 'courtesy stigma' which they may acquire (or feel they acquire) because of their relationship with the ex-patient. They may also have to cope with their own feelings of shame, guilt and anxiety. Family members may thus try to hide the fact of the ex-patient's hospitalization, and to distance themselves in various ways (Miles 1987).

Suicide and self-harm

One of the major dangers of mental disorder and mental breakdown is the risk of deliberate self-harm. Each year in Britain about 4500 deaths are recorded as suicides giving a comparatively low rate for an industrial country of 8 per 1 000 000 population (Fig. 8.2). These official statistics reflect only a relatively small proportion of self-harm. First, many 'suicidal' deaths are simply not recorded. Taylor (1982) found that only half the deaths of a sample of people who were seen to have 'jumped' under London Underground trains were officially recorded as suicides. This suggests the true suicide rate may be as much as double the official rate.

Second, a large number of people commit serious acts of self-harm which would lead to death without medical and nursing attention. Overdosing is the most common, and increasing, method of self-harm. In 1955 hospitals in England and Wales admitted 5000 overdoses, in 1990 the figure exceeded 100 000. Some researchers suggest that acts of deliberate self-harm may be as high as 200 000 a year, and according to

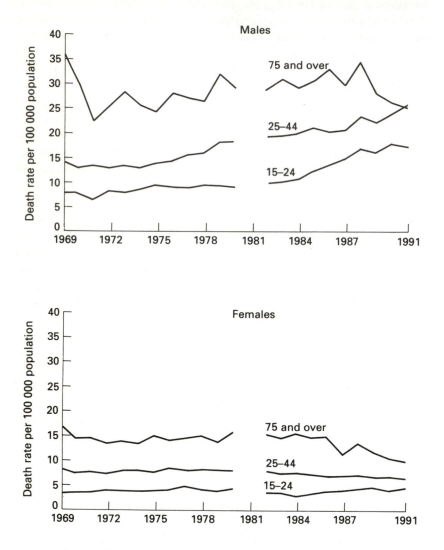

Fig. 8.2 Death rates, by age, for suicide and undetermined injury, England 1969–1991. (*Source* Department of Health (1992) *The Health of the Nation: A Strategy for England.* HMSO, London. (Reproduced by permission of the Controller of Her Majesty's Stationery Office, Crown copyright.))

the Samaritans on average someone in Britain attempts suicide every 2½ minutes.

A common error which people (including nurses and doctors) make in trying to understand suicidal behaviour is to assume that a clear distinction can be made between 'genuine' (the person wants to die) and 'false' (cries for help) suicidal acts. Detailed reconstruction of the circumstances of suicidal acts has proved this assumption to be false. In fact, the majority of acts of deliberate self-harm, including many that end in death, are desperate gambles with life and death where the result is decided by factors outside the individual's control. The term 'para-suicide' is used to describe this behaviour which is less than a deliberate suicide attempt but more than a suicidal gesture.

Most acts of deliberate self-harm are parasuicides, and the understanding of them owes much to Stengel (Stengel 1973). He argued that most suicidal acts were not simply aimed at death and dying, but also at life, survival and contact with others. In most cases suicidal individuals give warnings of their intentions and try to communicate their unhappiness and growing despair to others. For example, most suicidal acts take place in a setting (usually the home) where others are present, and use a method (usually poisoning) where rescue is possible.

The observation that most suicidal acts are undertaken with ambivalent intent and are preceded by attempts to communicate unhappiness and despair has implications for prevention and for nursing suicidal and potentially suicidal patients. The warnings that people give should be taken seriously, rather than believing the myth – which persists among nurses and doctors – that people who are really serious about suicide do not talk about it. As well as direct warnings there are more oblique indications of suicidal intent. These may include a preoccupation with death, expressions of worthlessness and of being a burden, dramatic mood swings, significant change in behaviour and giving away treasured possessions. Partly as a result of their mistaken beliefs about the intent of people who overdose, nurses and doctors tend to be impatient with overdose patients. They are often treated harshly in casualty, ignored on the wards, and made to feel they are wasting staff time. Such reactions are likely to reinforce the already negative self-attitudes of suicidal patients.

Suicide is a particular risk among those suffering from depressive disorders, especially those who are coming out of their depressive state. Yet, despite the association between mental disorders and suicide, most people who harm themselves do not have a long-standing (clinically defined) mental illness. Most are suffering from an emotional breakdown, often triggered by some (inter-)personal crisis. The tendency of some people to take their emotional problems to their doctors in the hope of a cure for their unhappiness (Chapter 3) can have disastrous consequences. Three quarters of those who overdose have seen their doctor in the two weeks before they harm themselves, and the majority overdose on medically prescribed drugs.

Suicide raises a number of ethical and moral dilemmas over people's right to end their own life and the responsibilities of nurses and doctors to protect people who may not be capable of making a rational decision for themselves. Some feel it is morally wrong to restrain a suicidal patient but legally a nurse who does not take reasonable care to protect a patient known to be a suicidal risk can be sued for negligence. A nurse who assisted a patient to commit suicide could be guilty of manslaughter.

Other less directly life-threatening but self-damaging conditions such as alcoholism and eating disorders pose similar dilemmas about the relative autonomy, responsibility and control of patients and staff. For example, the forced feeding of anorectics creates emotional and ethical problems for many nurses. These conditions also raise the question of whether such self-damaging behaviour is best viewed as a disease amenable to medical intervention.

Community care

Despite the move away from the treatment of mentally disordered and mentally handicapped people in hospitals since the 1960s, this is still a major place for treatment, with some 70 000 residents in large mental hospitals in 1990. Hospitals are likely to retain an important role in the care of people with mental disorders as sources of referral, as sites for assessment, treatment and rehabilitation, and to provide shelter and asylum. However, the disadvantages of institutional care, together with the introduction of psychotropic drugs, led to the strong pressures for more care in the community.

'Normalisation'

An important idea supporting this move has been the concept of 'normalisation', originally developed in connection with the care of the mentally handicapped (Race 1987). Severe mental handicaps are caused by a variety of organic impairments resulting from either genetic (e.g. Down's syndrome) or traumatic causes (e.g. brain stem injury). 'Mental handicap' was thus seen as a medical condition, and when medical intervention failed or was inappropriate, hospitalization was seen as a reasonable and acceptable method of 'treatment' – or at least care. However, mild mental handicap is linked to poverty and deprivation, and its genetic causes are uncertain in most cases. A growing body of opinion suggested that adopting the 'medical model' had serious negative consequences, leading to the infantilization and the inappropriate application of the sick role to people who were not sick, but had learning difficulties (see Chapter 6). Regardless of the cause, it seemed more appropriate to regard such people as suffering from learning disabilities, and to focus intervention on enhancing their cognitive and social skills. Further, the 'medicalization' of learning disability was one source of the negative attitudes towards the mentally handicapped, legitimating the negative expectations about ability and performance which lead to the negative spiral of exclusion and withdrawal from social life and low self-esteem described in Chapter 7.

'Normalization' strategies aim to enhance abilities (while recognizing enduring disabilities) in three main ways. First, by providing positive role models. Second, by providing a range of practical instruction and skill enhancement activities. Third, by integrating the mentally ill and handicapped into the community as valued social participants. According to Pilling:

'All models share two key components:
(1) The promotion of interventions which are aimed at helping individuals develop or re-learn skills and role competencies
(2) Modifications to social and physical environments in order to preserve or enhance functioning in spite of continuing disabilities.'
(1991, p. 16).

The success of both 'normalization' strategies and the community care of the mentally disordered, people with learning disabilities and others whose behaviour is unacceptable or difficult to relate to, depends upon their genuine integration into everyday social life. Their mere presence in a community does not equate to their *integration* into that community. The evidence is not encouraging. Neighbours and communities may not be welcoming, and so these people may be lonely and isolated in their 'home' in the community (Race 1987).

Components of community care

What constitutes 'community care' is not always clear. Three interconnected aspects seem to be involved:

- an alternative to institutional care (i.e. care *in* the community)
- the integration of the individual into the normal social world
- care *by* the community (e.g. by families and the 'lay public').

At a minimum, community care must provide a home for those who would previously have been catered for by the hospitals. A range of facilities have been developed ranging from highly staffed 'hostel wards' and group homes, through shared accommodation with some professional support, to single person flats with minimal support. The nature of such community provision is supposed to be related to the capabilities of people and their need for rehabilitation and support. However, many critics say that such provision has not kept pace with the loss of hospital places, and that their former residents are disproportionately found among the impoverished and homeless (Brandon 1991; Pilling 1991). This has consequences for the other two aspects of community care. Integration into the community seems at best patchy and to be less than wholehearted for some groups. The last meaning of community care – care by the community – seems largely unrealized for those persons without supportive partners or family to care for them.

Care or control?

Underlying the growth of psychiatric care for the mentally disordered was the assumption that many mental disorders are diseases which should be managed and treated by health care professionals. This assumption has been questioned. While many mental disorders are the product of diseases, it has been suggested that medical treatment has little to offer and may even be counterproductive in some circumstances, such as the care of people with learning disabilities.

With reference to mental illness, we have observed that some sociologists have argued that the definition of someone as mentally ill often owes more to social than to clinical considerations and that being labelled as 'mentally ill' can significantly affect that person's subsequent behaviour and self-image. Other critics go further. Szasz (1961; 1970) argues that the very notion of mental illness is a myth. He distinguishes between physical and mental illness. Symptoms of physical illness are objective signs (e.g. cancerous cells), whereas the symptoms of mental illness are that the patient's behaviour and communications deviate from what is considered normal in a particular society. According to Szasz, while the physician makes a scientific diagnosis about a patient's body, psychiatrists and psychiatric nurses make value judgements about a patient's behaviour. He does not deny that many psychiatric patients suffer psychological distress, but argues that these people have 'problems in living' and not mental illnesses. Thus it makes little sense to offer them medical treatment designed to correct deviation from biological norms. Furthermore, as long as 'mental illness' is blamed for so many of people's problems in living, it detracts attention from the real causes, which may lie in adverse life circumstances, moral conflicts, intolerance, or social injustices.

Szasz and other critics, such as Kennedy (1981), argue that by defining deviant behaviour as illness and offering to cure it, the psychiatric professions are helping to reinforce accepted ways of thinking and legitimizing the treatment, and sometimes the compulsory detention, of those who deviate from them. From this point of view psychiatry, psychiatric nursing and mental health legislation are much more about the social control of people whose behaviour is causing problems for *others* than they are about caring for sick people themselves. According to Szasz, the myth of mental illness persists in modern societies not because of its scientific validity, but because it is such an effective means of social control.

Although this view has been criticized both for underestimating the effectiveness of contemporary psychiatry and for overestimating its social control function, it does raise important ethical issues. At the core of nursing (and medical) work is the principle of always acting in the patient's interests. The fact that many people are being treated in hospitals not because they want to be there, but because others such as family members, managers of residential institutions or the courts want them there, strikes at the heart of this most fundamental principle. Practices such as the hospital treatment of alcoholics and those with eating disorders, the compulsory admission of patients, and the widespread administration of major tranquillizers, raise ethical issues which it is impossible for psychiatric nursing to avoid.

The medical profession and the courts have been sensitive to the charge that psychiatry and mental health legislation have been used as a means of social control. Doctors have become increasingly reluctant to use compulsory powers to detain patients and the overwhelming majority of psychiatric hospital admissions are now voluntary. This has been generally welcomed as a liberal and 'progressive' development. However, it can create a 'double bind' for psychiatric nurses. When medical staff refuse to implement the Mental Health Act but expect that disturbed patients will still be controlled, nurses sometimes feel obliged to resort to coercive detention. This may involve simply telling patients they cannot leave, removing their clothes or even locking them up for a time. The necessity for such *de facto* detention creates both moral and ethical dilemmas for nurses. In this context Cavadino suggests that, 'the more adequately patients' rights are protected, the more difficult the job of the psychiatric nurse is likely to be' (1989, p. 81).

The 'anti-psychiatry' of Szasz and some sociologist has raised important criticism of existing practices without suggesting what could be put in their place. Should people who are unable to look after themselves be left sleeping rough on the streets? Should people refusing to eat be left to starve? Should the people expressing murderous feelings towards others be left until they kill? Mental disorders seem to necessitate some form of social control and most psychiatric professionals are probably aware of the control elements to their work. However, it could be argued that despite all its well-documented shortcomings the kind of control offered by psychiatric care in hospitals or in communities is more humane than leaving the mentally disordered to fend for themselves or to face criminal punishment and possibly imprisonment. Rather than being 'for' or 'against' psychiatric care, the more important question may be how mental health resources are deployed.

Summary

Mental disorder covers a wide range of conditions from recognized diseases to behavioural problems which are assumed to be manifestations of some underlying disease. Explanations of mental disorder and models of treatment are mainly based upon biological and psychological theories. However, sociological research has drawn attention to the role of wider social influences. First, social epidemiology has demonstrated the extent to which the genesis, diagnosis and treatment of mental disorders are influenced by social variables such as gender, class and ethnicity. Second, interpretive sociology has drawn attention to the importance of the reaction of others (including health professionals) in shaping patients' experiences. Third, sociologists have examined the impact of institutional and community care. Finally, sociologists have contributed to the discussion of some of the ethical dilemmas arising from the responsibilities of nurses and doctors to care for those who are unable to make rational decisions for themselves. Flanagan (1986) argues that psychiatric nurses are in a position to act as powerful advocates for their patients. In this context, the crucial question is whether the 'medicalization' of human madness and desperation tends to serve the interests of the vulnerable patient or those of wider society in controlling those others find troublesome.

References

Bateson G., Jackson D., Haley L., & Weakland J. (1956) Towards a theory of schizophrenia. *Behavioral Science*, **1**, 251–64.
Brandon D. (1991) *Innovation without Change? Consumer Power in Psychiatric Services*. Macmillan Education, Basingstoke.

Brown G.W. & Harris T. (1978) *Social Origins of Depression: A Study of Psychiatric Disorder Among Women.* Tavistock, London.

Cavadino M. (1989) *Mental Health Law in Context: Doctors' Orders?* Dartmouth, Aldershot.

Department of Health (1992) *The Health of the Nation: A Strategy for England.* HMSO, London.

Dryden W. & Golden W. (1987) *Cognitive-behavioural Approaches to Psychotherapy.* Hemisphere, London.

Fernando S. (1988) *Race and Culture in Psychiatry.* Routledge, London.

Field D. & Taylor S. (1992) The Contribution of Sociology. In *A Textbook of Psychiatric and Mental Health Nursing* (Ed. by J.I. Brooking, S.A.H. Ritter and B.L. Thomas) p. 151, Churchill Livingstone, Edinburgh.

Flanagan A. (1986) A question of ethics. *Nursing Times,* Aug 27, 39–41.

Goffman E. (1991) *Asylums: Essays on the Social Situation of Mental Patients and Other Inmates.* Penguin, London.

Gove W.R. (1975) Labelling and Mental Illness: A Critique. In his *The Labelling of Deviance: Evaluating a perspective.* Wiley, New York.

Kennedy I. (1981) *The Unmasking of Medicine.* Paladin, London.

Krause I.B. (1989) Sinking Heart: A Punjabi communication of distress. *Social Science and Medicine,* **29**, 563–75.

Laing R.D. & Esterson A. (1964) *Sanity, Madness and the Family.* Penguin, London.

Miles A. (1987) *The Mentally Ill in Contemporary Society,* 2nd edn. Blackwell, Oxford.

Pilling S. (1991) *Rehabilitation and Community Care.* Routledge, London.

Race D. (1987) Normalisation: Theory and Practice. In *Reassessing Community Care* (Ed. by N. Malin) pp. 62–79. Croom Helm, London.

Rosenham D. (1973) On being sane in insane places. *Science,* **179**, 250–58.

Scheff T.J. (1966) *Being Mentally Ill: A Sociological Theory.* Aldine, Chicago.

Stengel E. (1973) *Suicide and Attempted Suicide.* Penguin, London.

Szasz T.S. (1961) *The Myth of Mental Illness.* Harper & Row, New York.

Szasz T.S. (1970) *The Manufacture of Madness.* Harper & Row, New York.

Taylor S. (1982) *Durkheim and the Study of Suicide.* Macmillan, London.

Towell D. (1975) *Understanding Psychiatric Nursing: A Sociological Analysis of Modern Psychiatric Practice.* Royal College of Nursing, London.

Wender P., Rosenthal D., Kety S., Schulsinger F. & Welner J. (1974) Cross fostering: A research strategy for clarifying the role of genetic and experimental factors in the aetiology of schizophrenia. *Archives of General Psychiatry,* **30**, 121–8.

Further reading

Ramon S. (Ed.) (1991) *Beyond Community Care: Normalisation and Integration Work.* Macmillan/Mind, London.

Chapter 9
Death, Dying and Bereavement

Death has real and symbolic significance in our society. It generates questions about the meaning of life and how death is defined. It raises moral questions about euthanasia and the duty to maintain life and poses ethical dilemmas about confidentiality and the 'right to know'. All these occur in the context of an ageing, multi-cultural society where groups have different beliefs, values and priorities in relation to death. These complex issues affect the professional decisions which nurses are called upon to make and especially the difficult decisions which have to be made about the delivery of individualized patient care within the constraints of limited resources. Nurses are the main group of staff directly responsible for the care of terminally ill people, and will become increasingly involved in the decision making and policies developed in this area of work. While people die at all ages, and miscarriage, stillbirth, and the deaths of infants and children are of concern, in this chapter we concentrate primarily upon the care of dying people in older age groups. We categorize the care of the dying into four main settings. We also examine coping with death and bereavement, and focus upon a key area of debate: disclosure and communication.

Death in modern Britain

In Chapter 2 we noted that Britain is characterized by an ageing population. One consequence of this is that whereas formerly people would experience a number of deaths among those they were closely associated with, in the present era children rarely experience the death of a close friend or family member, and even for adolescents and adults such deaths are uncommon events. Although the appearance of HIV/AIDS has altered this among some groups, the trend remains broadly the same. Associated with this has been an increase in the number and proportion of people dying in NHS hospitals and other institutions. In 1990 23% of deaths occurred in the person's own home, and 72% occurred in institutions: hospitals (54%), hospices (4%), or nursing or residential homes (14%) (OPCS 1992). Relatively few people in our society die suddenly and unexpectedly, and with the control of infectious diseases the majority of unexpected deaths affecting young people are caused by accidents on the road, at work, or in the home. Only a minority of these reach the hospital, and few progress beyond the accident and emergency departments. Other sources of sudden and rapid death, affecting older people, are heart attacks and strokes. Again, such deaths rarely occur in hospitals as most victims die prior to entry to the hospital, and those that do enter hospital may be treated in specialist units such as coronary care units.

A number of writers have suggested that as a consequence of these changes there are few of the collective family and community rituals which in previous eras made sense of death and supported the bereaved. Thus, when they are faced with coping with their own death or that of someone close to them people may have to come to terms with the unfamiliar without the help of clear collective rules, and with little support from the wider community. It is argued that death, dying and mourning have become highly individualized and are viewed with apprehension and fear by most members of our society (Aries 1983). Sontag (1979) argues that certain diseases such as cancer or HIV/AIDS are particularly feared, and that these act as metaphors for more general and widespread anxieties about dying and death. The solution for many people is to place the onus for dealing with death and dying upon doctors and nurses. Yet these workers themselves are likely to share the apprehensions and anxieties of the wider population.

The main settings of terminal care

The focus of this section, which is based on Field and James (1993), is the places where dying occurs. The great majority of deaths occur in hospitals, hospices, domestic homes or residential institutions, although some people die elsewhere. Figure 9.1 indicates the main sources of help for people who are terminally ill.

Dying at home

Most people would prefer to die in their own home, and even when people die in a hospital or hospice, most of their care will take place in their own homes with the help and unpaid work of their close family and friends ('lay' carers). People who die at home will normally do so as the

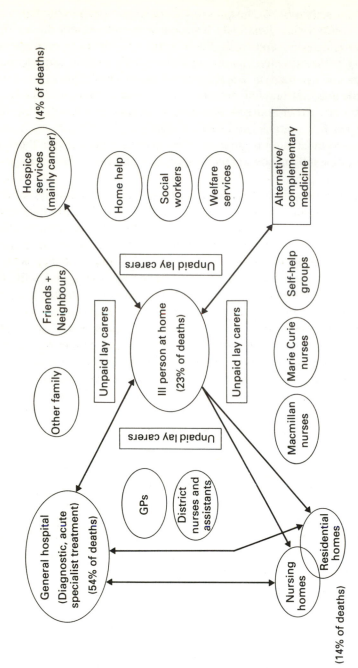

Fig. 9.1 Sources of help for people who are dying. (*Source* D. Field & N. James (1993) Where and how people die. In *The Future for Palliative Care* (Ed. by D. Clark) Open University Press, Milton Keynes. (Reproduced by permission of Open University Press.))

result of a long-term illness, often marked by persistent and distressing symptoms. It is thus highly likely that at some time they will have been admitted to a hospital or hospice for treatment of their condition. Since homes and families vary widely in their material, social, psychological and spiritual make-up, patterns of domestic care vary. The implementation by Parliament of the Care in the Community Act 1990 (Chapter 11) will lead to even greater emphasis on such unpaid lay care in the community.

Dying comfortably in one's own bed in the familiar surroundings of home with family and friends in attendance is deemed by many people to be an ideal way to die. A major advantage of dying at home is that the home provides a familiar environment within which the dying person may be better able to come to terms with his or her apprehensions and anxieties about their terminal illness. Being in a familiar environment can, of itself, provide psychological comfort, reassurance and support to the dying person. It is also likely that the dying person will be able to influence the quality of their life more easily and retain greater control than in an institution, at least during the time they retain mobility and mental clarity. There are also advantages for lay carers. Caring for the dying person may assuage feelings of guilt and enable carer(s) and cared for to maintain family ties. In particular it has been suggested that lay carers will cope better with their bereavement if they can take an active part in care, and this is easier at home than in a formal institution.

There are also potential problems with home care, such as the adequate control of symptoms. The desirability, and even the possibility, of a 'home death' depends primarily on the human resources available to help both with the control of symptoms, and the constant attendance and extra domestic work which such care entails. Although many families wish to look after their relative at home, they may be unable to do so, and may feel guilty as a consequence. Changes in population and social structure mean that there are now more people without family or relatives to provide unpaid home care than in previous times (Chapter 10).

The physical help and social support given by community nurses and their access to other resources is vital. Opportunities for respite care, home help services, and the support which is offered from the primary health care team may make all the difference between care at home or admission to a hospital (Cartwright 1991a). Having an outsider to talk to, or to ask advice from can help lay carers keep a sense of perspective. A community nurse may also be very important in negotiating in-patient care when it is necessary and in helping the lay carers to come to terms with the fact they can no longer manage on their own.

Dying in a hospital

The shift towards community care has meant that hospitals are increasingly becoming places where acute, intensive, short-stay treatment is given while the community (including local authority and private residential and nursing homes) is now the preferred place for long-term care. People typically spend the last few days of their lives in a hospital or hospice. The deaths which most hospital staff have to deal with are those where dying takes place over a long period of time as a result of a chronic condition, and in which death is anticipated by the staff. Further, the terminally ill people involved will typically be adults beyond middle life (82% of deaths in hospital are of people over the age of 65). Death is a rare occurrence in many hospital settings, and once past their training period nurses may be able to avoid settings such as oncology wards and intensive care units which are characterized by high levels of death. Nevertheless, a significant number of deaths in hospitals do occur over a relatively short period of time, and in settings which are primarily geared to deliver acute restorative therapy.

Different hospital units have different amounts and types of death and dying according to the nature and type of their patients (and their disease conditions). Thus, nurses working in a general hospital will have widely different experiences of nursing dying people. A death in a maternity unit, in an acute surgical ward, in an intensive care unit, in a young disabled unit, or in a ward for the elderly will involve different types of patients, whose lives are more or less highly valued in our society. Their deaths will be experienced very differently by the staff caring for them, e.g. as tragic, an unexpected shock, failure, release, or the peaceful end to a full life.

The period of *time* over which death occurs and its *predictability* are major factors affecting how staff experience terminal illness and treat dying patients (Glaser & Strauss 1965). In general, hospital staff have most difficulty in dealing with quick and unexpected deaths and are most comfortable with deaths which are predictable and which can be prepared for. Another important factor is the *age* of the patient. In our society people find it is easier to accept the death of old people than of young people. In particular nurses find it psychologically difficult to nurse infants and young children who are terminally ill, and people of their own age with whom they may identify such as those with cancer or AIDS.

The physical care of terminally ill people seems to vary widely not only between hospitals but also within hospitals. Although knowledge of effective pain and symptom control is being disseminated to the hospital sector, difficulties persist because of the complex nature of symptomatology among terminally ill patients. A further difficulty concerns the decision to move from therapeutic treatment aimed at cure and restoration of function to palliative care aimed at symptom relief. Nurses may become aware of the need for a shift to palliative care before doctors do because of the continuous and close nature of their contact with the dying person. One of the main areas of conflict between ward sisters and doctors is the care of terminally ill patients and decisions about resuscitation. It seems that it is often difficult for doctors to move from the aggressive management of disease towards a pattern of care where other needs of patients and their quality of life are seen as primary.

Within hospitals there are difficulties in delivering patient-centred care in accordance with the body of knowledge and expertise which nursing has developed. While the continuing development of technology and knowledge has led to sophisticated interventions into matters of living and dying, demands on nursing staff have increased, and the co-ordination of the various elements of the treatment of terminal conditions has become more complex. The number of staff involved in terminal care has increased, which means that the inter-disciplinary co-ordination of care is important. Nurses, who are at the centre of care delivery, may thus be confronted with delicate and difficult tasks of negotiating treatment with doctors and other staff. Their personal knowledge of and involvement with the patient may also place them in the role of patient advocate. Finally, other factors such as the changes in the pattern of nursing work and pressures on resources mean that there will be fewer trained front line nurses to deliver care.

The question of the degree to which hospital staff should become involved with their patients is unanswerable, and reflects personal preferences and beliefs. Given the nature of nursing work as emotional labour (James 1992; Smith 1992), some emotional involvement with long-term patients may develop over a period of time, with a sense of loss when the patient dies. There are positive and negative sides to both involvement and detachment. Over-involvement with patients is identified by Vachon (1987) as one source of stress. However, lack of involvement may also have negative consequences for nurses, and some nurses feel guilty if they do not have any feelings about the death of someone they have nursed (Field 1989).

Changes in the functioning of NHS hospitals are affecting the nature and forms of emotional involvement which develop between nurses and patients, perhaps making these more transitory and less intense. With shorter lengths of stay, higher patient throughput, less favourable nurse–patient staffing levels, and more complex disease conditions to deal with, the general levels of workplace pressure upon trained nurses have increased over the lifetime of the NHS. Vachon claims that it is not the dying person who is the main cause of stress for nurses, but aspects of the environment within which their care takes place. Despite these pressures, it is likely that some type of emotional involvement will still occur as long as nursing work is based on 'care' and 'emotional labour' (Chapter 12).

Dying in a hospice

Hospice care originally focused upon in-patient centres of excellence promoting holistic care of dying people in a homely environment, but now takes a variety of forms (Table 9.1), including a network of 800 Macmillan nurses working with primary care teams and pain and symptom control teams in hospitals (Griffin 1991; Seale 1989).

The very fact of referral to a hospice may be regarded as an important moment in a terminal illness, conveying a number of messages to those concerned. Patients do not always understand that admission to a hospice means that they are terminally ill, and although this will be understood by most, it is not uncommon for hospice in-patients to be unaware that they are dying at the time of their first admission. For relatives and hospice staff admission is a clear signal that death is imminent, and indicates that this is now an appropriate time to talk about their prognosis to the person who is dying.

Talking about the person's death and dying is expected to be one of the strengths of hospice staff. Through the teamwork which challenges traditional inter- and intra-professional hierarchies, the channels for disclosure are left open and are unimpeded by the proscriptions against disclosure found in so many hospital settings. Hospices specifically set out to improve the quality of life for those who are dying, particularly those dying from cancer. Because dying is recognized as a social and spiritual as well as a physical event, hospices preceded hospitals in taking account of the quality of life of their patients. The notion of 'total

Table 9.1　Hospice services in Britain.

Service	Number
In-patient hospices (2820 beds)	175
Day care hospices	186
Home care teams	360
Support nurse/teams in hospitals	160

Source　*Directory of Hospice Services (1992)* St Christopher's Hospice Information Service. (Reproduced by permission of Hospice Information Service.)

pain' means taking account of psychological, social and spiritual factors, in addition to physical symptoms. The hospice approach to dealing with this form of holistic care is to encourage the expression of all forms of pain so that they may be attended to, and the nurse's role in supporting the patient is based on an understanding of the patients' emotions and not simply a narrow focus upon their physical pain.

Hospice staff are given permission to express their own feelings, rather than to hide behind their uniform or their 'professionalism'. In practice, the implied intensity of emotional involvement is not as dramatic as it may at first appear. Though staff involvement is encouraged, it is also subject to individual and group regulation, so that although attachments may occur, the depth of a relationship is not the same with each patient. An important component in coping with loss is being given 'permission to grieve', something which may be denied to nurses in other settings. The supportive environment of the hospices and their focus on agreed goals of care should mean that there are fewer major difficulties of workplace stress and may make such stress easier to handle.

Dying in an institutional home

Residential and nursing homes are an increasingly important place of death, particularly for those over the age of 85, and research suggests that at least 14% of all deaths occur in these homes. Both types of institutional home are likely to play an increasingly significant role in the care of dying people during the 1990s. In some areas nursing homes have already largely replaced long-stay geriatric wards. Most people who are in institutional homes are there either because there were no lay carers available to support them when they lived in their domestic homes, or because such carers are unable to continue to do so. Those with no relatives to act as go-between or advocates for the old person are especially vulnerable to the values and approach of the staff who run the home (e.g. Hockey 1990).

Nursing homes have to have a trained nurse on the premises night and day, whereas residential homes do not because their residents are supposed to be largely self-sufficient and free from illness. However, in practice residential homes may contain many residents who are physically unwell, confused or demented (Willcocks *et al.* 1987). Old people dying in both types of homes are characterized by a different pattern of symptoms than those dying elsewhere. Cartwright (1991b) reports higher levels of mental confusion, greater loss of continence, more constipation, more bad temper, and greater difficulty in seeing and hearing among residents of communal homes. Old people in institutional homes are also more likely to be suffering from chronic and long-term

conditions than those living in their own or relatives' homes (Bury &
Holme 1990). Indeed these conditions, especially mental confusion or
incontinence, may have contributed to their admission to the home.

The basis of care for those who are dying in an institutional home is
dramatically different from the domestic home relying as it does on low
paid, largely part-time staff, and with a very variable quality of symptom
control. The use of community nurses in institutional homes is much
greater than by those old people in their own homes, and in residential
homes symptom control will depend on the involvement of the home or
client's GP and other specialist community services. In nursing homes,
the quality of symptom control will depend primarily upon the quality
and training of the nurses employed by the home, although it will also
depend upon the quality of medical care forthcoming from GPs. The
adequate management of symptoms thus depends upon the quality and
links with the primary care team and other health services, as well as
upon the quality and training of the nursing staff employed. A particular
problem for staff is the often high number of confused or senile residents, as it may be difficult to assess the severity of other symptoms. As
is the case with terminally ill people being cared for in the domestic
home, admission to hospital is likely when acute episodes or problems
arise, although it may be difficult for homes to negotiate admission to
hospitals for their residents because of the pressure of demand for
hospital beds.

There is an enormous range in the quality of care which is offered to
those dying in institutional homes, but for the most part special attention
to the care of dying people is minimal. In many homes death is 'mar-
ginalized' and seen primarily in terms of the practical problems which it
causes for staff. Most homes seem to operate with a policy of 'closed
awareness', keeping those who are dying in ignorance of their prognosis,
even if they are alert and able to cope with such news. Under such circumstances the processes of denial and withdrawal from the dying
resident by staff and relatives may occur leading to the 'social death' of
the resident. As in hospitals and hospices, the good intentions of individual nurses may help clients to know that someone cares for and
understands them. However, the normal practice of the institution may
overwhelm such individual efforts to provide personal care and attention.

The 'us' and 'them' divide between staff and clients bodes poorly for
emotional involvement, and under these circumstances the types of
relationship reminiscent of old-style psycho-geriatric wards can occur,
where a few clients are 'favourites', most go unremarked, and some
groups of clients are categorised as 'difficult'. If the significance of caring
for the dying goes largely unrecognized in nursing and residential homes,

so do staff needs. Workplace stress can be heightened by nursing caseloads of confused, demented and incontinent residents which may cause high levels of physical labour and stress.

Coping with dying and bereavement

Both dying and bereavement have personal and social aspects which are difficult to disentangle: not only are personal attachments lost, but also social relationships, connections and activities. Further, the experiences of dying and grieving, both before and after the death, are greatly affected by social and physical circumstances such as where dying and death take place, the types of communication between those involved, and the social support available (Littlewood 1992). For example, both the dying person and their partner will lose their relationship to each other and the shared social activities which they participated in as a couple. Attachment to others is a source of emotional and psychological strength and support, and a source of social cohesion (Chapter 5). But it is also a source of pain, loss and distress when attachments are under threat or severed. Thus it is not surprising that both dying people and their close intimates appear to experience broadly similar loss reactions.

Dying

The work of Kubler-Ross (1970) alerted those working with dying patients to the need to take account of the psychological reactions which dying people experience. She proposed that a number of stages could be identified in the psychological adjustment of hospitalized cancer patients to the knowledge that they were dying. The first reaction was that of denial ('it can't be true'). This can be seen as a response which allows people to control the impact of the bad news and come to an initial acknowledgement of it. Acknowledgement leads to the next stage: anger. This can be directed at anyone – doctors, nurses, partners, self – or anything – God, the world in general. Anger can be difficult for nurses and others to cope with, and so they may withdraw from or limit contact with the dying patient, leading to their isolation at a time when they may be in great need of contact and support. Anger is followed by the stage of bargaining aimed at gaining more time or symptom relief. Bargains are often 'silent' and private: 'If I promise to be nice to people God will let me see my next birthday.' As full realization sinks in, and bargaining is seen as futile, depression sets in. Finally, according to Kubler-Ross a stage of acceptance may be attained.

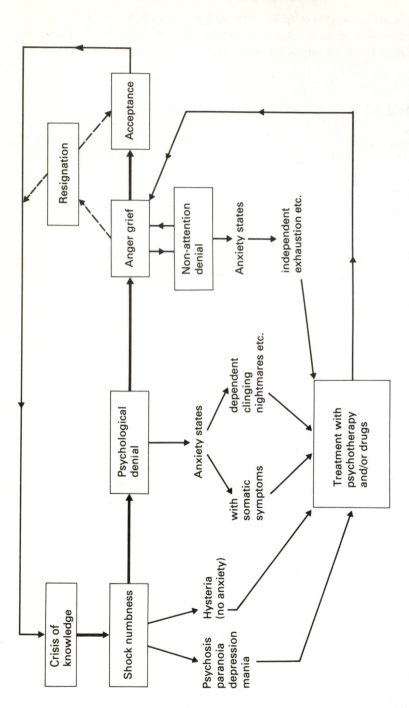

Fig. 9.2 Variations from Kubler-Ross's model of the psychological reactions to dying. (*Source* A. Stedeford (1984) *Facing Death: Patients, Families and Professionals.* Heinemann, London. (Reproduced by permission of Butterworth-Heinemann Limited.))

Despite the positive impact of Kubler-Ross's ideas in focusing nursing attention upon the isolation and psychological difficulties of dying patients her work can be criticized (Stedeford 1984). Most importantly, although the reactions she describes are found in dying patients, they are not unidirectional and sequential stages, and they vary from person to person. Fig. 9.2 shows the range of variations which are possible. Unfortunately some nurses have taken Kubler-Ross's work as prescriptive, rather than as a guide to what might be expected. Thus they might interpret anger as a positive sign, while neglecting to pay adequate attention to possible remediable causes of such anger (e.g. unrelieved pain or a justifiable complaint). Attempts may be made to 'move' the patient on 'to the next stage'. In some cases nurses may feel that they have failed if their patient dies without reaching 'acceptance'.

Bereavement

In hospitals the main focus of nursing work and concern with dying people is with specific individuals, with little sustained provision (or capacity) to care for the grief and mourning of relatives and friends. These are more likely to be the province of community nurses, although the research evidence suggests that most bereaved people have no sustained contact with professional carers.

We might ask whether it is sensible to view grief as a pathological rather than a normal condition. Nevertheless, it is helpful for nurses to be able to recognize the stages of grief, and understand the factors which aid or retard its resolution. For example, the care for parents bereaved by a stillbirth has been improved. It is now recognized that parents have difficulty in coming to terms with their loss without seeing the body, and so parents are now allowed to see and hold their dead infant (Roberts & Oakley 1990).

The loss through death of someone who is close is one of life's significant and stressful events. Loss of companionship and doing things together may lead to familiar activities losing their meaning simply because they are no longer joint activities. Loss of other activities and relationships may also result from the loss of a partner, as 'paired activities' are the norm in our society. In addition to the losses and changes in leisure activities and daily routines, some spouses may experience loss of income, and possibly the loss of their home as a result of their bereavement. Generally speaking the death of a spouse occurs in old age and, especially for elderly widows, results in a change of status and movement into an 'empty' role. To the extent that social support is available it may mitigate this generally negative picture (Chapter 5).

Normal reactions to bereavement have been described as occurring in four approximately sequential phases of grieving stretching over a couple of years (Bowlby 1981). The initial shock, disbelief, and 'numbness' may last from a few hours to a week. This is followed by a chaotic period characterized by anger, distress, restlessness, and active searching for the lost person. Denial may also occur. In this period of acute grief, the bereaved person vacillates between seeking reminders of the dead person to assuage their sense of loss, and avoiding them in order to escape from their grief (Stedeford 1984). Familiar places, activities and sounds may all vividly recall the dead person, and many people report talking with, hearing or seeing the dead person. This is a crucial stage in 'grief work' as the reality of the death becomes confirmed and accepted and the initial pain of loss is handled. The bereaved person may experience a number of physical symptoms, such as weight loss and sleep disturbance.

This period is followed by a time marked by disorganization and sometimes despair as the person comes to grips with their various losses and changes of activities, begins to learn new skills, and develops new patterns of living. Finally, a stable pattern of life may be achieved when the person has resolved the problem of retaining their connection with the dead person while 'letting them go' and continuing with their own life. Despite this apparently orderly progression, it should be emphasized that grief is dis-orderly and these emotions may be experienced at any time (Littlewood 1992).

It is claimed that rituals of mourning are important social mechanisms for helping resolve the core dilemma of acute grief because they provide a process which attenuates the death while affirming its reality. For example, both viewing the body and funerals serve to confirm the fact of death, and where the body is buried the thud of earth upon the coffin can be a dramatic and shocking confirmation that the dead person has indeed departed. Funerals and other rituals also serve to validate the social worth of the deceased and to confirm the relationship of the mourners to them and to each other. Elaborate rituals, which extend over a long period of time, may serve to limit and guide mourning and to shape social support by providing a structure in which there is a gradual tapering off of the connection of the bereaved with the dead person.

The most important functions of funerals and other rituals of mourning are twofold: to confirm and give reality to the fact of death and to mobilize social support for the bereaved. These are important functions because grieving often becomes complicated when the fact of death is denied, e.g. when there is no body, and social isolation and lack of support are associated with difficulties with grieving.

Communication and disclosure

The work of Glaser and Strauss (1965) can be seen as in many ways complementary to the insights of Kubler-Ross, as they focused upon the social circumstances which affected the care of dying hospital patients. They were particularly concerned with patterns of communication and awareness about dying. While for dying patients and their relatives their experience is unique and highly personal, for nurses the care of dying patients is part of their work, and the ways in which they define and perform such work has important consequences for patients and their relatives. One critical dimension in this is the knowledge which staff, the patient, and relatives have about the terminal prognosis. This is not necessarily straightforward, for the clarity and certainty of both the fact and the time of death have become blurred by the predominance of chronic disease and the capacity of modern medicine to intervene in disease processes to avert and retard the dying process. Certainty of death may develop slowly over a long period of time, and even when the fact of death is certain its timing may remain in doubt. 'Social death' and a process of 'social dying' as staff and others withdraw from social interaction with terminally ill patients may often precede 'biological' death.

It is still the case that some hospital consultants forbid nurses to disclose a terminal prognosis, even in the rare cases where a patient asks directly for confirmation of their suspicions that they are dying. However, 'open awareness', where a terminal prognosis is known by all persons involved, is an increasingly common situation in our hospitals. This is a situation which many nurses, patients and relatives see as desirable. There appears to have been a strong move away from the practice of keeping dying people in ignorance of their terminal prognosis towards a situation where the expectation (if not the practice) is that terminal prognoses will be disclosed to patients (Field 1989; Seale 1991). Where before, the needs of the dying patient as a person were ignored, now more active efforts to improve the quality of psychological and social care by responding to patients' unspoken apprehensions and questions can be seen in many places. One of the most compelling reasons for moving to a policy of disclosure of terminal prognoses is the evidence that most terminally ill patients eventually become aware that they are dying. For example, Hinton (1980) found that 66% of his sample of dying patients indicated to him that they knew they were dying, although they had not necessarily revealed this knowledge to hospital staff or to their relatives.

This move toward greater openness and responsiveness has brought with it many challenges (Buckman 1988). Most nurses and doctors find the task of actually transmitting this information very difficult and stressful, and few have received adequate training in appropriate communication skills. When nurses are uncomfortable about talking openly with patients about their likely death – even where they believe that this is the right thing to do – it is likely that they will avoid or limit their contact with them to a greater or lesser extent. This is especially likely to occur where nursing is organized in terms of tasks rather than by the allocation of individual nurses to particular patients, where death is uncommon, where there is little team support to nurses, and where there is no clearly formulated policy regarding disclosure.

Summary

NHS hospitals are, and will probably remain, the major place of death in British society, but most of the care of people who are dying takes place in their own homes. In both these settings, nurses are the main health workers involved in caring for those who are dying. Institutional homes for the elderly will become more important as places where people live and die. The quality of terminal (or palliative) care has improved with the dissemination of ideas and practice from the hospice movement and elsewhere. It is likely to be influenced positively by the incremental improvement of medical and nursing knowledge and practice and negatively by continuing problems of resource allocation. The pressure for open discussion with and full disclosure to patients will persist, especially in combination with wider societal pressures for greater patient involvement in the decisions made about their treatment. Nurses will continue to experience the rewards and difficulties of providing terminal and palliative care, and play a key role in the experiences of those who are dying and their close associates for the foreseeable future.

References

Aries P. (1983) *The Hour of Our Death*. Peregrine Books, Aylesbury.
Bowlby J. (1981) *Loss: Sadness and Depression*. Penguin, Harmondsworth.
Buckman R. (1988) *I Don't Know What To Say*. Papermac, London.
Bury M. & Holme A. (1990) *Life After Ninety*. Routledge, London.
Cartwright A. (1991a) Balance of care for the dying between hospitals and the community: Perceptions of general practitioners, hospital consultants, community nurses and relatives. *British Journal of General Practice*, **41**, 271–4.

Cartwright A. (1991b) The role of residential and nursing homes in the last year of people's lives. *British Journal of Social Work*, **21**, 627–45.

Directory of Hospice Services (1992) St Christopher's Hospice Information Service.

Field D. (1989) *Nursing the Dying*. Tavistock/Routledge, London.

Field D. & James N. (1993) Where and how people die. In *The Future for Palliative Care* (Ed. by D. Clark). Open University Press, Buckingham.

Glaser B. G. & Strauss A. L. (1965) *Awareness of dying*. Aldine, Chicago.

Griffin J. (1991) *Dying with Dignity*. Office of Health Economics, London.

Hinton J. (1980) Whom do dying patients tell? *British Medical Journal*, **281**, 1328–30.

Hockey J. (1990) *Experiences of Death*. Edinburgh University Press, Edinburgh.

James N. (1992) Care = organisation + physical labour + emotional labour. *Sociology of Health and Illness*, **14**, 488–509.

Kubler-Ross E. (1970) *On Death and Dying*. Tavistock, London.

Littlewood J. (1992) *Aspects of Grief: Bereavement in Adult Life*. Tavistock/Routledge, London.

OPCS (1992) *Mortality Statistics: General Review of the Registrar General on Deaths in England and Wales*. HMSO, London.

Roberts H. & Oakley A. (1990) *Miscarriage*. Penguin, London.

Seale C. (1989) What happens in hospices: a review of research evidence. *Social Science and Medicine*, **28**, 551–9.

Seale C. (1991) Communication and awareness about death: A study of a random sample of dying people. *Social Science and Medicine*, **32**, 943–52.

Smith P. (1992) *The Emotional Labour of Nursing: How Nurses Care*. Macmillan, London.

Sontag S. (1979) *Illness as Metaphor*. Allen Lane, London.

Stedeford A. (1984) *Facing Death: Patients, Families and Professionals*. Heinemann, London.

Vachon M. C. S. (1987) *Occupational Stress in Caring for the Critically ill, the Dying and the Bereaved*. Hemisphere, Washington.

Willcocks D., Peace S. & Kellaher L. (1987) *Private Lives in Public Places: A Research-based Critique of Residential Life in Local Authority Old People's Homes*. Tavistock, London.

Further reading

Dickenson D. & Johnson M. (Eds) (1993) *Death, Dying and Bereavement*. Sage, London.

Open University (1993) *Death and Dying*, Course K260. Open University, Milton Keynes.

Part IV
Caring for the Sick

Chapter 10
Family, Community and Health

One of the objectives of sociology is to gain a more detached view of ourselves and of others than can be achieved by personal experience alone. From this perspective the joys, dreams and despairs of individuals are in no way diminished but they are seen in the context of broad patterns and trends within families, communities, institutions, and nations. With this in mind, this chapter considers family relationships, community ties and their implications for health. Its predominant themes are diversity and change in the development of family life in modern Britain. For this reason it dwells on some types of families that have become more common in recent decades as well as those with longer histories.

The popular image is still of a 'nuclear' family in which a married couple bring up their natural children. It is found in soap operas and TV commercials. More seriously, it also informs political debate, moral teaching and social policy. This family is widely regarded as the 'average' family, the 'natural' family and the 'ideal' family to which all should aspire. Other types of households, such as one parent families or step-families, are often portrayed as flawed, deviant or at best pale imitations. They are even sometimes perceived as a threat to 'normal' family life, as in debates about 'family values' which have been prominent in elections in Britain and the USA. In reality, however, the late twentieth century has witnessed a transformation in the way people conduct their private lives. The outcome is a shifting mosaic of different types of family relationships, including both traditional and new forms. Some long established values and ideals are being questioned; others are retained but pursued in new contexts. We should no longer refer to 'the family', as if it were a single and fixed entity, but rather we should speak of 'families' (Elliott 1991; Kiernan & Wicks 1990).

Developments in family relationships

Changes in marriage are the key to recent changes in family relations more generally. Leaving aside short-term fluctuations, for the first two-thirds of the twentieth century the underlying trend was for numbers of marriages, and the proportion of the population getting married, to increase. This reflected changes in the ratio of men to women in the population. In the late nineteenth century women considerably out-numbered men and there was no option for many but to remain spin-sters. As this imbalance gradually disappeared, marriage became an aspect of almost everyone's life.

Recently, however, new trends have emerged (see Table 10.1). In the last two decades there has been an overall fall in numbers of marriages. Marriages in which neither partner has been married before (known as first marriages) have declined particularly steeply. In contrast, weddings that are second, or subsequent, ceremonies for one or both parties (known as remarriages) have increased dramatically. Over a third of all marriages are now remarriages. About one-fifth of people born in mid-twentieth century Britain will have married two or more times before the year 2000.

In part these changes reflect a tendency to postpone marriage; thus, teenage marriages declined sharply in the 1980s. This too was a reversal of trends in the 1950s and 1960s, when age at marriage was falling. Another factor has been a marked growth in the numbers of cohabiting couples and of cohabitation as an accepted part of the process of household or family formation. By the mid-1980s there were estimated to be about 900 000 cohabiting couples in Britain. Some of these relation-ships are short-lived, others are a prelude to marriage or remarriage. Some people regard cohabitation as a long-term commitment in its own right and not as a preliminary to something else. An increasing number of couples live together, share possessions and bring up children but do not get married. By the mid-1980s there were over 400 000 children living

Table 10.1 Marriage in the United Kingdom.

	1961	1971	1981	1989
First marriage for both partners (in thousands)	340	369	263	252
Second, or subsequent, marriage for one or both partners (in thousands)	57	90	135	141
Total marriages (in thousands)	397	459	398	393
Remarriages as a percentage of all marriages	14%	20%	34%	36%

Source Adapted form Table 2.14 of Central Statistical Office (1992) *Social Trends 1992*. HMSO, London. (Reproduced by permission of Central Statistical Office.)

with cohabiting parents. Some of these children were from previous marriages of one or both partners.

In the early 1990s divorces were running at about 150 000 per annum, six times the levels of the early 1960s. Of every ten couples getting married, four could expect subsequently to find themselves in the divorce courts (although five could expect to celebrate their silver wedding anniversaries). The numbers caught up in divorce proceedings each year have doubled since 1970. If current trends continue, within a decade or so fewer than half of all children will have natural parents who are married at the time of their birth and remain married until they are grown up.

Divorce is particularly prevalent when the couple are very young, have had a brief courtship or when the bride is pregnant. Divorce rates are highest amongst those with unskilled manual occupations and lowest among those in professional and managerial backgrounds. This may, in part, reflect financial factors. For the well-off, divorce is likely to result in a sharp decline in living standards and a division of valuable possessions (houses, cars, furnishings, and so on). Families living on low wages, experiencing frequent periods of unemployment and dependent to a significant degree on social security entitlements have few capital goods to lose. In these circumstances, divorced mothers may derive an income from welfare benefits comparable to that previously available to them within marriage.

There are estimated to be well over a million one parent families in Britain, about one in five of all families with dependent children. Their numbers have doubled since the 1970s. Over 90% of lone parents are women, most of whom are divorced, separated or unmarried mothers. Some 1.9 million children are living in such families, representing one-seventh of the under-sixteen age group. One parent families are less likely than two parent families to be owner-occupiers and more likely to live in local authority or privately rented accommodation. As a result, they tend to be found in poor quality accommodation in inner city areas and council estates, where they may constitute a substantial proportion of all households.

High rates of remarriage mean that being a divorcee, or a member of a one parent family, are often temporary conditions. This suggests that people still value and seek a happy marriage; indeed, the increasing divorce rate could be said to indicate the high regard in which people hold the institution of marriage and the high quality of marital relationships which they expect with their partners. One consequence of the rise of remarriage, however, is that a growing number of adults and children belong to stepfamilies (also called 'reconstituted families') at some stage in their lives. Other stepfamilies are formed as a result of cohabitation. About one-tenth of all children are currently living in stepfamilies.

A century ago families including five children were commonplace. By the 1960s a remarkable transformation had occurred with three-quarters of married women having two children or less. In the 1970s birth rates fell still further and, although they subsequently recovered slightly, in the early 1990s were well below earlier periods. Numbers of births are also well below the figures of thirty years ago (Table 10.2). Even more remarkable has been the decline in numbers of children born within marriage and the very dramatic increase in extra-marital births. In the 1950s the proportion of extra-marital births was much the same as it had been at the turn of the century, that is, about one in twenty five. Today well over a quarter of British children are born outside marriage. In addition, the numbers of extra-marital births that are jointly registered by both parents have risen very sharply. Joint registration is usually taken to indicate a continuing close relationship between the parents, often including financial arrangements and emotional support. This is further evidence of long-term cohabitation as an emerging form of family life.

These trends should not be taken to indicate that the family is a declining institution. Rather, they suggest a rapidly developing range of different types of family relationships which children and adults may enter and leave for various periods. Some of this fluidity is captured in the following fictitious, but entirely plausible, biography which spans eight different households:

When Bill was ten, his parents separated. He lived with his mother and saw his father every Saturday. Four years later, his mother remarried,

Table 10.2 Live births in the United Kingdom.

	1961	1971	1981	1990
Total of all live births (in thousands)	944	902	731	799
Total live births within marriage (in thousands)	887	830	636	575
Total live births outside marraige (in thousands)	57	72	95	224
Extra-marital births as a percentage of all live births	6%	8%	13%	28%

Source Adapted form Table 1.13 and Chart 2.22 of Central Statistical Office (1992) *Social Trends 1992*. Central Statistical Office HMSO, London. (Reproduced by permission of Central Statistical Office.)

and Bill added a stepfather to his family. At eighteen, Bill left home to attend college, and after graduation he and his girlfriend moved in together. A year and a half later they married and soon afterwards they had a child. After several years, however, the marriage began to sour. Bill and his wife eventually separated with Bill's wife retaining custody of the child. Three years later Bill married a woman who had a child from a previous marriage and together they had another child. Bill's second marriage lasted 35 years until his death. (In Elliott 1991).

Private lives and health issues

This section will briefly explore some of the implications of recent changes in family relationships for health and health care. It should be emphasized that we are dealing here with general trends and that not all individuals or families will experience the same situations or constraints.

Divorce, marital breakdown and health status

Married people have lower levels of mortality, physical morbidity and psychological distress than the divorced, the widowed and also the single (Chapter 5). This holds true for both men and women, although most studies suggest that husbands derive greater levels of health benefit from marriage than wives. Generally speaking, parents appear to enjoy better health than non-parents, although mothers with young children and lone parents run particular risks with respect to mental health (Macintyre 1992). The effects of marital breakdown on mortality are particularly apparent where psychological welfare and social support play an important role in the causes or cure of disease. Stress, loneliness and hazardous life styles are reflected in raised mortality from suicide, accidents, cirrhosis of the liver, cancer of the lung and heart diseases. Failure to maintain therapeutic regimes may be reflected in raised mortality from diabetes and TB.

Marital breakdown may entail a loss of emotional closeness, social prestige, economic resources, accommodation, friendships and contacts with children. To this may be added that many people experience the public world of bureaucracies and markets as cold and heartless; they seek to forge a sense of personal destiny and identity in the private spheres of courtship, sexuality and marriage. The sense of loss entailed in bereavement or divorce, then, may reflect the breadth and depth of marital relationships. It may be a loss of a utopian ideal as well as a present reality.

A great deal of concern surrounds the effects of divorce on the welfare of children. These appear to be variable and to depend on specific circumstances. However, most studies suggest that, even when there has been considerable stress and tension in the home, children wish to see their parents stay together. Few children react to the breakup with relief or see it as a solution to problems. The immediate separation appears universally to be a time of profound emotional disturbance. Young children may blame themselves for the separation. Older children may understand better but feel rejected, deeply anxious and have strong feelings of anger. Wallerstein and Kelly (1980) identified long-lasting distress among a substantial minority of the children in their study. The way parents handle these emotional problems can be of vital significance for the future development of the child (Parkinson 1987). It appears to be very important that children do not feel abandoned by one or both parents and that both parents discuss and explain what may be very painful matters with their children. Children who maintain continuous contacts and open communications with both parents are more likely to weather the emotional storms.

One parent families

Within one parent families the pressures and worries of domestic routines, child-rearing and financial management fall on just one adult. Further, such families may arise from emotionally difficult circumstances such as separation or divorce. There are few opportunities for lone parents to be 'off duty' or to share their cares and burdens. What is more, members of one parent families tend to be more socially isolated than two parent families, having fewer friendship ties, kinship visits and social 'outings'. In some communities there may still be a social stigma attached to membership of such families and it is possible that adults or children may feel a sense of personal failure or responsibility for the breakdown of the marriage. As time goes on, lone parents may find themselves adopting roles and relationships with respect to their children which incorporate aspects of the traditional roles of both mother and father. Fathers who see their children for relatively brief visits or trips may increasingly adopt an avuncular role. As a result parent-child relationships may have a somewhat different dynamic to those of the two parent family.

All these are reasons to believe that members of one parent families face distinctive emotional difficulties and pressures. Nurses should be aware of these, both as potential sources of health problems and as a context of illness behaviour. A good deal of research has suggested that, on average, children brought up in one parent families experience higher rates of delinquency, problems of psychological adjustment and educational underachievement than those in two parent situations (Amato & Keith 1991). It is important, however, not to jump to unwarranted conclusions from these observations. Some of the older medical and social work literature characterized one parent families as inherently pathological or deviant groupings. They were described as incomplete or disorganized fragments of 'proper' families: the phrase 'broken home', still widely heard, captures this view. For many years a popular policy option was that of 'restoring normality', either by the reconciliation of the marriage partners or the fostering of children in two parent families.

Pressure groups representing lone parents reacted against such views, asserting that they stereotyped their families and failed to address the specific features of their difficulties. Detailed and systematic research, as opposed to poorly designed studies or outright speculation, has indicated that the relationship between membership of a one parent family and other forms of behaviour, such as crime or educational failure, is far more complex than once supposed (Macintyre 1992). Many of the difficulties faced by such families, including many emotional stresses and anxieties, can be traced to the great economic hardships that most one parent families face.

A very high proportion of one parent families are living in poverty. In 1990, 53% of one parent families lived in households with a weekly income of £100 or less, compared to just 4% of two parent and cohabiting families. Many lone parents find employment is a difficult and unprofitable option. Reliable child care has to be arranged and paid for from the relatively low wages available to many working women. Alimony, or maintenance payments, offer a notoriously unreliable and low level of income. Very few ex-husbands earn enough to maintain two households adequately. In these circumstances, a high proportion of one parent families rely on state welfare benefits as a main source of income (Popay *et at.* 1983). Benefit entitlements are often complex, fragmented and means-tested, leading to under-claiming. Moreover, there are very few benefits specifically designed with one parent families in mind (Bradshaw & Millar 1991). Many depend on Income Support. In 1989, some three-quarters of a million one parent families (representing two million adults and children) were receiving Income Support. Nearly three-quarters had been on Income Support for over a year; nearly half for three years or more.

The relationship between poverty and health is very well established (Chapter 4). Deficiencies in diet, housing, heating, environment and opportunities for recreation exact a heavy, and well-documented, toll in the form of physical disease, accidental and non-accidental injuries and psychological distress.

Stepfamilies

Adults and children entering stepfamilies may have experienced divorce, separation, single parenthood or bereavement. Adult members may have been married one or more times before. Children from one or more previous marriages may reside permanently, temporarily or occasionally within the stepfamily. Once again, then, we encounter diversity and variation.

Financial problems encountered by lone parents may be eased by remarriage, with consequent benefits for health. However, where partners still derive income from a previous marriage (for example, maintenance payments) or have a financial stake in another household (for example, part ownership of a house) financial transactions can remain complex and may be a source of friction. These monetary questions are but one aspect of broader ambiguities or tensions surrounding the boundaries of social relationships within stepfamilies (Burgoyne & Clark 1984, Clulow 1991).

Uncertainties arise partly because both adults and children in stepfamilies may have emotional commitments to members of family units other than the one in which they live most of the time. These external bonds may remain of great emotional significance over long periods, even within a successful stepfamily. Ambiguities concerning boundaries may be heightened when additional children, who reside in other households, come into the stepfamily for more or less temporary visits. The complexity of family bonds is further increased when wider kin are taken into account. Will ex-grandparents continue to keep up close relationships? What bonds do children feel to newly acquired aunts and uncles whom they have not grown up with and know little? All this has to be negotiated in the context of potential difficulties concerning the nuclear core of the stepfamily. Children may find themselves with a new set of siblings, whose character, histories and family traditions are unknown to them. They are faced with accepting a new parental figure into their family circle whilst maintaining a relationship with a mother or father elsewhere. The sexual basis of family bonds between adults may be brought home to children, who may also be forced to recognize that there is now no chance of a reconciliation between their natural parents.

The resentments, rivalries and anxieties that can easily arise in this situation may be exacerbated by difficulties surrounding the exercise of authority and control between generations. Children may resent being disciplined by a step-parent. Step-parents and natural parents (both inside and outside the step family) may come into conflict over appropriate forms of punishment and control of children. Children may play one party off against another. Step-parents may even feel that the relationship between their partner and their partner's children is exclusive and threatening. Tensions can take a further twist if, as is not uncommon, the new partners decide to cement their relationship by having a child of their own.

In part, stepfamilies are up against the beliefs, norms and values which surround traditional notions of family life, including assumptions about life-long monogamy, 'wicked stepmothers' and the exclusive nature of blood ties. Their members have to negotiate new forms of family bonds which are more open-ended and complex than traditional notions have allowed. Health professionals need to be aware of the emotional framework of stepfamilies. Thus, for example, the provision of informal health care or social support between stepfamily members may well be influenced by these issues.

Extra-marital births and infant health

There is an established relationship between extra-marital births and infant ill health. Official statistics have long recorded considerably raised levels of infant mortality for babies born outside marriage. Births outside marriage have also been associated with low birth-weight, raised incidence of birth complications and raised levels of non-accidental injury during the first year of life. In addition, unmarried mothers have made less use of health care services, both for themselves and their babies. They have, for example, tended to present late for antenatal care.

Babies born outside marriage, and their mothers, commonly suffer from multiple deprivations and multiple risks. Very young mothers face enhanced health risks for themselves and their babies, and a high proportion of lone mothers are in this age group (Cooper 1991). Furthermore, available evidence suggests that extra-marital births are more common in lower income groups, where poverty is likely to affect the survival chances of the child. In addition to these disadvantages, unmarried mothers may encounter prejudice and discrimination in housing, employment and in more informal contexts.

Recent years have witnessed new developments in extra-marital conceptions and infant health which add to the complexity of the picture. An increasing number of mothers giving birth outside marriage belong to older age groups. Many of these older women already have other children, born within marriages that subsequently broke up. Frequently, they are cohabiting prior to, or instead of, remarrying. As a group, they tend to have greater social skills, more experience of child care and greater material resources than teenage mothers. A linked trend is the rise in joint registration of extra-marital births, noted earlier. This suggests an increasing proportion of unmarried mothers have a close and continuing relationship with the father of their child. Many of these mothers are members of households with regular incomes and have partners with whom they can share the practical chores and emotional pressures of family life. Some children born outside marriage, it seems, are now brought up in less straitened or disadvantaged circumstances than formerly. This appears to be reflected in infant mortality statistics. The lowest rates of infant deaths occur among babies born inside marriage, closely followed by those born outside marriage jointly registered by parents with the same address. The highest rates are for those born outside marriage registered by mothers alone.

Families and informal care

Families are a major source of health care, often referred to as 'informal care' (Dalley 1988; Parker 1990). One estimate (Green 1988) suggests there are 6 million carers in Britain (one adult in seven), 1.4 million of whom devote twenty or more hours per week to caring. The old, chronically sick, terminally ill, mentally and physically handicapped and mentally ill are particularly likely to receive family care on a long-term basis. Some of these patients are bedridden, incontinent, confused, paralysed or of limited faculties. In the case of chronic long-term illnesses, routine attention to therapeutic regimes and monitoring of symptoms may be required.

Informal carers are unpaid and are rarely professionally qualified or technically trained. They become eligible, or obliged, to adopt the role of carer largely as a result of ties of family and kinship. Similarly the sick become eligible for such care not as a result of formal citizenship rights (as in the NHS) or monetary payments (as in private medicine) but largely as a function of specific family bonds (for example, mother-daughter relationship). Informal carers typically have responsibility for most or all aspects of their patients' welfare. Whilst many carers are 'their own boss' and can develop idiosyncratic routines, this also accentuates the open-ended and demanding nature of their task. Many are 'on call' at all hours of the day and night.

Informal caring commonly entails a range of costs. These may be financial, such as extra heating, special diets, specialized equipment or wages and job opportunities foregone by the carer. Carers also often experience a loss of personal mobility, a heavy round of daily tasks, a reduction in their social lives and increased social isolation. They are frequently cut off from other carers and from the formal health care system. There are few pressure groups to represent their interests or opportunities for them to meet others in like situations.

Informal care has been described as 'a labour of love' (Finch & Groves 1983). It is a moral responsibility, a personal commitment and a social duty. As a result, caring relationships may be highly charged emotionally. They may represent personal affirmations of identity, meaning and loyalty. Carers may receive great emotional rewards from caring in the form of intimacy with a loved one. By the same token, they may also experience a burden of anxiety, worry and guilt. They may find it difficult to accept or express negative feelings about the social, psychological and financial costs of caring. They can be affected by a sense of self-recrimination that seems to outsiders to be undeserved. Their commitment can lead them to sacrifice their own health, possibly resulting in a crisis in which both carer and patient become in need of emergency treatment. In addition, tensions, rivalries and resentments can be generated or surface within families providing care. Such stresses may be eased by opportunities to get away from caring for a few hours or days, self-help networks, involvement of wider family members, and sensitive support from health professionals, domiciliary services and day-care services.

Although a substantial proportion of carers are middle-aged, a significant number are themselves quite elderly, many looking after a spouse or very aged parent. Green (1988) found more men involved in informal care than had been anticipated. Nevertheless, most commentators agree that female family members are far more likely than males to accept responsibility for, and commit time to, informal care (Parker 1990). Where men are involved it is often in indirect or supporting roles. Gender stereotypes typically portray women as the nurturing sex within domestic settings. As a result, providing care to other family members is sometimes regarded as a 'natural' or taken-for-granted aspect of being a wife, mother or daughter. Moreover, many aspects of informal care are embedded within domestic labour more generally, still widely regarded as 'women's work'. Gender differences in employment opportunities may also mean there is a financial incentive to forego the earnings of female, rather than male, household members. For these reasons, women from all walks of life are likely to face responsibilities for informal care at some point in their lives.

When informal health care is wholly or partially incorporated into 'housework', performed by women, it can often remain unrecognized or unappreciated. Such work entails far more than just nursing the sick (Graham 1984). Domestic routines determine the quality of the environment, accommodation, diet and leisure time of household members, all with direct implications for health. Material, and health inequalities between household members may reflect divisions of gender or age within families. For example, working-class women have traditionally given priority to their menfolk and children in stretching out limited food budgets. It is in families that the values, beliefs and attitudes which constitute health cultures are transmitted across the generations, shaping sexual conduct, personal hygiene, folk remedies, illness behaviour and attitudes to professional medicine. Family members often mediate between the sick and health professionals. At times of health threatening crises, such as unemployment or bereavement, it is with family and kin that many people talk through their anxieties and seek support.

Research has consistently disproved the popular myth that families no longer care for their dependents (Parker 1990). However, there have been developments in the twentieth century that put increasing strain on family care. The numbers and proportions of elderly people in the population have risen substantially. In 1901 over-75s were 1.3% of the total population; by 2001 they will comprise 7.5%. Government policies have, since the 1950s, emphasized a shift away from institutional provision for the long-term sick towards what has been called 'community care'. Much evidence suggests that this policy has been characterized by a woeful gap between intention and resources as well as a lack of co-ordination between the agencies involved. All too often it has been a euphemism for unsupported care provided by women within a family context.

Although demand for informal care has increased, other changes have reduced the availability of those who have traditionally taken up these roles. At the beginning of the century many carers were middle-aged spinsters, remaining at home to look after ageing parents. This group has substantially declined in numbers as explained above. In addition, a far higher proportion of married women are now in paid employment, shouldering new burdens and responsibilities. Furthermore, the effects of changes in patterns of family life have to be taken into consideration. Will members of stepfamilies, cohabiting couples or divorcees feel obligations to care for sick or aged relatives and ex-kin? As yet it is difficult to identify precisely what the impact will be on informal care. What we do know is that people are rethinking traditionally conceived family relationships and loyalties.

Kinship, community and lay referral systems

Family and kinship ties constitute a critical element of most 'lay referral systems', that is, the chain of advice-seeking contacts which the sick make with other lay people prior to, or instead of, seeking help from health care professionals (Chapter 6). Such consultations can be extensive and elaborate, or truncated and simple. Lay opinions expressed in these networks may be in tune with, or antithetical to, professional medicine. In this way, family relationships can influence access to and use of formal health services.

Where lives are focused around inward-looking nuclear family units, lay referral systems are often limited in extent and patients may find their way into the formal health care system relatively quickly. In contrast, extended families recognize and celebrate relationships with a much wider range of relatives, such as aunts, uncles, cousins and grandparents. These bonds are typically maintained by visits, feasts, rituals, the exchange of services and the transmission of wealth. Members of such lay referral systems may expect their diagnoses and folk remedies to be accorded a significant degree of respect. This may keep the patient from the doctor's surgery, either temporarily or permanently.

McKinlay's (1973) study of two samples of mothers in Aberdeen, from unskilled or semi-skilled working-class backgrounds, provides an illustration. One group had booked into antenatal care relatively late and had made little use of available services. The other consisted of mothers who had made regular visits to antenatal clinics from a early stage in their pregnancies. Under-utilizers were found to have more frequent and intense contacts with their extended kin. They relied heavily upon their kinship networks for financial support, health advice, emotional guidance and access to housing and labour markets. Many were suspicious of professionals, and other sources of authority, from outside their close-knit families and local communities. In contrast, women who made greater use of antenatal services tended to socialize with friends rather than with kin, obtained accommodation and employment independently of relatives and had fewer contacts with their wider families. Their main confidants were their husbands, with whom they had relatively co-operative and sharing marriages. Their lay referral systems rarely extended outside the nuclear family and their spouses encouraged them to consult health professionals.

Nuclear family relationships characterize growing numbers of skilled manual and routine white collar workers, although even here aspects of wider kin contacts are often maintained. Extensive kinship bonds are more often found among older working-class communities, based around 'smoke stack' industries. In the latter, extensive contacts between female kin, especially mothers and married daughters, provide the basis for a strong sense of collective identity and the exchange of practical support. Some ethnic minority communities in Britain also sustain cohesive corporate family or household units.

Lay referral systems have implications for the design of formal health care systems. If health professionals wait for the sick to present themselves at centrally located clinics, patients with locally based kinship networks may be disadvantaged. Formal health care services which reach out to families and local communities are more likely to have a high take-up rate among such patients. These include services brought physically close to families and communities, for example, mobile units located on the street or at the workplace. Their effectiveness can be enhanced when spearheaded by professionals who already have extensive local knowledge and contacts, such as community nurses. Attempts can be made to win the hearts and minds of key members of kin and community networks, who may then go on to recruit other family members. In this way, the formal health care system can work with the grain of family and community relationships, adapting services to the life styles of the sick.

Research evidence suggests that family and community support networks have a positive effect on the health of their members (Oakley 1988). Individuals with close-knit and cohesive family ties are better able to cope with health-threatening life crises (such as unemployment or bereavement). They are less likely to engage in health-damaging behaviours (such as smoking or excessive drinking) and they are less likely to suffer from depressive illnesses or poor mental health. Many health problems faced by divorcees, lone parents and single mothers arise from the disruption of their family support networks. These effects cut across other social divisions, such as class, ethnicity and gender. Awareness of such processes may help health professionals identify those who are 'at risk'. Moreover, therapeutic interventions might, in part, take the form of bolstering and facilitating support networks (Oakley 1985).

The State and family surveillance

Many aspects of legislation and social policy shape and constrain the form and development of family relationships. They not only set limits or boundaries to family ties but, in addition, influence their character and contents. Thus, programmes with respect to education, welfare, social security, taxation, pensions, housing, the elderly and the sick are formulated and implemented on the basis of assumptions about the way in which 'normal' family relations operate. Statutes establish the terms and conditions under which family relations can be made and broken. Factory acts, schooling provisions and training policies shape the position and roles of children within families. Policies with respect to child support, maintenance, child abuse and family violence institutionalize the family as a locus of certain kinds of caring.

Nurses become part of this process of surveillance and shaping of family life through the 'medicalization of social control'. Social control is the process in which those who occupy key positions of power within a society punish transgressors of, and mobilize general consent for, the ethical, legal or moral codes of a society. The term 'medicalization' refers to the way in which more and more areas of social control have become subject to medical jurisdiction. Thus, for example, the naughty and disruptive child is redesignated as hyperactive, suffering from the disease hypokinesis. Similarly, persistent drunkenness is transformed from a moral failing or weakness of character into a disease (alcoholism) with medically defined symptoms and therapies. In this way, doctors and nurses become drawn into defining what is socially normal and morally acceptable behaviour. Issues such as drug use, sexuality, child-rearing and family violence become technical medical problems rather than matters of moral or political debate. Thus, nurses on paediatric wards, and in accident and emergency departments have become increasingly involved in the search for signs of abuse and battering among children and old people. Within the community, health visitors are required to make similar judgements (Chapter 3).

The medicalization process has touched many aspects of family life. Ever increasing numbers of medical experts, many of whom are state salaried and state licensed, appeal to medical or quasi-medical theories to legitimate their interventions in family life. They include health educators, doctors, health visitors, community nurses, social workers, case workers, psychotherapists, counsellors and educationalists. Ironically, the more families are charged with the provision of health and other services, as in the community care programme, the more state agencies seek to monitor and regulate their members. The more scope for family care, the more need for family surveillance and education.

Summary

The study of families is of critical importance to those who wish to understand health and health care. Family relationships may be implicated in the causes and the distribution of disease as well as in shaping forms of illness behaviour. Family ties influence access to, and use of, formal health services whilst providing informal health care. We have also seen that all these processes are shaped by the increasing diversity and complexity of family life. An understanding of the diverse and changing patterns of family life in modern Britain is of particular relevance to nurses. The work of community nurses and health visitors especially will need to be responsive to the variety of household structures and family relationships discussed in this chapter.

References

Amato P. R. & Keith B. (1991) Parental divorce and adult well being: a meta-analysis. *Journal of Marriage and the Family*, **55**, 43.

Bradshaw J. & Millar J. (1991) *Lone Parent Families in the UK*. Department of Social Security Research Report No 6, HMSO, London.

Burgoyne J. & Clark D. (1984) *Making a Go of It: A Study of Stepfamilies in Sheffield*. Routledge & Kegan Paul, London.

Central Statistical Office (1992) *Social Trends 1992*. Central Statistical Office, HMSO, London.

Clulow C. (1991) Making, breaking and remaking marriage In *Marriage, Domestic Life and Social Change* (Ed. by D. Clark). Routledge, London.

Cooper J. (1991) Births outside marriage: recent trends and associated demographic and social change. *Population Trends*, **63**, (Spring) 8–18.

Dalley G. (1988) *Ideologies of Caring: Rethinking Community and Collectivism*. Macmillan Educational, London.

Elliott J. (1991) Demographic trends in domestic life, 1945–87. In *Marriage, Domestic Life and Social Change* (Ed. by D. Clark). Routledge, London.

Finch J. & Groves D. (Eds) (1983) *A Labour of Love: Women, Work and Caring*. Routledge & Kegan Paul, London.

Graham H. (1984) *Women, Health and the Family*. Wheatsheaf Books, Brighton.

Green H. (1988) Informal Carers. In *General Household Survey 1985*. HMSO, London.

Kiernan K. & Wicks M. (1990) *Family Change and Future Policy*. Family Policy Study Centre, London.

Macintyre S. (1992) The effects of family position and status on health. *Social Science and Medicine*, **35**, 453–64.

McKinlay J. (1973) Social networks, lay consultations and help-seeking behaviour. *Social Forces*, **53**, 255–92.

Oakley A. (1985) Social support in pregnancy: the 'soft' way to increase birthweight? *Social Science and Medicine*, **21**, 1259–1985.

Oakley A. (1988) Is social support good for the health of mothers and babies? *Journal of Reproductive and Infant Psychology*, **6**, 3–21.

Parker G. (1990) *With Due Care and Attention: A Review of Research on Informal Health Care*, 2nd ed. Family Policy Studies Centre, London.

Parkinson L. (1987) *Separation, Divorce and Families*, Macmillan Educational, London.

Popay J., Rimmer L. & Rossiter C. (1983) *One-Parent Families: Parents, Children and Public Policy*. Study Commission on the Family, London.

Wallerstein J. S. & Kelly J. B. (1980) *Surviving the Break Up: How Parents and Children Cope with Divorce*. Grant McIntyre, London.

Further Reading

Graham H. (1984) *Women, Health and the Family*. Wheatsheaf Books, Brighton.

Macintyre S. (1992) The effects of family position and status on health. *Social Science and Medicine*, **35**, 453–64.

Chapter 11
Health Policy in Britain

In the preceding chapters we have seen that people's health is subject to a number of important influences, such as living standards and working conditions. We have also seen that their experience of illness and their capacity to cope with it are affected by the nature of the families and communities in which they live. In this chapter we consider another set of influences upon health, namely the kind of formal health services which are available. We begin by outlining the development of health policy in modern Britain, examining the origins and development of the NHS. We then look at the current 'crisis' in the NHS. Finally we look at recent government reforms of health policy and consider some of their implications for nursing.

Health policy and the role of the State

In modern Britain the State accepts wide responsibilities for the health and social welfare of its citizens, thus leading to the characterization of Britain as a 'welfare state'. Before 1945 the responsibility of both national and local government for individuals' health and welfare was much more limited. There are differing opinions about the reasons for the development of the welfare state. Some suggest that the widespread provision of education, health services, social security benefits and the like followed on more or less inevitably from the development of industrial societies. For example, it is argued that industrial societies 'need' a literate and numerate population, and so education systems develop. Similarly, they need fit and healthy workers, so a health system appears. Others argue there is no such inevitability in the development of welfare services. The USA, for example, is a striking case of an industrial society which has refused to bring its health services under state control. British attempts in the 1980s and 1990s to limit the welfare state suggest that there is nothing inevitable about the *amount* and *range* of services which are provided.

'Health policy' is simply the term used to describe how the State

(central government, local authorities, the NHS) works with other
bodies (the medical and nursing professions, pharmaceutical industries,
health insurance companies, etc.) to provide health services and to
influence the health of individual people.

To appreciate the strengths and weaknesses of the British system and
our approach to health policy, it is useful to see it in comparison with
other countries. All modern industrial societies have developed complex
arrangements for health and social security. What differs is the degree to
which the State is involved in providing these services. In the USA and
Japan, private and 'occupational' welfare (e.g. company health insurance) are important. Both are countries which have resolutely refused to
bring health services into a 'welfare state' kind of provision. In western
Europe we have 'welfare states', but in terms of who runs and pays for
health services there are differences. In Britain the State has a near-
monopoly over the provision of health services, whereas in Germany
there are both state-run and private health insurance schemes.

Such differences in health policy show that the 'NHS style' of delivering health care – i.e. 'free' services for the patient at the point of use –
is rather unusual, if not unique. We should not take the NHS and 'free'
medical care for granted, but try to see it as the outcome of historical
changes and political compromises (Klein 1989).

The NHS: origins and aims

As we saw in Chapter 2, the role of the State in health policy before the
NHS can be seen as one of growing 'collectivism'. The term 'collectivism'
does not necessarily mean 'socialism' or 'becoming more socialist'. It can
be defined simply as growing state intervention. For example, the limited
collectivism of the Liberal Government of 1911, which brought in state
health insurance for the first time, was designed to counter socialist
demands for a more comprehensive health service and insurance
scheme. It was a landmark because it showed for the first time that
government was prepared to compel people to insure themselves against
the risk of *individual* illnesses. No longer was the State restricting itself
to a background role of public health laws and policies, as in the nineteenth century (see Chapter 2) (Fraser 1984).

The 1911 Act introduced the principle of payment of GPs by 'capitation' – that is, an annual fee payable to the doctor for each person (per
capita) on the GP's list of insured patients. This is still the main method
of funding GPs today. For this and other reasons, the early legislation by
the Liberal Government before the First World War is sometimes considered to be the foundation of the modern NHS. However, this is a

misleading assumption. The NHS was founded on a principle of access to 'free' services which are largely paid for out of taxation, not insurance. The original aim of the NHS was to move away from any hint of a system in which treatment is conditional upon the ability to pay, or having insurance cover. Though this philosophy has strong advantages it also has drawbacks, as we will try to show below. Before looking at this it is important to understand why there was pressure for a unified system of health services provided by the state.

The failings of the pre-NHS system

A number of shortcomings can be identified in the pre-war health services: first there were weaknesses in the insurance system of funding health care, which left dependants (mainly women and children) and the unemployed without cover. Second, costs of medical treatment were rising rapidly, as today, but in those days middle-class families on modest incomes were often hit as hard as those in the working class by medical bills. Third, there was growing dissatisfaction among doctors, some of whom were also finding times hard (especially during the depression years of the 1930s) and who wished the 'market' of available patients to be opened up. A rising demand for personal medical treatment was not being matched by ability to pay.

However, these factors on their own cannot 'explain' the arrival of the NHS. Similar problems existed in other countries, which then went on to establish quite different kinds of health service. The Second World War, and the particular British experience of it, goes a long way towards explaining the gathering momentum of the 'NHS idea'.

The Second World War and its impact on health policy

The war provided a stimulus to plan and organize a nationally funded health system – the Emergency Medical Service – through which the government initially extended free medical treatment to service personnel. Gradually, other categories of patients were included, such as evacuees and workers in strategically important occupations. Thus a 'free' service took shape in embryo. Also, consultants and medical advisers from the prestigious teaching hospitals in the voluntary sector began, as a result of wartime duties, to understand just how sub-standard conditions were in many other hospitals. This fuelled later demands for more public investment in hospitals and for better remuneration of hospital doctors.

Largely as a result of the wartime experience, then, the basic idea of a state-funded, public health service 'free' at the point of use gained acceptance. Prospects for a health service funded by social and/or private insurance (the main method of paying for health services in Europe) correspondingly diminished, especially as Britain after the war was administered by a Labour Government strongly committed to state intervention.

The NHS: a product of compromise

In 1946, the Government introduced its NHS Bill to Parliament. Between then and 1948, fierce arguments about key aspects of the new service raged among politicians, and between Aneurin Bevan, Minister of Health, and the medical profession. These shaped the basic structure of the health service, which is still with us. Compare 'what might have been' – leading suggestions for organizing the service, which won support among some quarters at the time (the right-hand column) – with what was finally agreed in 1948 (the left-hand column) (Fig. 11.1).

To sum up, the NHS as it emerged in 1948 was the product of conflict and compromise, mainly between the Government and the medical profession. The Government gained its objective of providing a health service for all, 'free' at the point of use and without any kind of means test. It was also successful in moving the country away from a mainly insurance based system of paying for health services to a tax based system. But as we noted in Chapter 2, the medical profession exacted a price for its co-operation (in early 1948, the British Medical Association had threatened not to co-operate with the plan). Consultants were won over to the NHS plan in 1948 by 'stuffing their mouths with gold', as Aneurin Bevan put it, in a reference to merit awards – the system of paying substantial bonuses to senior doctors for advances in medical

What was implemented	Alternative proposals
A service controlled mainly by the medical profession, accountable to a central Ministry of Health	A service run by existing local authorities (as with education), accountable to city/county councils.
GPs become 'independent contractors' to the NHS, not salaried employees	All doctors to be paid salaries, as employees of a local health service
Separate hospital, GP and community health services	Hospitals, GPs and public/community health services to be co-ordinated by local authorites
Service funded mainly by taxation	A service to be funded by a state insurance scheme

Fig. 11.1   The introduction of the NHS.

treatment and research. Doctors were given a large say over how resources were to be distributed in the NHS and, though many were initially opposed to state medicine, it was quickly realized that the NHS could become a strong protector of the medical profession.

Has the NHS failed?

In many respects it has proved to be a success. For example, it was clearly an improvement over the inadequate and highly unequal jumble of hospital and GP services provided before the war. It has provided access to health care without the barrier of having to pay fees for services. It has cut out the administrative costs that would have been incurred if Britain had chosen an insurance based health service. The NHS has established itself as the most popular part of the welfare state. However the NHS did have a number 'design faults' – flaws which have continued to cause problems to the present day.

The NHS: a service for sickness

The focus of the NHS has always been the care and treatment of sick people, but it was never clearly established who would co-ordinate the management of the service. Doctors were granted a great deal of management power, but were also given professional freedoms as well. This has often meant that individual consultants or teams of doctors have striven to defend their particular interests (for example, giving priority to high-prestige areas of medicine such as heart surgery over other areas such as geriatric medicine). Management often appeared to be based on medical professional concerns rather than the needs of patients.

Some observers remarked at the time the NHS was introduced, that Britain gained a 'National Hospital Service' rather than a comprehensive health service. By maintaining divisions between hospitals, GPs and preventive or community health services, the NHS perhaps exaggerated the importance of hospital care and neglected the less glamorous community and preventive services. From this point of view, Britain lost an opportunity to start building a service based less on curative medicine and more on helping people to stay well. It is only recently that health promotion has been given a higher priority (Ashton & Seymour 1988).

Health expenditure

One of the main worries people had about the 'NHS idea' in the 1940s was that it would lead to abuse, over-use of the medical services and, as a result, soaring costs. If patients could walk into any surgery or hospital and obtain services free of charge, surely it would be impossible to contain costs? While spending on the NHS has risen, compared to the health care systems in other developed countries, expenditure on the NHS has been low. Britain spends less of its national wealth, or 'Gross National Product' (GNP) on health care than most other comparable industrial countries. In 1987, for example, the UK spent under 6% of GNP on health compared with over 11% in the USA, 9% in Germany and Sweden and 8% in France (Office of Health Economics 1989). As Britain is less wealthy (per head of population) than these countries, the differences in the actual amount of money spent on health are even wider, as Table 11.1 shows.

One reason for Britain's lower expenditure on health services lies in the way the NHS is funded. Most of the money for the NHS is drawn from taxation. This means that health spending is funded directly from the Treasury, and every year the Government must decide how much to spend on items such as schools and roads as well as on health. In other words, health spending must compete with all the other demands on the public purse. Though the NHS has regularly received increases in the amount devoted to it, there is always a strong pressure to economize and to contain costs. If health services were funded differently – for example, by a state insurance scheme or private health insurance – there is no doubt that people would have to pay more than they do now. As a result, though, more income would come into health care and it would be earmarked for health – the Government would not be able to spend it on other things.

Table 11.1 Health care expenditure (public and private services) per person in selected countries (1987).

	£
Switzerland	1233
West Germany	1006
Sweden	1002
Norway	860
France	758
Austria	600
Italy	507
United Kingdom	423
Eire	338

Source Adapted from Table 2.2, p. 8 of Office of Health Economics (1989) *Compendium of Health Statistics*, (7th edn). Office of Health Economics, London. (Reproduced by permission of Office of Health Economics.)

A second reason for the 'success' of the NHS in holding down costs is the way GP services are paid for. The 'capitation' system rewards GPs whether or not a patient enters the surgery, because the doctor receives a set amount per registered patient every year, irrespective of whether any treatment has been given. Therefore there has not been much financial incentive for the doctor to find out whether additional medical treatments are needed, or to extend consultation times beyond a few minutes per patient, though the recent reforms have attempted to make the system more responsive than before. Traditionally, the capitation method of funding did avoid the abuses of other systems – for example the American – where there are strong financial incentives for doctors to provide expensive or lengthy treatments, and where a certain amount of unnecessary surgery and therapy takes place. However the flaw in the British system is that it can lead GPs into a rather complacent attitude towards patients' problems.

Thirdly, British spending on health has been contained by relatively gradual increases in wage costs. As mentioned in Chapter 2, wages account for a huge bill of almost three-quarters of total NHS spending on hospitals and community health (Office of Health Economics 1989). Health services are highly labour-intensive. However pay increases for nurses, other health workers and therapists have usually been at an average or below-average level since the war.

Reform of the NHS

As we have seen in Chapter 2, rising expectations of health services coupled with advances in medical treatment and the growing need for treatment from an ageing population have contributed to something of a crisis in health care. In addition to these trends are the flaws in man-agement of NHS medicine we mentioned above and problems in the way the NHS is funded and organized. In response to these critical problems the Government passed the NHS and Community Care Act in 1990 (which came into effect in April 1991). The aims of this legislation were to increase managerial control over health professionals, to make health care organizations more accountable for the resources they used, and to introduce more competition within the NHS (Ham 1991).

Some argue that far-reaching changes have been introduced. By comparing the NHS post-1991 with the NHS of 1979 and before, it can be seen that the policy changes of the 1980s were incremental. Each step taken – the management reforms, increasing privatization of certain hospital services, the introduction of 'community' care – has been quite large, so that although each one has followed on from the other, the amount of change if we were to jump from 1979 to 1991 in one leap is perhaps greater than is often realized. Although it will take time for the full effect of the reforms to be felt, it is possible that they will have all sorts of unforeseen consequences, not only on the management structure but also on the 'culture' of the health service. For example, it is suggested that doctors, nurses and other health workers will increasingly put priorities of 'cash' or spending targets before patient needs. Will the ideals of altruism and public service, which some believe were the hallmarks of the 'traditional NHS', be whittled away?

Others believe that the changes, although substantial, are not a *fundamental* change in British health policy. The NHS remains the near-monopoly state provider of health services, and although private health insurance has gained some ground, most patients still receive 'free' medical services which are mainly funded by taxation. There are four main changes, which we now consider.

Purchasers and providers

A distinction between 'purchasers' of health care and 'providers' has been introduced (see Fig. 11.2). Health authorities now have a new role of purchasing health services for the populations in their districts. They must assess needs and are responsible for making sure those needs are met within a defined budget. In the pre-1991 NHS, District Health Authorities were above units and their hospitals and other services, but now they are in more of a partnership with them: 'Districts are the purchasers ... while hospitals or other health care facilities are the providers or suppliers' (Levitt & Wall 1992, p. 80).

Contracting for health care

A system of 'contracts' for providing health care was introduced. For example, District Health Authorities must, as purchasers, ensure that

Strategic decision-makers and central funding	Secretary of State and Department of Health Regional Health Authorities Family Health Service Associations		
Purchasers	District Health Authorities		Fund-holding GPs
Providers	Hospitals (Directly Managed Units)	Hospitals (Trusts)	GPs (Fund-holding and non fund-holding)

Fig. 11.2 The new NHS – purchasers and providers.

they have drawn up contracts with local hospitals to guarantee the supply of a comprehensive range of services and medical operations. Each contract stipulates the cost, quantity and quality of the services to be provided over a year. Equally, fund-holding GPs must draw up contracts with providers (see Fig. 11.3).

The contract idea is vital to the reforms because it is the key to organizing the process of buying and selling in a state-run health system. It is a way of making sure that equipment, materials and labour are costed, as they would be in private business. As a result there has been a major change in the way hospitals are funded: formerly, they were resourced largely on the basis of their size and previous budget – that is, how many staff a hospital employed, what its running costs were calculated to be, etc. Now funding is directly related to the number of patients treated. Hospitals are expected to compete with each other, and

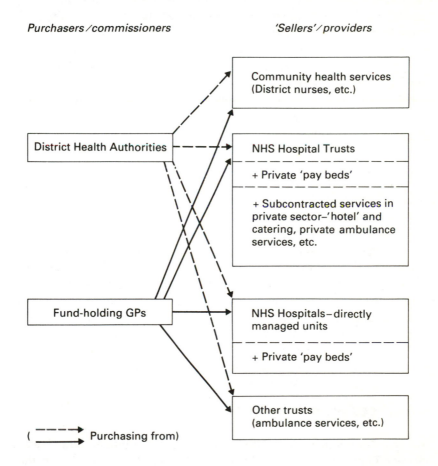

Fig. 11.3 The purchaser-provider relationship.

it has been made easier for GPs to refer their patients to hospitals outside their area if services are provided more cheaply elsewhere.

Trust hospitals

Although some hospitals remain within local health authorities, in the 1990s an increasing number may become independent NHS Trusts. That is, they are still NHS hospitals, but are accountable to their own management boards which are modelled on industrial management. Self-governing trusts (SGTs) are funded by central government (the Department of Health), but have considerable freedom to decide how to spend or invest their money and how to plan services.

Changes in medical general practice

GPs in larger practices (over 11 000 patients) may apply to become 'fund-holding' or 'budget-holding' GPs. This means that they are allocated funds from the Regional Health Authority. With this money they are expected to purchase services for their patients from the relevant District Authorities and other providers such as hospitals. The aim of the new approach is to introduce some competition into the supply of hospital based treatments and other services because budget-holding GPs are able to negotiate with Districts over the costs of hospital treatment and to choose the most competitive offer.

In addition to the introduction of budget holding, general practice as a whole has been affected by reorganization. As part of a drive to enhance the role of the GP and to bring in new goals in primary health care, the Government scrapped the former 'Family Practice Committees' and introduced Family Health Service Authorities. These authorities, which are accountable to Regional Health Authorities, must oversee certain key reforms: for example, the monitoring of GPs' drug prescriptions to ensure that doctors keep a rein on drug expenditure. FHSAs will also check upon the success of GPs in meeting recently introduced preventive health targets (such as the percentage of children immunized against common diseases, or the proportion of female patients screened for cervical cancer). More generally, the reforms have tried to make GPs become both more 'customer friendly' than before and more financially efficient – two goals which are not always compatible.

A market for health care?

The changes outlined above are a reflection of the long-running battle between Government on one hand and the health professions on the other. The attitude of doctors to the Government's reforms in 1990 was well illustrated by a poster campaign, organized by the British Medical Association, which featured a picture of a steamroller: with the picture was the caption, 'The Government's Plans for the NHS'. The medical profession saw all sorts of ways in which their professional freedoms would be limited by the reforms. The Government, and to some extent health service managers, saw in the reforms a way of making the professionals more fully aware of the costs of services. For too long, it was argued, health professionals had recommended treatments without thinking of cost or value for money. Thus the Government countered the argument that the NHS is 'cheap to run' and relatively efficient by pointing out that spending on the NHS had risen substantially year by year, and that in return the NHS had remained a rather unresponsive service – patients' complaints were sometimes ignored and waiting lists were still a significant problem.

There are doubts, however, about the value of market-style changes in public services and the ability of such a policy to improve services. Critics have suggested several major flaws. First, does the patient or 'consumer' in a public health service really choose or purchase treatments in the same way as a fee-paying consumer? Patients have greater freedom than before to switch from one general practice to another, but in the case of fund-holding GPs it will be the doctor who initially decides where the patient will go for treatment (according to the contracts previously drawn up), even if this is somewhat inconvenient for the patient. In such cases the GP is more of a purchaser or consumer than the patient.

Second, even if patients do have a greater say over what kind of treatment they should have or where they should have it, the increased freedom they have may run directly counter to other aspects of the reforms which are designed to reduce expenditure. Restriction of the choice of drugs to be prescribed for NHS treatment may mean that some drugs will only be available to patients who are able to pay for them. There may be pressures on budget-holding GPs to discriminate against the long-term chronically sick and 'expensive' patients, many of whom will be elderly.

Third, it is argued that market-style goals of efficiency can lead to a preoccupation with *output* (how many hospital patients processed in a given time, or how many adult women screened for cervical cancer) at the expense of *outcome* – that is, the number of people who have experienced detectable health gains. Also, in areas such as palliative care the *process* of care may be as important as the outcome of care. Many aspects of the psycho-social care of patients, which are central to nursing, cannot be measured by reference to financial cost. To counter this, the Government built various measures of 'quality of care' into the contracts to be drawn up with service providers, though some still believe that health service managers will have more incentive to fulfil the short-term quantitative side of contracts than the 'quality' aspects.

Fourth, there is a danger that in a system which is semi-commercialized but is not a 'true' market, providers will be able to push purchasers around rather than supply them with what they want. In fact this often happens in a 'true' or private market where there are relatively few suppliers. The consumer has to 'like it or lump it', and there may be a danger of this in a considerable number of health districts (Levitt & Wall 1992, p. 81).

Finally, there is a prospect of increasing disorganization in the NHS. Recent governments have shown concern with the slowness and inflexibility of NHS management. However, their dislike of cumbersome planning mechanisms has perhaps led to a new set of problems – a lack of co-ordination of health services, as self-governing hospital trusts and GP fund-holding practices operate increasingly independently. And there is the possibility that, as in the commercial world, some semi-independent trusts will face financial ruin. Whether such 'market disciplines' will eventually benefit health care in the long run is very much open to doubt. The procedures for dealing with failed trusts are as yet unclear, as Levitt and Wall point out (1992, p. 88).

Changing health policy, management and nursing

So far we have largely viewed the problems posed by the health reforms and the 'crisis' of health care from the point of view of the patient, or the doctor, or government. However, there are also very important policy implications for nurses. Their role in the health service has undergone marked changes, especially as far as the management of the NHS is concerned.

The introduction of the NHS, as we have seen, accelerated the move to a hospital based service. This had great significance for the future direction of nursing. The basic power hierarchy operating within the 'new' (1940s) NHS hospitals was largely unchanged from the nineteenth century. Nurses were seen as very junior partners to doctors in the hospital system. Nursing had always been primarily a 'female' job and this often enabled the male-dominated medical profession to behave in an authoritarian and often dismissive way to nurses.

Growing management power in nursing

By the 1960s two developments altered this traditional situation. First, Britain was in a period of economic growth and full employment, and nursing was competing for applicants with other, better paid jobs. Secondly, the need to recruit was increased by a programme of hospital building. Many of the old Victorian hospitals were replaced by large, 'high-tech' buildings which needed more and better qualified staff. One way to ease staff shortages had been to recruit enrolled and auxiliary nursing staff from outside the UK, mainly from Ireland and the Commonwealth. There was also a growing trend towards the 'professionalization' of nursing (Dingwall *et al.* 1988).

In 1966 the Salmon Report recommended that nursing be given new managerial responsibilities. The new post of nurse manager was created. In practice, the relatively small percentage of male nurses began to dominate these posts. Currently, half of all senior nurse managers are men, but men make up less than 10% of the nursing workforce. Because of the new managerial emphasis and increased career opportunities in nursing, the profession made some gains in rewards and status. As the 1970s drew to a close, however, Britain faced recurring economic problems. Unemployment, and disappointingly slow economic growth challenged previously accepted views on the cost and efficiency of the NHS. In 1979, the newly elected Government of Margaret Thatcher brought debates on the future organization of the whole welfare state, and of the NHS in particular, into the forefront of the political arena. Government began to plan to reorganize the NHS on a more 'business-like' basis. Ideas about a 'value for money' service and the need for financial efficiency were heard everywhere.

Undermining nurse management

As a part of this re-think, the Griffiths Report on NHS management was published in 1983. It recommended that a new managerial structure be introduced, challenging some of the entrenched powers of the medical profession and giving strong executive powers to hospital general managers. As part of the 'business' approach, wages and staffing levels needed to be kept to the lowest level possible. New ways of testing nurses' performance were introduced. By 1988, many nurses were highly discontented about both their pay levels and staff shortages. Some groups of nurses even began taking forms of industrial action and political protest. As a response to this, a grading system was introduced. Grades ranged from Scale A (nursing auxiliaries) to Scale I (unit managers) and were based on qualifications and management views of nurses' responsibilities. The new system was not without its faults; during 1989 alone 100 000 appeals were made by nurses against their grading.

Nurse training – increasing professionalism?

Another example of rapid policy change in the 1980s is the educational direction taken by nursing. The enrolled nurse grade was phased out, and many sought to upgrade their enrolled status to that of registered nurse via the many 'conversion' courses made available. Nursing education started to be centred in higher education, with the development of Project 2000 courses. A 'rush for qualifications' began, and is still very much a feature of nursing today. However, the proportions of qualified staff still vary greatly among the specialities. The most highly qualified field is primary health care (85%), while the 'Cinderella' field of mental handicap has the fewest qualified nursing staff (40%) (see Table 11.2).

Reflecting the traditional nature of the NHS, nursing is still largely based in hospitals. In 1991 173 000 nurses worked in general hospitals, 58 000 in psychiatric hospitals, 42 000 in geriatric units and only 42 000 in community services. Nursing is a costly part of NHS expenditure, representing nearly a quarter of the total budget. However government policy is moving in the direction of replacing hospital care with care in (or by) the community (Griffiths 1988).

Community care and related trends

In 1989, the Secretary of State for Health presented a document, *Caring for People – Community Care in the Next Decade and Beyond*, which set out far-reaching policy changes. As far as possible, it was argued, people should be cared for in their own homes or in a 'homely' environment. This will mean changes in the work of community based nurses, and a trend towards teams of neighbourhood nurses to care for people in given localities. As a result of the NHS and Community Care Act (1990) much more co-operation with local social service departments will be required and, while there will be difficulties, there will also be new opportunities to extend the role of nurses.

Table 11.2 Qualified and part-time nursing staff by speciality.

Speciality	% Qualified	% Unqualified	% Learners	% Part-time
General	57	15	28	31
Geriatric	54	46	0	58
Mental illness	56	31	13	21
Mental disability	40	51	9	24
Primary health care	85	12	13	41

Source V. Beardshaw & R. Robinson (1990) *New for Old? Prospects for Nursing in the 1990s*. King's Fund Institute, London. (Reproduced by permission of King's Fund Institute.)

From 1993, it is proposed that health visitors and district nurses will have the right to prescribe certain medications to their patients. At the time of going to press this change had been postponed because of concerns about how the expenditure by nurses on prescriptions could be monitored. This marks a break from the traditional system of doctor control of prescribing and as many GP practices are becoming 'budget holders' this will change the working relationships between GPs and community nurses even more radically. GPs will have to purchase the services of community nurses from the health authorities (see Fig. 11.2).

Despite some possibilities for enhanced status among nurses, however, the overall picture as far as nursing is concerned is likely to be one of a continuing erosion of their managerial functions and of the gains made in the 1960s and 1970s. While on one hand nursing represents an increasingly highly qualified and expensive occupation, on the other there are significant pressures to 'de-skill' the work and to hold down pay: for example, there is much discussion currently of moves by health authorities to employ increasing numbers of unqualified staff for certain tasks. The projected system is called 'skill mix' and some think that it represents one of the greatest dangers to the enhancement of nurses' pay and working conditions. Secondly, we should not forget that self-governing hospital trusts are free to settle the pay and conditions of their own staff. They may override national pay agreements and, while the Government argued that this could mean nurses and other staff will be awarded above-average settlements by some trusts, the likelihood is that a greater number of nurses will face depressed pay awards.

Summary

While health policy includes a range of issues, such as government policies on smoking, poverty, environmental safety and pollution (Chapter 3), this chapter has concentrated on the distinct role of the NHS. We have seen that the NHS was a product of political and professional compromise, which continues to affect its organization and the delivery of health care. The reforms of the NHS in the 1990s are a response to continuing pressures for more health care, and perceived inadequacies in the way health care is organized. They also reflect a change in philosophy. Recent governments have been committed to a set of values which stress the benefits of the market and of free enterprise in meeting human needs. This shift in health policy means that the work of nurses and other health professionals will be increasingly evaluated in terms of cost-effectiveness. Much will depend on the way these changes are implemented; however, the case for concluding that Britain's health services are set to follow a radically different path is a strong one.

References

Ashton, J. & Seymour H. (1988) *The New Public Health*. Open University Press, Buckingham.
Beardshaw, V. & Robinson R. (1990) *New for Old? Prospects for Nursing in the 1990s*. King's Fund Institute, London.
Department of Health (1989) *Caring for People: Community Care in the Next Decade and Beyond*. Cm 849. HMSO, London.
Department of Health (1989) *Working for Patients*. Cm 555. HMSO, London.
Dingwall, R., Rafferty A.M. & Webster C. (1988) *An Introduction to the Social History of Nursing*. Routledge, London.
Fraser, D. (1984) *The Evolution of the British Welfare State*. Macmillan, London.
Griffiths, R. (1983) *Report of the NHS Management Inquiry*. DHSS, London.
Griffiths, R. (1988) *Community Care: an Agenda for Action*. HMSO, London.
Ham C. (1991) *The New National Health Service*. Radcliffe, Oxford.
Klein, R. (1989) *The Politics of the National Health Service*, 2nd edn. Longman, London.
Levitt, R. & Wall, W. (1992) *The Reorganized National Health Service*, 4th edn. Chapman and Hall, London.
Office of Health Economics (1989) *Compendium of Health Statistics*, 7th edn. Office of Health Economics, London.

Further reading

Ham C. (1992) *Health Policy in Britain: The Politics and Organisation of the National Health Service*, 3rd edn. Macmillan, London.
Harrison S.J., Hunter D.J. & Pollitt C. (1990) *The Dynamics of Health Policy*. Unwin Hyman, London.

Chapter 12
Nursing as an Occupation

In this chapter we consider the occupation of nursing, beginning by looking at past and present images of nursing. We then consider nursing work in hospitals and in the community, and look at nurse-patient relationships. A number of innovations associated with the 'new nursing' and Project 2000 are described in terms of the redefinition of nursing knowledge and practice. The relations between doctors and nurses are examined through considering the applicability of the concept of 'profession' to nursing. Alternative views of the occupation are then discussed. Finally, a number of questions designed to evaluate the current and future prospects for nurses are posed.

Images of nursing

The Nightingale nurse

The most common image of nursing is that of the hospital nurse in full uniform tending the needs of doctors and patients. She is usually white, female and middle-class. This historical image originates from the mid-nineteenth century. Scientific discoveries associated with disease processes led to the rapid development of medical knowledge and practice and an increase in medical schools and hospitals. Doctors needed a supply of 'suitable clinical material' for teaching purposes and 'a reliable assistant who was constantly in the wards and could be relied upon to distribute the medicine and apply the poultices as desired' (Abel-Smith 1964). Florence Nightingale on her return from organizing a nursing service in the Crimea in 1856 was well placed as an upper middle-class woman of means to set up training schools for others of similar background, to be those 'reliable assistant(s)'.

Nightingale had to counter the prevailing image of nursing as a disreputable profession, typified by Dickens' character, Mrs Gamp:

'Like most persons who have attained to great eminence in their profession, she took to [spirits] very kindly; insomuch that, setting aside her natural predilections as a woman, she went to a lying-in or a lying-out with equal relish and zest.'

(Dickens 1843).

She also countered nursing's negative image by arguing that it was a vocation rather than a profession. Long hours and low pay kept the nurse in her rightful place and preserved her respectability. Mrs Gamp's relish and zest were replaced by subservience and obedience.

According to Doyal (1979), nurses were employed to provide efficient patient care based on the 'sanitary idea'. This is demonstrated in Nightingale's observation that the assumed effects of disease were often because 'of the want of fresh air, or of light, or of warmth, or of quiet, or of cleanliness, or of punctuality and care in the administration of diet, of each or of all of these'

(Nightingale 1859).

Contemporary images

Salvage (1985) identifies three modern images of nurses – angels, battle-axes and sex symbols – derived from nurses themselves, the public, and

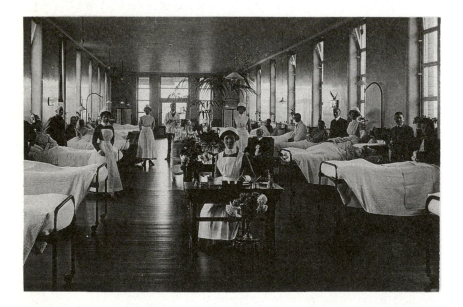

Fig. 12.1 Ward at Northampton General Hospital, c. 1906. (*Source* O'Neill C. (1991) *A Picture of Health.* Meadow Books, Oxford. (Reproduced by permission of Meadow Books.))

the media. According to Oakley (1986), the most enduring public image remains that of the good woman and her 'alertness to the needs of others'. Recent advertisements for cancer charities, in which the nurse is shown to be aware of not only the patient's needs, but also the family's, draw on this image (Smith 1992). In research undertaken during the mid-1980s, in a large teaching hospital, students were found to fit the image of the nurse as 'young lady' or good woman. As such they could also be typified as Nightingale's direct descendants, in that they were white, middle-class and female (Smith 1992).

The changing image of nursing is reflected in the photographs of nurses shown in Figs. 12.1 and 12.2. More recent changes are seen in the photographs and text in college prospectuses. In the late 1960s nursing was clearly presented as a female occupation. Even ten years ago the prospectus portrayed nursing as an occupation for women who were young and white. Images of male and black nurses were noticeably absent, even though nationally ten per cent of the workforce are men

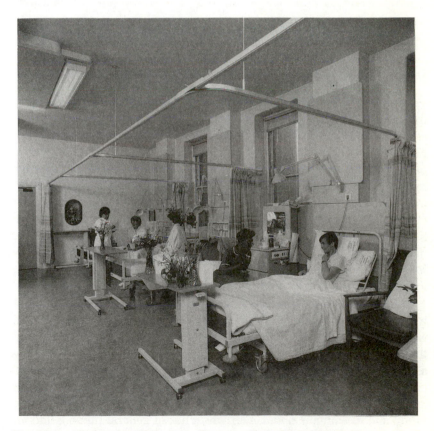

Fig. 12.2 Modern hospital ward. (*Source* Chris Priest/Magpie.))

and nine per cent of nurse recruits are from developing countries (Pearson 1985).

The story of Mary Seacole, a Jamaican nurse and contemporary of Nightingale's in the Crimea, illustrates how images of black nurses have been hidden from history. Seacole was as famous among the troops as Nightingale, but on her return to England sank into oblivion because she was of neither the right class nor race. In the 1990s however, the college prospectus, like the national recruitment campaigns, emphasize the need for a diverse work-force and applications from 'minority groups' and 'mature' entrants are said to be particularly welcome.

In the earlier prospectus, the white, female nurses are carefully coiffed and neatly dressed in traditional nurses' uniforms complete with crisp caps and aprons. By 1990, the photographs are quite different. Gone are the caps and aprons which may partially explain why the stance of the nurses, black and white, female and male, is much more informal both in the classroom and in the field. The recruitment literature suggests that the single image of nurses as white, young, female and working in acute general hospitals, is no longer the only one. If we look at what has happened both within nurse education and the health service since the late 1980s we can see why.

Nursing in the 1980s

The health service reforms (Chapter 11) are said to shift priorities away from acute hospital care to the needs of patients and clients in the community. Project 2000 has been a response to meet the changing needs of the population. More and more patients, including psychiatric patients and people with learning difficulties, will expect to be cared for in the community as the large mental hospitals and institutions are closed (Chapter 8). The Project 2000 'aims to prepare nurses for the 21st century by providing a system of education geared to meeting future health needs' and a 'simpler pattern of preparation' (UKCC 1986). This means that students will undertake a common foundation programme followed by a choice of one of four specialisms: general, mental health, mental handicap and paediatrics.

Traditionally psychiatry has attracted more men than women and until recently men were unable to become midwives. The opening up of a variety of specialties to both men and women may help to break down the gender stereotypes attached to particular types of work, especially as the model of custodial care requiring physical strength becomes less important. In Salvage's view, the low profile of men as general nurses leads to assumptions and stereotypes that there must be 'something funny and effeminate' about men who choose general nursing and an assumption that they are likely to be homosexuals. She suggests that this may be so, but 'there are no figures to prove it'. Although there are also many lesbians in nursing, they are even more invisible than homosexuals, being subsumed under the 'battleaxe' image.

In summary, it appears that nurse recruiters in the 1990s are attempting to appeal to a more varied population, to reflect the needs of the community, the changing role of women, and demographic changes. It is still too early to tell whether the combined effects of introducing Project 2000 and the changes within the health service will attract a more varied work-force which in turn will change the predominant image of nursing as women's work and of nurses as young, white and female, based in hospitals.

Nursing work

At the present time, the majority of nurses work in hospitals. This is reflected in Table 12.1. Whether working in hospital or community however, the central focus of nursing work is through direct contact with patients, clients and their families and/or 'significant others'.

Hospitals

Traditionally, hospital nursing was organized around the execution of tasks as part of the medical division of labour (Fig. 12.3). In the 1960s, task allocation was still strong. The most junior and least experienced

Table 12.1 Number and composition of the nursing work-force in 1988.

Work-force	Number (in thousands)	%	Change, 1981–88 (%)
Registered	133.1	44	+21
Enrolled	69.5	23	+6
Midwives	19.2	6	+17
Health visitors	10.7	3	+12
District nurses	9.4	3	−9
Students basic	51.3	17	−2
Pupils basic	6.2	2	−71
Student midwives	4.0	1	−16
Other	1.4	1	−29
Total	304.8	100	

Source V. Beardshaw & R. Robinson (1990) *New for Old? Prospects for Nursing in the 1990s.* King's Fund Institute, London. (Reproduced by permission of King's Fund Institute.)

nurses undertook tasks perceived as basic or simple, such as dusting the ward furniture or cleaning the bedpans. As the nurse became more senior s/he graduated through a series of tasks from giving bedpans, doing the bed baths, taking the temperatures and blood pressures, and finally the dressings, drug rounds and injections. In all, a patient could be looked after by at least five different nurses in a day, and their needs were – and to some extent still are – governed by that routine.

Although the organization of nursing care in hospitals has become more patient-centred in line with the nursing process, many tasks and routines shaped by medical diagnosis and treatment are still apparent. These tasks and routines include doctors' rounds, diagnostic tests and therapies on and off the ward. There are many reasons why hospitals maintain these routines and institutional ways. Davies (1990) and other writers believe that competing rationalities underpin institutional care work. Scientific and technical-economic rationalities correspond to what Davies calls male-orientated doctors' and administrators' 'assembly-line care of the sick'. Costs are kept to a minimum and as many patients as possible are processed through medical diagnosis and treatment in the minimum time possible.

Another factor that has shaped hospital routines and work organization has been the use of untrained staff as the main work-force in direct patient care. In many hospitals, ward sisters and charge nurses may be responsible for the care of some 20 patients with 15 nurses, two-thirds of whom are untrained. The reasons for task-orientated nursing become evident. Many sisters find it easier to supervise students and auxiliary nurses by adherence to tasks and routines – rather than giving them responsibility for planning their own patient-centred care.

A famous study undertaken by Menzies in the late 1950s to find out why students were leaving nursing believed that high anxiety levels were partly responsible (Menzies 1960). Menzies saw the task-orientated way in which nursing care was organised as a defence against that anxiety. She wrote:

'The nursing service attempts to protect the nurse from the anxiety of her relation with the patient by splitting up her contacts with them. The total workload of the ward or department is broken down into lists of tasks, each of which is allocated to a particular nurse.'

Moves were made during the 1960s and 1970s in both the USA and Britain to redefine nursing as distinct from medicine and task-orientated care. In 1972, the influential Briggs report was concerned with emphasizing the nurse's caring role as distinct from that of cure. It stressed that nursing was not subservient to medicine but complementary to it. The subsequent development of the nurse practitioner role, the growth in the number of university nursing degrees, clinical nurse specialists and the introduction of the 'nursing process' all reflect the report's recommendations.

Salvage (1990) examines the appearance of this 'new nursing' (Fig. 12.3). It clearly challenges the predominance of the bio-medical model (Chapter 3) by seeking new ways of defining nursing knowledge and practice, independent of medicine. Salvage traces its origins to the work of Henderson (1960) in the United States. Henderson sought to define the unique contribution of the nurse as assisting individuals whether sick or well in activities which contributed to health, its recovery or a peaceful death. Nurses were to assist patients in fourteen activities of daily living and these activities have been the framework that has underpinned the nursing process. In 1977, Henderson's activities of living and the nursing process were recommended as the basis of the general nursing curriculum.

Primary nursing, which also originated in the US, goes even further than the nursing process. It emphasizes continuity of care by the same nurse for the same group of patients from admission to discharge, therefore setting out an explicit emotional involvement between nurses and patients. Calliandro and Judkins (1988) write: 'Primary nursing is holistic care. It begins with the premise that a person is a psychological, physical, spiritual, social and cultural unity'. Traditionally primary nursing is associated with hospital nursing, but these authors suggest that as it is a philosophy of care it 'does not depend upon a setting. It may be practised anywhere at any time'.

The differences between 'traditional' and 'new models of nursing are best seen in terms of a continuum. In practice there are many 'mixed' models. Developments such as clinical nurse specialists and nurse

Traditional nursing	*New nursing*
task-oriented	patient-centred
hierarchical	egalitarian
shared responsibility	individual accountability
nurse implements orders	nurse initiates care
fragmentation of care	continuity of care
'assembly line' care	holistic care
distance from patient	closeness to patient
physical and technical care given priority	integration of physical, technical and psycho-social care
low visibility of psycho-social care	high visibility of psycho-social care
many nurses: many patients	few nurses: few patients
disease/physician-defined care	nurse/patient-defined care

Fig. 12.3 The continuum between 'traditional' and 'new' models of nursing.

practitioners, reflect certain trends within nursing to develop its medico-technical and curative aspects which may run counter to the 'new nursing's' emphasis on holism and caring. These trends are also evident in a recommendation made in Project 2000 to develop a range of nurse specialists (UKCC 1986). Similar tensions were evident in Smith's (1992) study of nurse training. Students preferred technical nursing associated with medical specialities which they identified as valuable for their learning. They also recognized the importance of care in terms of their physical and 'emotional' labour for patients and each other, but took this for granted as something 'natural' rather than a skill to be learnt.

The community

In midwifery and community care, midwives, district nurses and health visitors would argue that they have always operated a person-, rather than a task-orientated service. District nurses are involved in keeping disabled and/or elderly people living at home instead of moving to hospitals or institutions. Their training emphasizes the whole person, and like health visitors they work closely with general practitioners rather than hospital doctors. However, many district nurses with high workloads may of necessity adopt a task-centred approach to their care focused on dressings, injections and patient hygiene.

Health visitors work somewhat differently to nurses. They emphasize health promotion and advice, and have fewer explicitly technical tasks to perform, other than child development examinations and immunizations. Many health visitors specialize in advising the elderly and educating the public on major killer diseases such as cardiovascular disorders and cancer. Advice on and promotion of healthy eating, stress management, accident reduction/safety and healthy life styles are key activities.

Nurse–patient relationships

Nurse–patient relationships are clearly a central feature of nursing work (Chapter 6). Strauss and colleagues (1982) describe how medical legitimation shapes the nature of the work that nurses and others do in the 'technologized hospital'. Different tasks are distributed amongst workers and involve two types of relationships: one is instrumental for carrying out physical and technical tasks with patients; the other is expressive, concerning patients' psycho-social care. They describe psycho-social care as 'sentimental' work, i.e. where the recipient being worked on is alive, sentient and reacting.

Strauss and his co-researchers found sentimental work changed according to the patient's diagnosis, their individual medical history and the predominant ward ethos. Nurses were more likely to undertake certain types of sentimental work such as explaining to and comforting patients following medical interventions and interactions. Because staff were not held accountable for undertaking sentimental work, it was not always documented in the patients' notes nor verbally reported between staff members. Therefore, it often remained invisible.

In Britain, the introduction of the nursing process emphasized the central role of the nurse in undertaking 'sentimental work' with patients. A key component of the nursing process, was an explicit commitment to raising the profile of emotional care through the development of relationships between nurses and patients. Armstrong (1983) observes that once the nursing process was adopted as a philosophy and work method the textbook presentation of the nurse's role changed. Patients were no longer described in strictly biological terms. Psychology and communication skills were emphasized and 'subjectivity' and emotions were encouraged as part of the nurse–patient relationship.

The 'new nursing' leads to a reappraisal of the relationship between nurse and patient, in the wake of what Doyal called the 'destruction of the patient's autonomy' by medicine (Doyal 1979). 'New nursing' seeks to re-define nurse–patient relationships in terms of partnership rather than one in which the nurse is in a position of power. For example, Morse (1991) describes the nurse–patient relationship as a negotiating process, demonstrating the complexity of this 'taken for granted' aspect of nursing and emphasizing the patient's input as a key factor. These person-centred approaches to care are reflected in current government policy which declares in 'The Patient's Charter' that all patients and clients must have a named nurse, midwife or health visitor.

Nursing: profession or occupation?

Defining a profession

Oakley (1986) suggests that a profession is a 'superior type of occupation' which requires greater formal entry qualifications and training. A profession may be characterized as an occupational group which regulates and controls itself and requires its members to undergo advanced education so they acquire a specific and exclusively owned body of knowledge and expertise. Occupational groups wishing to become a profession, may adopt the strategy referred to as 'professionalization'. Salvage (1985) suggests that nursing's preoccupation with professionalism is partly a bid to discard the submissive attributes associated with its image.

Much of the early work on professions and professionalization used medicine as its 'template' (e.g. Freidson 1970). According to sociologists, some occupations, such as nursing, teaching and social work may never attain full professional status and consequently have been dubbed the 'semi-professions'. Oakley (1986) argues it is not by chance that these 'semi-professions' are predominantly female occupations. Shorter and less academic training courses, lower status work and questionable commitment to long-term education and career, traditionally associated with a female workforce, are all reasons why these occupations are said to be unable to attain full professional status.

In the case of nurses, Freidson (1970) also believes that they can never be other than 'semi-professionals' because their knowledge and skills are dependent on the medical model of cure. Doctors control the admission of patients, their diagnosis and treatment and many nursing tasks must be explicitly authorized by them. Freund and McGuire (1991) illustrate how in the USA medicine has used its professional dominance to prevent serious competition from nurses, midwives and other predominantly female health care occupations. For example, until recently, obstetricians have successfully opposed nurse-midwives delivering babies and subsequently limited the conditions under which they are able to practice.

Parallels can be drawn in Britain, especially in relation to midwifery. Doctors have used their professional dominance and power to regulate and control practice and effected a virtual take-over of the specialty. Although the Midwives Act, in 1902, set up the means by which midwives became independent practitioners, since that time until the present, doctors have increased their control over pregnancy and childbirth. The number of births taking place in hospital as opposed to the home and the growth of high-technology intervention during delivery, are testimonies to their success. However, despite medical dominance, both countries have seen a growth in the numbers of independent midwives.

Application to nursing

Medicine and law, with their prolonged training periods, male domination, high earning capacity and social status, have dominated thinking on professionalization. Medicine is based on knowledge that is seen as both 'objective' and 'abstract'. By inference it is male and associated with intellectual work, science and the mind, and was the model, in the past, that many nurses strove to emulate. Both professions (especially at the top) are largely male preserves.

O'Brien (1989) a feminist sociologist and former nurse, describes 'male-stream' thought as the outcome of male-dominated thinking which views knowledge as 'objective' and 'abstract' and associated with science, intellectual work, the mind and men. Common sense, manual and domestic work, and the body are associated with women. The setting up of opposites in this way, implies that women are inferior to men, as are activities such as manual and domestic labour that use the body and common sense rather than the mind and intellectual work. Such systematic polarization also leads to a belief that the mind and body are separate from each other and that the activities associated with each are totally unconnected.

Feminist scholars have begun to challenge the set of 'male-stream' assumptions by which an occupation is judged. If, for example, we apply Freidson's argument that nursing knowledge and skills are dependent on medicine's, then it seems nursing cannot fulfil the criteria for being a 'full' profession. It may be, however, that there is a need to apply an alternative approach to defining nursing knowledge and expertise.

Alternative frameworks

Oakley (1986) shows how women's psychology and social roles are based on the assumption that women serve others and derive fulfilment from doing so. By implication, the 'basic' aspects of nursing (like any care work) are taken for granted as something that women automatically do and enjoy (Smith 1992). As Ungerson (1983) points out, care work is 'imbued with sex-role stereotyping' and may be devalued because of this. But as Oakley's research on housework has shown, women have accumulated a significant knowledge base and set of skills (such as mothering) that are largely unrecognized by society (Oakley 1974).

Salvage believes that the women's movement has contributed to the development of the 'new nursing' described above by challenging both the domestic and occupational domination of men over women. In the case of nursing, male (i.e. doctor) subordination of traditionally female nurses resulted in the predominance of bio-medicine over more person-centred approaches to care (Salvage 1990). As we have seen, the 'new nursing' succeeded in questioning the bio-medical approach, as the only legitimate basis on which nursing was organized.

The importance of seeking alternative frameworks for nurses to define knowledge and practice in their own terms – rather than medical, male-stream ones, is illustrated in further evidence from the study of nurse training cited above (Smith 1992). The nurse training programme was organized over three years during which students passed through modules organized around medical specialties. Informally they were pressurized by the rhetoric of the nursing process to care for people rather than treat diseases.

As already noted, students valued technical nursing associated with medical specialities rather than physical and 'emotional' labour which they took for granted as something 'natural'. However, their perceptions changed as they progressed through their training. As new students they described nursing in terms of practical (e.g. bed-making, bathing, toileting) and psycho-social activities (e.g. talking and empathy). They were critical of their introductory programme which emphasized anatomy and physiology 'all cells and bits that don't connect with the patient' and were surprised at how little was said about 'care'.

By the end of their training they no longer saw nursing in these terms but distinguished between building up their skills through experience, and formal in-depth bio-medical knowledge about 'diseases, drugs and therapy'. The students felt they required this knowledge to practice effectively as qualified nurses. That is, in the absence of an alternative framework (now encapsulated by the 'new nursing') student nurses defined their formal knowledge, in 'male-stream' biological terms. Caring work associated with communication and interpersonal skills which are the hallmark of the 'new nursing' were undervalued and seen as part of their personal and experiential package as women which brought them in to nursing.

Students learnt about 'care' informally, through watching and working with more experienced nurses on the ward:

'You see how the nurses sort of manage patients and talk to them and you "just" pick things up. It's "just" their general attitude; you think that's a really nice way to treat someone...they show an example.

'The more you come in contact with patients in difficult situations you learn how to cope, because that's how the seniors have learnt ... "just" through experience.'

These comments might be interpreted in a number of ways. On the one hand students may have been minimizing the learning of care by their repeated use of 'just' picking things up or 'just' learning through experience. On the other, they might have regarded these skills as 'natural' which did not require particular skill or effort to acquire. In other words, the students saw knowledge as facts which they were formally taught as opposed to the skills they acquired through their experiential learning and in many cases, their socialization as women.

Benner's alternative framework for defining nursing as a 'caring' profession 'grounded in practices rather in a set of abstract principles' can be seen to offer possibilities for broadening out the knowledge base of nursing beyond factual knowledge to include those skills described by the students as acquired by observing and giving direct patient care. She defines nursing as a 'caring profession' based on a different set of premises to those traditionally used to distinguish a profession. She says: 'Caring and caring practices must be located in a community, in a shared world of members and participants ... They are grounded in practices rather than as a set of abstract principles' (Benner 1988). The Project 2000 course that most student nurses now undertake aims to change the structure and knowledge base of nurse education away from the treatment of patients and diseases in hospitals to health promotion and people-centred community care (UKCC 1986).

Relevance of professionalization and professionalism to nursing

The answer to whether professionalization and professionalism are desirable as a way of emulating medicine, remains equivocal on a number of counts. First, the medical commitment to cure and the aggressive treatment of disease is no longer seen to hold the answers (Chapter 3). In relation to nurses and their status, Oakley puts her view very firmly: 'The current crisis of confidence in medical care should tell us that professionalization is not the answer, that it may indeed be positively damaging to health' (1986).

Salvage sees professionalism to have negative effects within nursing. It may divide the 'professional' nurse from untrained carers, such as hospital auxiliaries or patients, relatives and friends. According to Salvage, professional nurses need to exclude such groups in order to 'prove' their own status and the worth of their skills and training. Also, professionalism treats nurses as a homogenous group with a shared view of nursing, but the occupation has a diverse history and is made up of a variety of activities. For Salvage, professionalization is 'not the only or necessarily the best direction in which nursing could move. It is a move to try to win all sorts of goals ranging from better care to better pay, which may be linked but not necessarily the direct and inevitable result of using such a strategy' (1985).

An alternative strategy to professionalism is trade unionism and the use of collective bargaining to improve pay and conditions. Traditionally the Royal College of Nursing (RCN) as a professional association was less interested in these issues and remains opposed to strike action. Despite claims to represent the majority of trained and learner nurses, the RCN was seen by many as an organization for elite managers and nurses from the teaching hospitals. Nurses, especially the 'rank and file' from the 'Cinderella' services and non-teaching hospitals, favoured the health service unions, COHSE and NUPE (soon to amalgamate with NALGO as UNISON). During the 1970s and 1980s pay campaigns and as a response to clinical grading (1987) health service union membership increased from all sectors.

Overall, however, the last thirteen years of Conservative government dramatically changed the membership situation. On the one hand, legislation has reduced trade union power generally. On the other, the RCN has responded to rises in unemployment, health service cuts and wage restraints by acting as an independent trade union and becoming increasingly vocal on issues of pay and conditions. The nurse membership trends in COHSE, NUPE and the RCN appear in Table 12.2.

The 'new nursing', practice developments and professionalization

Hierarchy is strong within nursing, and professionalism traditionally has discouraged nurses from questioning their seniors and the established way of doing things. These hierarchical traditions permitted the development of 'managerialism' as another professionalizing strategy within nursing (Chapter 11). The origins of this strategy can be traced to the 1960s when the 'matron elite' representing the Nightingale tradition were replaced by up to five grades of senior nurse managers. The structure was complex and hierarchical but gave senior nurses with professional

Table 12.2 Trends in nurse membership of the health service unions and the RCN.

	1978–79	1992
RCN	122 000	297 719
COHSE	110 000	150 000
NUPE	80 000	90 000

Sources 1978–79 figures   C. Hancock, (1979) Special Industrial Relations Problems in Nursing. In *Industrial Relations in the NHS* (Ed. by N. Bosanquet). King's Fund, London.
1992 figures   RCN Membership services, NUPE Research Department.

NB Some nurses have membership of more than one organization. RCN figures do not include nursing auxiliaries who are excluded from membership.

Overall trade union membership in the UK has declined by 25% since 1979.

In aggregate terms it is likely that union density in nursing in the NHS is at least as high as the hospital 'average' of 66%.

Source   J. Buchan (1992) State of the Unions in the Health Service. *Nursing Standard*, 12 August, p. 31.

aspirations a career structure. This structure was particularly advantageous to male nurses who were committed to nursing as a lifelong career unlike women who were expected to marry and have children. By the early 1980s up to a third of all senior administrative posts were occupied by men.

Since the mid-1980s the introduction of industrial-style general management into the NHS with a chief executive able to make unilateral decisions has weakened the role of nurses as managers. This is particularly evident in the membership and composition of executive management boards in the newly formed NHS trusts and commissioning teams (Chapter 11). This move away from 'managerialism' in the early 1980s, briefly benefited the clinical nurse. The complex management hierarchies began to be disbanded and replaced by senior nurses with both management and clinical responsibilities, particularly in hospitals. The rationale for this restructuring was to devolve power to nurses in the clinical areas through new style 'nurse consultants' who were able to act as the link between field-level staff and senior managers. They were also able to develop their clinical specialties, and the number of clinical nurse specialists increased.

Within this context of devolving nursing management to the bedside, primary nursing as part of the 'new nursing' emerged from its US origins to become a key issue for 1980s nursing. Associated with the emergence of primary nursing were other innovations including nursing development units, nursing beds in which nurses rather than doctors admit and care for patients. Such innovations have allowed nurses to experiment with alternative paradigms of healing, holism and complementary therapies such as massage and aromatherapy (Pearson *et al.* 1992).

The 'new nursing' represents not only explicit attempts at professionalization by moving away from an occupational-bureaucratic model but also offers a wider impetus for change. The emphasis on practice and the improvements it brings to patients is appealing to generalists and to the elite groups of nursing specialists and academics. Aspects of the 'new nursing' are also congruent with the general management ethos which emphasises nurses' individual accountability.

Current and future prospects

In this final section a number of questions are raised in order to evaluate current and future prospects for nurses in the light of occupational and societal change. What effects will the introduction of Project 2000 and the innovations discussed in this chapter have on nursing and nurses? To what extent are nurses able to seize the initiative to develop their own

skills and knowledge independently of doctors and to work in partnership with patients and clients? Are traditional ways of emulating professionalism being challenged?

Doctors and nurses

When the nursing process (and later primary nursing) was introduced in
the 1980s, there was an outcry from doctors. The nursing and medical
press was filled with letters and editorials expressing doctors' dismay
that nurses were shedding their traditional roles. One of the pre-
occupations appeared to be that doctors felt uneasy at the nurses' new-
found voice and assumed that this would lead to open confrontation
over patient care.

Another development which led doctors to take notice of nurses was
the expansion of nursing roles to take on skills and expertise which in
the past were medicine's sole preserve. For example, the development of
nurse practitioners means that in certain situations nurses are able to
diagnose and treat diseases. The doctors' reactions to these developments may be interpreted in two ways. Were doctors truly concerned
with maintaining standards or were they more concerned in safe-
guarding their own professional practice? The example of their control
of nurse-midwives described above, and more recently their promotion
of a new kind of technical assistant accountable to them, suggest the
latter.

Nurses' attitudes and behaviour seem to sustain their domination by
the medical profession. Hart, a nurse researcher, found that when nurses
talked to her about their work and their effects on patients, they were
eloquent and articulate. When they were in the presence of doctors, they
remained silent on two accounts. On the one hand they felt intimidated
by a 'superior' occupational group and on the other they harboured a
belief that what they did was less important than doctors' work (Hart
1991).

Nurses and patients

The proposed nursing strategy being formulated in the Department of
Health promises to be patient- and client-focused, 'developing new ways
of delivering care which are more responsive to need' (Department of
Health 1992). It is pointed out, however, that nursing is the largest single
item of NHS expenditure but that its impact on health outcomes remains
to be explored.

Care has become a political issue as concerns for cost-effectiveness and efficiency sweep the British health service, and budgets are finely tuned to respond to the market place (Chapter 11). Caring is threatened in two ways. First, qualified nurses are expensive and may be seen to be expendable. Second, emotional care is not easily measured. Furthermore its costs are not only financial. Only when nurses can demonstrate the uniqueness of their interventions and their effects on outcomes, will they be able to counter cutbacks and limits to their autonomy.

Until recently most accounts of the effect of nursing upon patients have been anecdotal, but largely thanks to pioneering work in the Nursing Development Units (NDUs) this is changing. The view of nursing as simply supportive of (medical) therapy is challenged by research at the NDU at Burford (Pearson *et al.* 1992). Quality of care in the NDU was judged to be higher than in other wards, patient dependency was lower, and satisfaction with care expressed after discharge was higher. This research demonstrates the importance of nursing interventions in producing beneficial therapeutic effects by attending to the emotional care underpinning technical care and curative procedures. Similarly, Higgins and Dixon (1992) showed that qualified nurses were important to patients' recovery. Such findings go against the current trends for training fewer qualified nurses and substituting their care with health care assistants.

Summary

In this chapter we have examined the image of nurses as young, white, middle-class and female, and of nursing as women's hospital based work. The introduction of Project 2000 and health service re-organization are yet to demonstrate whether nursing will attract a more varied work-force. The key element of nursing work in hospital and community is the nurse-patient relationship. Innovations associated with the 'new nursing' aim to emphasize and support this key element by organizing work around people rather than tasks, and by promoting care rather than cure. Alternative ways of defining nursing knowledge based on promoting health and independence rather than on bio-medicine, have also been sought. The discrepancy between this view of nursing work and the view of nursing as a profession have been explored. Issues of power and control within the health care division of labour remain. Doctors still maintain professional dominance over nurses, while managers exercise new found power and control over both groups. The effect of promoting partnership (as advocated by the 'new' nursing models) on power relations and control between nurses and patients, still requires evaluation.

Acknowledgement

I am grateful to Gill Black for her insights into the 'new nursing' as an occupational versus a professionalizing strategy.

References

Abel-Smith B. (1964) *The Hospitals, 1800–1948.* Heinemann, London.

Armstrong D. (1983) The Fabrication of Nurse Patient Relationships. *Social Science and Medicine,* **17,** 457–60.

Beardshaw V. & Robinson R. (1990) *New for Old? Prospects for Nursing in the 1990s.* King's Fund Institute, London.

Benner P. (1988) *Nursing as a Caring Profession.* Working Paper for the American Academy of Nursing, Kansas City, Missouri, October 16–18.

Calliandro G. & Judkins B.L. (1988) *Primary Nursing Practice.* Scott, Foresman and Co., Glenview, Illinois.

Davies K. (1990) *Women, Time and the Weavings of Everyday Life.* Avebury, Aldershot.

Department of Health (1992) *Revitalising the Strategy for Nursing.* NHS Management Executive, London.

Dickens C. (1843) *Martin Chuzzlewit.* Clarendon (1982), Oxford.

Doyal L. (1979) *The Political Economy of Health.* Pluto Press, London.

Freidson E. (1972) *Profession of Medicine: A Study of the Sociology of Applied Knowledge.* Dodd Mead, New York.

Freund P. & McGuire M. (1991) *Health Illness and the Social Body: A Critical Sociology.* Prentice Hall, Englewood Cliffs.

Hart E. (1991) Ghost in the Machine. *Health Services Journal,* December 5, pp. 20–22.

Henderson V. (1960) *Basic Principles of Nursing Care.* International Council of Nurses (Revised edn 1979), Geneva.

Higgins M. & Dixon P. (1992) Skill Mix and the effectiveness of nursing care. *Nursing Standard,* **7,** (4) 18–21.

Menzies I. E. P. (1960) A Case Study of the Functioning of Social Systems as a Defence against Anxiety. A report on the study of a nursing service of a general hospital. *Human Relations,* **13,** 95–121.

Morse J. (1991) Negotiating commitment and involvement in the nurse-patient relationship. *Journal of Advanced Nursing,* **16,** 455–468.

Nightingale F. (1859) *Notes on Nursing.* Blackie (re-issued 1974), Glasgow.

O'Brien M. (1989) Reproducing the World. In her *Reproducing the World: Essays in Feminist Theory.* Westview Press, N.J.

O'Neill C. (1991) *A Picture of Health.* Meadow Books, Oxford.

Oakley A. (1974) *The Sociology of Housework.* Martin Robinson, London.

Oakley A. (1986) On the Importance of Being a Nurse. In her *Telling the Truth About Jerusalem: A Collection of Essays and Poems.* Basil Blackwell, New York.

Pearson M. (1985) *Equal Opportunities in the NHS. A Handbook.* Training in Health and Race. Cambridge.

Pearson A., Punton S. & Durant I. (1992) *Nursing Beds: An Evaluation of the Effects of Therapeutic Nursing.* Scutari, Harrow.

Salvage J. (1985) *The Politics of Nursing.* Heinemann, London.

Salvage J. (1990) The Theory and Practice of the New Nursing. Occasional Paper, *Nursing Times,* **86**, (4) 42–5.

Smith P. (1992) *The Emotional Labour of Nursing. How Nurses Care.* Macmillan, Basingstoke.

Strauss A., Fagerhaugh S., Suczek B. & Wiener C. (1982) Sentimental work in the technologised hospital. *Sociology of Health and Illness,* **4**, 254–78.

UKCC (1986) *Project 2000. A New Preparation for Practice.* UKCC, London.

Ungerson C. (1983) Women and caring: skills, tasks and taboos. In *The Public and the Private* (Ed. by E. Gamarnikov, D. Morgan, J. Purvis & D. Taylorson). Heinemann, London.

Further reading

Robinson J., Gray A. & Elkan R. (Eds) *Policy Issues in Nursing.* Open University, Milton Keynes.

Index